NOEL STREATFEILD

NOEL STREATFEILD

A Biography by
Angela Bull

COLLINS

William Collins Sons & Co Ltd
London · Glasgow · Sydney · Auckland
Toronto · Johannesburg

First published 1984
© Angela Bull 1984

ISBN 0 00 195044 4

Set in Linotron Bembo by
Rowland Phototypesetting Ltd
Bury St Edmunds, Suffolk

Made and printed in Great Britain by
William Collins Sons & Co. Ltd Glasgow

Illustrations

Contents

Introduction

On 28 September 1936 *Ballet Shoes* was published, and a new children's classic was born. Noel Streatfeild, a former actress and author of several acclaimed adult novels, had produced, at her first attempt, a children's book which was to sell ten million copies, and win the hearts of hundreds of thousands of children.

By a strange coincidence I was myself born on the day *Ballet Shoes* appeared. It was one of the most important books of my childhood. I remember poring, entranced, over the illustations in a cousin's copy before I was old enough to read the story; and, when I did read it, the Fossil sisters were firmly established as favourite characters in my day dreams.

I was in my teens when Noel Streatfeild came to lecture at a local literary society. I went to her talk, and heard for the first time the fascinating story of her Vicarage childhood. Afterwards my parents invited her back to our house for coffee, and I remember her striking appearance, her unusual looped cigarette holder, and the glow of her personality. That was why, later, I dared, like many other aspiring writers, to send the manuscript of my first children's novel to her, for her comments. 'Too Dickensian' was the verdict; but at least she had read it, and thought about it.

Yet even then, somewhere around 1960, I was tempted to think of Noel as a writer whose career must be virtually over. As I, the representative of a younger generation, began to write, she, I believed, would naturally retire, as her contemporaries, Arthur Ransome, Kitty Barne, and Joanna Cannan, had done. I could not have been more wrong. Noel did not retire. All through the 1960s, and well into the 1970s, she went on – not just publishing, but delighting her readers with books like *A Vicarage Family*, *The Growing Summer* and *Thursday's Child*. More than thirty years after *Ballet Shoes* she could still produce bestsellers. Other writers, from Enid Blyton to C. S. Lewis, might come and go. Noel's career more than spanned theirs.

This constant evidence of unquenchable imaginative vitality interested me greatly. And Noel's vitality, I discovered, was not just confined to the writing of her books. In the late 1960s I heard how she had triumphed over a severe stroke, to lead an almost normal life again. In the early 1970s I learned that she appeared at Puffin Club children's parties, not as a faded figure from the past, but as an exciting, up-to-date writer, more widely known than ever through the paper-back editions and television adaptations of her books. Her position in the children's book world was unique, solidly established, and endur-ing.

Late in the 1970s I was gathering material about writers who had lived in Vicarages, and I turned back to Noel's autobiographical books, which I had read years before, and half forgotten. The personality that emerged from those books – warm yet rebellious, sometimes aim-lessly drifting, sometimes fiercely disciplined – fascinated me. Living in a Vicarage myself, I was able to identify with some of the stresses which she had undergone, and which had moulded her writing. The sense of identification awakened in me an urge to explore more fully her life and achievements.

By the time I had formulated the idea of writing about her, Noel was confined to a nursing home. She was pleased to know that there was to be a biography, but she was too ill to give much help. Her family, however, came to my rescue by lending me a stack of boxes, full of papers and documents which Noel had collected over a lifetime.

On this treasure trove of personal papers, which form a kind of continuous, if fragmentary, autobiography, much of my book has been based, and I am deeply grateful to Hugh Stubbs, Noel's literary executor, for the generous loan. I am equally grateful to other members of Noel's family, especially her sisters, Ruth Gervis and Richenda Stubbs, and her sister-in-law, Ursula Streatfeild, for all the help they gave me, and for lending the family photographs, which have been used as illustrations.

I must also record my gratitude to the many friends of Noel's with whom I was able to talk or correspond, particularly her former secretaries, June Allen and the late Con Boret; to all the people in Eastbourne who sent me accounts of the Streatfeilds, still a well-remembered Vicarage family; and to the members of the Puffin Club who wrote to tell me how much they enjoyed Noel's books. I would like to thank Noel's several publishers, and her literary agent, Osyth Leeston, for the loan of books which have now gone out of print. And finally I must thank my husband and children for bearing with my absorption in Noel Streatfeild for the last three years, and for encourag-ing me, as always.

Angela Bull
October 1983

I

A Sussex Idyll

Noel Streatfeild was born on Christmas Eve 1895. She was a rebel from an early age, and few things provoked her rebellious feelings more sharply than this disastrous birthday. It seemed so unfair that while her sisters and brother celebrated their birthdays in the summer, with proper cakes, and piles of presents, and the privilege of choosing – within limits – what they would like to do, hers was overshadowed by Christmas, the birthday of the One Person who, in their Vicarage home, was bound to be considered more important than herself.

'What a lucky little girl you are, to share the birthday of Our Lord!' her father's parishioners, or her pious relations, would tell her in hushed, reverent voices. Noel knew quite well that she was not lucky. Christmas Eve at the Vicarage was a day of hectic preparations, and no one had time to spare for Noel. She had to make do with combined birthday-and-Christmas presents, and such hasty meals as the harassed Cook could manage. Even her cake had its candles briskly removed, and reappeared, with a robin on top, as the Christmas cake. Always Noel longed to be special, the centre of the household, and her uncelebrated birthday came round every year as a cruel mortification.

None of her grown-up relations seemed to notice how much she minded; or, if they did, they may have believed that such disappointments were a valuable training for the soul. Noel was descended from generations of devout Christians, who would naturally have thought in those terms. Her father, and both her grandfathers, were Anglican clergymen; and, among her more distant ancestors, there were, on her mother's side, the Rev Henry Venn, who founded the Church Missionary Society, and the Rev John Venn, a leader of the Clapham Sect, which campaigned for the abolition of slavery; while, on her father's side, there was her great-great-grandmother, Elizabeth Fry, the famous prison reformer. It was a weighty heritage of piety and self-sacrifice.

In 1895 Noel's father, William Champion Streatfeild, was curate to his father, another William Champion Streatfeild, who was the Rector of Frant, near Tunbridge Wells. Previously he had been a curate to Henry Venn, the Rector of Sittingbourne, and here he had met and married the Rector's daughter, Janet Venn. William was thirty when Noel was born, Janet was twenty-three, and they already had an elder daughter, Ruth.

The Streatfeilds were a Kentish family, country gentlemen as well as clerics. They had owned land in the county since the twelfth century; and although, for five hundred years, their chief home was Chiddingstone Castle, near Edenbridge, younger members of the family had gradually bought adjoining properties, so that by the beginning of the nineteenth century it was possible to walk for miles over land belonging solely to Streatfeilds. To raise a Streatfeild cricket eleven was easy, and frequently done. (Noel, no cricket-lover, would steal into the tea-tent, during the matches, and solace herself with glasses of iced coffee and cream.) There was even one occasion, which the family liked to remember, when a hundred and fifty-seven Streatfeilds had sat down to luncheon together. Their most memorable ancestor, apart from Elizabeth Fry, was a Royalist Streatfeild, who visited Charles I the day before his execution, and was given a piece of the King's garter ribbon, long preserved as a family relic. For Noel, her sisters and brother, he was interestingly balanced by a Venn ancestor who had signed Charles I's death warrant.

In spite of the family's Kentish ties, Noel's first allegiance was to Sussex. Frant, where she was born, was only just inside the northern border of Sussex, close to the places where Streatfeilds had always belonged; but in 1897, before she was two, her family moved right away from the Streatfeild orbit. Her father was appointed Vicar of Amberley, and he, his wife and daughers, moved south-westwards into the heart of Sussex, to a tiny country village, sheltered by the Downs, and looking out over the flat, desolate marshes of the river Arun.

There was not much to Amberley; just a Norman church, a ruined castle, a cluster of cottages in small, well-tended gardens, some outlying farms, and an ancient, inconvenient Vicarage. It was idyllically peaceful and remote. The narrow lanes, linking it to other villages, were thick with dust in summer, and almost impassable with mud or snow in winter, while at any season, after heavy rain, the marshes might flood, isolating Amberley completely. It was so difficult to get about that the villagers seldom went far from home. A carrier drove to a nearby town once a week, when he could, and shopped for the whole village. William Streatfeild walked around his parish, or visited more distant parts in a donkey cart; and there were occasional railway trips to Arundel to buy shoes or coats for the children.

'It is extraordinary today,' Noel wrote half a century later, 'to imagine a village so remote from the world as that village was. It was a remarkably self-contained unit. It even administered its own justice, rather than call in the police. The justice took the form of what was called "rough music". The men of the village would turn out at night, and march round the cottage of an offender, beating on pots and pans. The noise would carry to the nearest village, and the shame of being "rough music-ed" was often sufficient to turn evil-doers from their ways.'[1]

Crowded into the old-fashioned Vicarage, the Streatfeild family expanded rapidly. Janet had two other children, Barbara and William Champion, and then she almost died giving birth to a fragile baby, Joyce, who succumbed to tuberculosis before she was two. There was the usual complement of servants thought essential for even the poorest clergyman – a cook, a housemaid, a nannie, a gardener, and a village girl to push the pram. Noel's earliest memory was of walking round Amberley castle with this girl, holding tightly, as commanded, to the pram handle, and wearing a green velvet caped coat, a green velvet bonnet, and white leggings. It is entirely characteristic of Noel that she should remember her clothes.

Within its own circle, family life was isolated. For the first time William and Janet were living far away from all their relations, and they never made friends easily. To begin with, Noel was very dependent on her adored elder sister, Ruth, but the dependence was broken when Ruth had to be sent away from Amberley. She was a delicate child, and the coldness and dampness of the old Vicarage, in its marshy setting, brought on alarming attacks of bronchitis and asthma. Chest infections were dreaded by Janet. Her own mother had died of tuberculosis when Janet was five, and her father worried constantly about Janet's health, twice sending her to Switzerland to convalesce after illnesses, in the hope that mountain air would strengthen her lungs. Much as Janet loved pretty little Ruth, with her sweet face and long fair hair, she dared not risk keeping her in Amberley. Ruth spent the next four years with her Streatfeild grandparents, an interlude which she remembered as very happy.

Left behind, two-year-old Noel found herself quite on her own. Luckily no one needed to worry about her. She looked thoroughly healthy, a sturdy rather than a pretty child, with a round face, thick brown hair, and widely spaced blue eyes. She seemed to make no particular demands, and Janet thankfully left her to her own devices. Nothing could have been better for a future writer. Undistracted, Noel quickly discovered the solitary pleasures of day-dreams and stories.

When she looked back on that quiet life in Amberley Vicarage, Noel often saw herself with a book in her hands. The house might be damp and old-fashioned, with dark rooms and awkward corners, but there was a cosy nursery where a fire blazed in the grate; and while the younger children were bathed and put to bed by Nannie, Noel would settle down on the hearth-rug, shielded from the blaze by a heavy steel fireguard hung with airing nappies and warming nightgowns, and pore over the magic pages of Beatrix Potter, or *Little Black Sambo*. She could not read, but the pictures fascinated her. She gazed, enchanted, at the courtly mice in *The Tailor of Gloucester*, trying to repeat the words to herself, and shivering with apprehension in case the Mayor of Gloucester did not get his cherry-coloured coat in time for the wedding. Noel knew how she would have felt about that.

Another book which stirred her imagination was *The Seven Little Goslings* by Laurence Housman. It was her own special book, a Christmas present, and she sniffed it ecstatically, relishing the smell of new paper and ink. There were pictures here too, to be enjoyed, and a charmingly wicked fox who tried to fool the geese by covering his tongue with chocolate creams, to make his voice soft and sugary. 'I adored this story,' Noel recalled, 'but so, alas, did everyone else, and I and a small boy cousin once came to blows over the book, during which a page was torn. I can still remember my mother's horror, and that, as a punishment, I was sent to bed. I thought this harsh at the time, but forever it impressed on me that it was a crime to treat a book badly.'[2]

A good deal of reading aloud went on in Amberley Vicarage. William read Noel *Tanglewood Tales*, a book of Greek myths, retold by Nathaniel Hawthorne. In Noel's memory it was always associated with the dark dining room at Amberley, with howling wind and rain outside, flames dancing in the fireplace, and her father's voice going steadily on and on, uncovering the riches of those wonderful stories, which fed her vivid imagination.

'I do not remember being Cinderella or the Beast in the nursery,' Noel wrote, 'but I distinctly remember being Circe. "Wretches," I shouted, glaring round at the baby in the cot, the children playing on the floor, and Nannie going about her business. "You have abused a lady's hospitality. Assume your proper shapes, gourmandizers, and be gone to the sty."

'I remember too, an artist who was painting under a tree on our lawn, asking whether a wheelbarrow could be moved. "Certainly not," I answered grandly. "Can't you see that that wheelbarrow is a white bull, and I am Europa getting on his back?" '[3]

Such anecdotes show the powerful effect stories could have on Noel. Already she had begun – in Ruth's words – to 'live in her imagination.' When Ruth came home on visits, Noel had endless stories to tell her, but most of the time she told them to herself, acting out the most dramatic scenes. Perhaps it was the strength of her imagination, her ability to live in unreal worlds, which led to her finding an unexpected companion.

Ruth was away, Barbara and Bill, her younger brother and sister, were engrossed in each other, and so Noel often found herself in the garden alone. It was an old garden, really quite small, though to Noel it seemed enormous. She was always discovering new corners, or making tiny footpaths under the low boughs of the bushes. Growing by itself, far from the house, was a most unusual rose tree, called a York and Lancaster, because each flower was half white and half red. At first Noel considered this rose her personal property, but gradually she came to realize that she shared it with another child, a little child in a crinoline skirt and long pantalettes.

That the Vicarage was haunted was well known in the village, although William and Janet never seemed aware of it. Noel, quite unafraid, took the strange little girl as a matter of course. She knew why, when there were visitors in the spare bedroom, the door handle would turn, the door creak slowly open, and footsteps patter across the floor. The little girl wanted to see the guests – who could seldom be persuaded to make a second visit of Amberley Vicarage. With the reticence of childhood, Noel never mentioned the little girl to her parents; and nor did the servants, although they sometimes had to endure the most provocative behaviour in the kitchen, when the little girl chose to throw plates and saucepans about. The servants knew too, as did the villagers, that the little girl was often accompanied by a woman, but Noel never saw her. After the Streatfeilds left Amberley, the cook was reported to have said that she did not tell Janet about 'the people', because she did not want to frighten her when she was pregnant.

In a way it was curious that Janet never saw the woman and child – or never admitted that she had done. Her father was later to live in a haunted house in Canterbury Close where he regularly saw the ghosts of some Huguenot refugees who had died there. But Janet was sceptical by nature, and Noel must have known instinctively that it was useless to confide in her mother about the little girl with the interesting clothes.

There was a strange sequel to Noel's encounter with the ghost. The wife of the Vicar who followed William at Amberley, decided that the house needed modernizing. In particular she wanted alterations made to the low-beamed, crooked staircase, and some workmen were brought in to open it up. Under the boards of the second stair, they uncovered two skeletons, a woman's and a little girl's. How they had got there nobody knew, but after the discovery, the haunting ceased.

Life for Noel at Amberley was not all stories, ghosts and solitary imaginings. Sometimes Noel went to stay with her grand-parents, and was joyfully reunited with Ruth. There were occasional parties too, in neighbouring Vicarages and big houses. Noel remembered one of particular grandeur, where an enormous Christmas tree towered in the drawing room, hung with presents for the children. Noel circled it, gazing bemused at the wonderful toys. Although there were plenty of books at home, playthings were scarce, and she longed for something really remarkable.

The hostess smilingly approached her.

'Noel – it is Noel, isn't it? – what would you like off the tree?'

Quick to seize so unusual an opportunity, Noel pointed upwards. 'That doll, please.'

The hostess lifted down, and placed in Noel's hands, a gutta-percha boy doll, in a black velvet suit with a white frilled shirt. Noel clutched him ecstatically. She was not, on the whole, fond of dolls, but a boy doll in velvet and frills was a treasure not to be resisted.

Other social occasions were the family weddings. William was the eldest of ten children, Janet had younger sisters and half brothers, so uncles and aunts got married with agreeable frequency. Ruth and Noel would be bridesmaids, and Noel could indulge her passion for clothes with dainty dresses of white satin and chiffon. The dresses were made in the village by a Miss Souter, whose fascinating gossip enlivened the visits for fittings. She had known another dressmaker, she told them, who had been asked to make twelve pairs of drawers for Queen Victoria. 'Very long and plain, beautifully sewn, of course, but just feather-stitching – no lace,' Miss Souter explained: and Noel felt scornful of the queen for ordering such boring underwear.

Queen Victoria was connected, too, with one of Noel's last memories of Amberley. After she had died at Osborne on the Isle of Wight, the queen's coffin was ferried to the mainland, and, on 2 February 1901, taken on by train to London. Since the railway line ran past Amberley, William Streatfeild decided that Noel should see the train. The marshes were flooded, but he squelched along a raised path, carrying Noel, until they reached the fence beside the railway. A little knot of people, all dressed in black, had gathered there, waiting and watching. At last the train puffed slowly into view, its engine decorated with green laurel branches, and a bow of purple ribbon. 'Never forget you have seen this train,' William told Noel solemnly. 'It carries Queen Victoria's body. Never forget that you have seen it.' Noel never did.

She was only six when the family left Amberley, but the years there were probably the happiest of her childhood. Of course the Streatfeilds were poor. Out of a low stipend William had to keep his wife, children and servants, and both he and Janet recognized the imperatives of charity, and gave away all they could spare. There was never much saving of money in the Streatfeild family. But poverty is relative, and in Amberley Noel had no one to compare herself with. She still needed very little. Books, day-dreams and the garden kept her contented; nice clothes were extra treats.

The pace of country life was gentle. William had time to work in the garden and read to the children. It was over their shared stories that Noel's strong bond with him was forged. Janet was reasonably free, for the only time in her married life, from the conventional burdens of a clergyman's wife. The Amberley villagers accepted her for what she was – a young wife and mother – and made no special demands on her. Isolated in their quiet Vicarage, the family was a compact little unit, buttressed by all the securities of their class, their age, and their religious tradition. Neither the absence of Ruth, nor the tragic fragility of Joyce, troubled Noel unduly. She had freedom, solitude, and endless leisure.

The particular charm of the Sussex countryside imprinted itself lastingly on her spirit. Its pastoral tranquillity – cottages with trim, flower-filled gardens, trees, the river, the downs with their soft, springy turf – represented for her the ideal landscape; and long after she had grown up, and moved to London, she retained a nostalgic love for it. She put this love into her first novel, *The Whicharts*, where the three heroines, enjoying a holiday on the Downs, decide that the word 'Sussex' epitomizes all the nicest things in life. 'Such Sussexly chocolates,' they remark; and, 'I do think my new frock's Sussex.' Perhaps Noel had done the same herself. She certainly drew on her recollections of the Amberley years when she wanted to create a picture of happy family life.

2

Family Life at the Vicarage

In 1902 William Streatfeild was instituted as the Vicar of St Peter's church in the parish of St Leonard's on the south coast. It was a residential area, holding itself a little aloof from adjoining Hastings, whose dubious gaieties of pier and bandstand and theatre drew crowds in the summer. Holiday-makers and their pleasures were not regarded with favour by the Streatfeilds. 'I was brought up at the seaside,' Noel was to say, 'and at that time there was a distinctly snobbish attitude about summer visitors. We were never allowed on the sea front at all during a bank holiday; in fact I grew up with the illusion that people who did go out on bank holidays were taking their lives in their hands. In the summer we would be sent down to the beach, but whoever took us had strict injunctions that it was to be a nice quiet beach, with no nasty trippers about.'[1]

Class barriers were strongly marked in 1902, with the Streatfeilds on the side of the middle classes and the gentry. Poor though they were, there were always servants to run the house, and middle class customs were observed, like drawing room tea, with delicate china and a silver teapot. Nice manners were considered the touchstone of good breeding. The Streatfeild children were expected to shake hands with visitors, to look up and smile when they were greeted, and to behave politely at table. Food and money, Noel was told, were two subjects a lady never mentioned.

Their new home must have seemed very unlike Amberley. The church, the parish hall, and the Vicarage formed three sides of a quadrangle round a narrow strip of garden. The church was modern, built only in 1885, a lofty brick barn of a place, with neither tower nor spire. The Vicarage was brick too, three

18

storeys high, with many sharp gables and bristling chimneys. 'Bare and bleak', Noel remembered it, 'with yards and yards of linoleum covering the hall, and people sitting on benches on either side, waiting to see father.'

Two changes in the family marked the early months at St Leonard's. Because the climate was healthy, Ruth was able to come home, but it was too late to save consumptive little Joyce, who died soon after the move. Noel was delighted to have Ruth's companionship again, and, in the characteristic manner of child-hood, quickly accepted her baby sister's death. Indeed her chief recollection of it was being taken by an aunt to plant forget-me-nots on the tiny grave, dressed in a new holland smock and sailor hat, whose charms easily banished the grief of the occasion.

William's new parish was much larger and busier than Amber-ley, and it was soon apparent that it would make enormous demands on his time and energy. There were innumerable activities to organize, and difficulties to solve. Those people whom Noel recalled sitting in the hall were waiting for the help which, in those days, the church provided; help in supplying food, or clothes, or coal; help with family and spiritual problems. William was never a man to hold back, and all too soon he was sucked into an unending round of duties.

Ever since he was a small child he had dedicated himself to God. Now his family began to realize that this dedication meant involving himself utterly in the cares of his parish, seeing each as a challenge to his own personal efforts. He had a strong, charac-teristically Victorian belief in individual acts of charity, without ever concluding that the real need was for a radical change in the social order. 'Everyone in God's eyes was equal to him,' Ruth wrote, 'but in many ways he was conservative, and, although I do not think he would ever had said so, he was for "the rich man in his castle and the poor man at his gate", only he felt that the rich man must be more than generous to the poor man.'[2]

As an example of this generosity from rich to poor, there were the soup kitchens. Outwardly respectable though St Leonard's seemed, with its terraces of solid houses rising above prim gardens, plenty of people lived in squalor, and often went hungry. Local shopkeepers were persuaded to give bones and vegetables, and Janet sold nourishing soup at a penny a jug all through the winter months. 'Fill that jug to the top,' Noel heard her say to her assistant, 'and give the children extra bread. That family never has enough to eat.'[3]

There had been no need for soup kitchens in Amberley. Noel described, in *A Vicarage Family*, how once her mother, feeling it was the duty of the Vicar's wife, made broth for a sick woman, and was astonished to receive in exchange a basket of vegetables. 'Don't you try to give things to the likes of us,' the woman had said. 'You've got all you can do to fill the bellies of your own.' But the poor people of St Leonard's did not think like that. Day after day they sat in the Vicarage hall, coughing and shuffling their feet on the linoleum, waiting for the Vicar to do something for them.

William was only too eager to respond. The more that was asked of him, the more he was ready to give. The old pleasures of games and stories with the children were crowded out; their needs were subordinated to the needs of the parish. 'As a father he was very loving,' Ruth remembered, 'but always very busy, and rushed, and over-tired. Though I loved him, I did in many ways feel more remote from him than his parishioners.'[4] Soon it was accepted that he would be the last to come in to a meal, and the first to jump up from it. He walked everywhere so that people could easily waylay him, and he was seldom in bed before midnight.

The strength to cope with this taxing life came from his ardent Christian faith. Being a high churchman he expressed his devotion to God in a complicated pattern of religious observances – daily Matins and Evensong, and daily celebrations of Holy Communion, with much additional prayer and fasting. Prayer seemed to him the answer to every difficulty, and it was all too easy for him to believe that any problem he had earnestly committed to God was as good as solved. Fasting meant the opportunity to offer his own suffering to Christ as a sacrifice for his people. Believing as passionately as he did in these spiritual exercises, it was impossible for him to stand back from them, and assess coolly the effect they might have on family life. Photographs of this time show him with a withdrawn, brooding expression that suggests an intense inner life – something which Noel inherited, though hers was differently directed.

William's Christianity had been nourished in the warm, loving atmosphere of his childhood home. Janet's early experiences had been very different. She had been brought up in a narrow-minded and zealous clerical household. There had been family prayer meetings when some stern, elderly relation would abruptly address Janet and her sisters with the words – 'Won't a little child raise a prayer to Jesus?' which froze them into horrified silence. There had been the equal embarrassment of being driven into the country on Sunday afternoons, and commanded to hand out tracts – popular pamphlets of moral and religious advice – to farm lads, who would laugh rudely in their faces. So it was hard for Janet to view the church with William's enthusiasm.

She had had little experience of family love. Her mother had died when Janet was five, an irreparable loss, for she had been gay and charming, with a light-hearted approach to life very different from that of her husband and his relations. Janet had inherited her delicate, dark, small-boned prettiness, but, sadly, not her talent for happiness.

Left with four small daughters and a son, her father had married again, a dour Scotswoman. 'I found her,' Ruth recalled, 'a snob, and an intimidating woman, with a long sour face, and an exceedingly bitter tongue, sitting in the bow window at Canterbury, and saying unpleasant things about everyone who passed. I think she did her duty by her stepchildren, but that was all. The boy ran away, and all the girls hated their stepmother, so it was not a very happy home.'[5]

Minor resentments scarred Janet's soul. One Christmas Day there were no presents on the table, and when the little girls at last, daringly, crept to their stepmother, murmuring – 'It's Christmas Day, Mama,' she replied offhandedly – 'Oh, yes; look in that cupboard,' where they found four workboxes, identical except for different coloured linings, lying unwrapped together. As a Scot, Mrs Venn may not have appreciated English Christmas customs, but to Janet it symbolized her hard-hearted indifference. And there was the time she was sent back to boarding school with an old week-day hat retrimmed to pass for a Sunday one – a trifling incident, but it rankled.

She grew up feeling unloved, cool towards religion, poorly educated in spite of the boarding school, uninterested in her own appearance. Yet she was very pretty – some people even remembered her as beautiful – and it was that prettiness which attracted her father's curate, William Streatfeild. She was only seventeen when he fell in love with her over the dining table at Sittingbourne Rectory. He proposed to her while they were skating, one cold winter's day, and married her as soon as she was twenty-one. Distrusting what little she knew of the world, shy, introverted, and prone to self pity, she was a wife and mother before she had had a chance to develop her personality.

Her role as Vicar's wife inevitably meant absorption into a system which was not entirely congenial. Her Evangelical ancestry made her unsympathetic towards William's Anglo-Catholic practices. Not for her the crossings and genuflexions, the devotion to the Blessed Sacrament. 'A curt nod at the name of Jesus was as far as she would go,' Noel recalled.[6] A tickly little cough afforded her a perennial excuse for missing the Good Friday three hours' services, while the cup of tea she said she needed to stave off the cough saved her from having to go to early Communion fasting, as William did.

Within the wider spheres of parish life there were some areas which interested her, and others which did not. She had as little as possible to do with running all the church functions and organizations, which could conveniently be left to the enthusiastic band of ladies, known collectively to the Streatfeild children as the 'parish pussies'. Jumble, Janet claimed, made her faint, so she never helped at the jumble sales put on for good causes. She attended the weekly Mothers' Union working parties, but instead of sewing she read aloud, brilliantly condensing a whole novel into an afternoon's session, and thus avoiding the obligation to chat. She did not find social relations easy. Someone who knew her well remarked to Ruth – 'We became friends, but I had to make all the running.'

But for causes that were close to her heart, she was prepared to work tirelessly. She was a regular visitor at the local hospital and the workhouse; and by delivering parish magazines, she kept an eye on many of the poorer homes. She knew exactly who would benefit most from her soup kitchens.

By far the greatest pleasure in her life was her garden. There was always a gardener to do the rough work, but she cherished her flowers and plants, and knew them all. Inside the Vicarage, she left as much of the domestic arrangements as she could to the servants, with frequently unsatisfactory results. Good cooks were rare, and expected ruinously high wages, so the Streatfeilds managed with poor cooks, who served monotonous, and sometimes deplorable meals. The rooms looked bleak, for Janet had neither the ability nor the money to furnish them attractively. It did not matter to William, who never cared what he ate, and had little time to sit in the drawing room; but Noel was later to notice, and condemn, the unhomeliness of her home.

That was in the future. While their parents mapped out paths for themselves in the new parish, and Janet, no doubt, grieved over Joyce, the four elder children were settling down in the nursery. When Ruth had been sent to her grandparents, Barbara had been a baby, and Bill had not been born; so, for the first time, they were all living together. They were curiously unalike.

Ruth was everyone's darling, a good, gentle, obedient child, with the long fair hair and blue eyes of a story-book princess. Art absorbed her. Their Streatfeild grandfather was a skilled amateur painter, and he had taught and encouraged Ruth. It was an ideal pastime for a delicate child. With her asthma she could not run about and play much, but she was happy to sit at the nursery table for hours, drawing and painting. She and Noel shared a bedroom, and quickly resumed their old alliance.

Relations between Barbara and Noel were very different. Barbara was lively, quick-witted and mercurial. Like her mother she was slight and dark, and so pretty that people would turn in the street to gaze after her. She seemed to dance beside the sturdier Noel like a slim, bright elf; teasing, maddening, provoking violent quarrels with her sharp-tongued repartee. Her particular affection was given to Bill, the youngest of the four.

In spite of being the only boy, Bill never seems to have been spoiled. Ruth and Barbara were both petted by their mother,

Ruth because of her delicacy, Barbara because of her affinity with
Janet; but Bill maintained a calm emotional independence from
everyone except Barbara. Good, clever, brave, he was an admirable child in every way. All his sisters recognized that.

Noel's position in such a quartet was difficult. She must soon
have discovered that she was the least pretty and the least clever,
and possibly she had already divined that she was the least valued
by her mother. In those early years, while Janet had been
occupied with sickly Ruth, with the babies, with her own ill
health – for the birth of Joyce had left internal complications from
which she did not fully recover for many years – she had
somehow, fatally, lost touch with Noel. Left to herself, Noel had
become much the most imaginative of the children, but at six she
could hardly appreciate the importance of that. Bright, good-
looking children were admired in the nurseries of St Leonard's.

School was now essential for the two elder girls. Both had so
far been taught at home, and Ruth had shown herself to be
extremely intelligent, reading the whole of *Little Women* to
herself when she was only six. In this, as in so much else, Noel
lagged behind. Her mother had tried to teach her to read from a
little book, mis-named – from Noel's point of view – *Reading
Without Tears*; but the attempt had been disastrous. 'As I remember,' Noel wrote, 'tears streamed down my cheeks at every
lesson. I learned in the dining room at Amberley, which looked
out over the garden. There, I remember, my father snatched time
to garden. And as I laboured with cats on mats, I heard my
younger sister prattling to him. "Lucky, lucky her," I thought.
"Miserable me!" It was during one lesson that my father dug up a
penny, which he gave to my sister. I can still remember the
feeling of hopelessness and despair that swept over me. A penny
in those days was riches. And here was my little sister being given
the penny, while I, a prisoner, slaved at reading and writing. I put
my head down and sobbed.'[7]

The school chosen for Ruth and Noel was the Hastings and St.
Leonard's Ladies' College. (The title 'College' was supposed by
the pupils to convey a special distinction.) It occupied an impos-
ing, red brick building, with light, airy classrooms, and a huge
assembly hall. The founders had thought much about education,

but little about recreation, for there was only a small yard, and no playing fields. Its purpose was serious. Girls went there to learn, and there was a good, well-qualified staff.

Noel started in the kindergarten, and here at last she mastered reading. Her teacher was Sheila Kaye-Smith, who later became well-known as a novelist. Some of her books – *The Children's Summer* and *Selina is Older* – show great sympathy for imaginative, awkward children, so perhaps she understood better than Janet how to handle Noel.

Nevertheless, Noel rapidly gained the reputation of a difficult, disruptive pupil. The change which, somewhere around the time of the move to St Leonard's, turned her from a basically contented child into one over whom everyone shook their heads despairingly, came from the wounding realization that she, the heroine of so many glorious games and day-dreams, was now out in the harsh, cold world, being judged, and found wanting.

She was born with a deep psychological need to be the centre of attention, but how could this be achieved when she was sandwiched between two unusually attractive sisters, and was rather a dunce at school? She had all the instincts of the actress she was to become, but no theatre to shine in. It was a problem she had to face on her own. No help could be expected from her parents; indeed they were part of the trouble. They certainly did not share Noel's belief that she was someone special.

Inwardly, perhaps barely consciously, Noel must have revolved all the possible ways of becoming important. Could she too be beautiful? At that time there was a popular cult of pretty children. Little girls with tumbling curls, and wide-eyed, wistful smiles, were photographed for magazines and Christmas annuals, sometimes in innocently erotic poses, their lacy garments slipping down from their dimpled shoulders. But Noel was honest with herself, and, examining her round face and straight brown hair in the mirror, she must have known that she could never compete.

At home she would have been assured that beauty was not really important. The child who was most precious to God and her parents was the good child. But all the children they knew, it seemed to Noel, were boringly good. What was the point of being merely one of the herd? A more subtle message was conveyed through many of the books and attitudes of the time; goodness was a mark of class. Little ladies and little gentlemen did not – could not, it was claimed – tell lies or boast, show off, speak roughly or rudely. The child who misbehaved, degraded herself in the eyes of society as well as in the eyes of God; and for a clergyman to have a naughty daughter was a double disgrace. 'People would be very surprised at your behaving like that, living in a Vicarage,' Noel was told when she was bad.[8]

'People would be very surprised' – perhaps that was the key. It must have dawned on Noel that naughtiness might not just be something which happened when she was cross. She might deliberately use it to her advantage, and make those dull, well-behaved children stare.

'She really was an imp of mischief,' Ruth recalled. 'I was sixteen months older than her, so I was always in a senior class, but when we first went to school I think the kindergarten and Form I shared a room. I remember seeing Noel flick small paper pellets dipped in ink at the spotless white sailor top of the boy in front. I also remember his mother turning up in a rage next day with the sailor top in her hand.'

On another occasion the headmistress, Miss Bishop, appeared in the classroom. She was a formidable woman, quelling most of the pupils by her mere presence. As she walked majestically up and down the room, inspecting the children's work, there was a gentle ripple of suppressed laughter. Miss Bishop swung round, and there was Noel, following her, and copying every gesture.

'Noel Streatfeild, you naughty child!' she exclaimed, and Noel folded her hands and lowered her eyes in a parody of penitence. 'Come to my study at once!'

Noel strutted out after her quite unabashed, grinning cheekily, and pushing out her small chest in a ridiculous imitation of Miss Bishop's large bosom.

'In spite of my mortification,' Ruth remembered, 'I did realize how funny she was, and how the other children delighted in her.'

Notes of complaint were sent to Noel's parents, and if William had not been a respected clergyman, he might have been asked to remove his daughter. Noel was not punished at home, but she was summoned for a long, sorrowful talk with her father. 'How can you be so naughty?' he asked despairingly, but Noel could not explain. She knew he would never understand what fun it had been to make the class laugh, to know that everyone was watching and admiring her devilry.

The ironic fact was that she derived her taste for the dramatic at least partly from her parents. William was a genuinely humble man, but each Sunday his position as priest made him the focus of attention for a large congregation. Week after week Noel saw him impressively spotlighted, as he prayed, preached and cele-brated the sacraments. On Sunday afternoons he held children's services, and Noel watched him standing on a box so that he would be visible to the tiniest toddler, keeping his audience spellbound with wonderful stories. Janet too had histrionic talents. She read aloud marvellously, to her children as well as the Mothers' Union; and she was a gifted raconteur when she chose to be, embroidering minor incidents into exciting tales. To dramatize her life, to crave the limelight, was inherent in Noel's character.

In spite of quarrels with Barbara, scoldings from Miss Bishop, and remonstrances from her father, Noel's early years at St Leonard's were by no means all gloom. There were pleasures too; simple ones, because the Streatfeilds had neither the means nor the inclination for anything extravagant, and frequently connected with Janet's love of nature.

There was Snowdrop Day in early spring, when a large house on the outskirts of Hastings opened its gardens for charity. Janet would take the children, and they would gaze in wonder at the great white drifts of snowdrops. On Good Fridays a picnic, with hot cross buns, would be packed up after the children's morning service, and they would be taken to a wood near Crowhurst where primroses grew in profusion. This was not a time for gazing. The church was decorated with primroses for Easter, and when the picnic had been eaten, the children filled their baskets with flowers. On Easter Day Janet hid eggs wrapped in coloured paper all over the garden. She hid them so well that half the day might pass – interrupted, of course, by the Easter services – before they were all found. They picked fruit in September, and gathered walnuts in October. 'I shall never forget those walnut afternoons,' Noel wrote. 'The walnuts had fallen off the trees, and you found them with your feet; for walnut gathering we always wore thick boots. Walnuts with their cases decaying give off a delicious smell; a smell which hung about us for days, as did the brown dye clinging to our hands.'[9]

Christmas, once Noel had swallowed her disappointment about her birthday, was fun too. The children made their own paperchains to decorate the nursery, linking strips of coloured tissue paper together with homemade paste. The rooms downstairs were smothered in ivy; the clock, the picture frames, the ornaments, half buried under evergreens. Janet would hang a few sprigs of mistletoe in the hall – surreptitiously, because William did not approve. Was he afraid one of the parish pussies might try to kiss him, Noel wondered, or was it that a curate might kiss one of his daughters?

One pleasure lasted all the year round – the pleasure of stories read aloud. In the evening quarrels and scoldings would be forgotten as the children settled down in the drawing room beside their mother's chair. Janet did not expect them just to sit still; she let them do things with their hands, to help them to concentrate. The books she read were chosen to suit the eldest child, and the younger ones gleaned what they could, which was often a surprising amount. Dickens and Jane Austen were tackled, as well as *Treasure Island*, *King Solomon's Mines* and *The Prisoner of Zenda* – stand-bys of the Edwardian nursery.

'When I think of my mother,' Ruth wrote, 'it is reading to us for at least an hour every evening. All the standard books were read to us in this way, with us sitting round the drawing room fire, drawing or sewing. Much of our education was shaky, but to have so many classics read in such happy surroundings was a good educational start.'[10]

3

The Odd One Out

When, many years later, Noel looked back on her childhood, she always claimed that she had been unhappy and misunderstood. Her sisters, on the whole, accepted their simple, uneventful lives, and found their own fulfilment inside the limited routine of the Vicarage; but as Noel grew older, she chafed furiously against all the restrictions which fettered her developing personality. 'I didn't belong to the environment in which I was born,'[1] she was to say; but it was an environment from which no escape seemed possible.

To begin with there were the physical restrictions. Middle class girls were kept as far as possible inside the sheltered world of home. Bill was sent away to school when he was eight, as was the tradition for boys, but Ruth, Noel and Barbara had virtually no independence. 'We were never allowed out of our Vicarage, except for short distances on well defined missions, unless there was a grown-up with us,'[2] Noel wrote. A maid or nursery governess walked to school with them in the morning, and fetched them home in the afternoon. A solitary shopping expedition was never even dreamed of.

There were restrictions too on making friends. Janet vetted all her children's acquaintances, and passed judgement on their suitability. 'No,' she might say, if they wanted to invite a particular school friend to tea. 'I don't think you can ask her. I don't call on her mother.' For the rules about 'calling' in Edwardian England were strict. Ladies paid formal afternoon calls on people who were socially acceptable to them. In St Leonard's the Vicar's wife would call on the wives of other professional men considered to be of equal rank with her husband – doctors, perhaps, or lawyers. Dentists, school teachers, even bank managers, were thought to be on a lower level, and were not visited by Janet; and she would certainly never call on the wife of a shopkeeper, unless he held some office in the church.

Although such fixed conventions no doubt smoothed the path of a shy woman like Janet, Noel found them vexatious in the extreme. She was always curious about other children, and there were so many with whom acquaintance was absolutely forbidden. She gazed longingly at them, the children whom she would never know, whose lives seemed much more interesting than her own. There were the rich children she glimpsed on train journeys, travelling grandly in first class carriages, while the Streatfeilds went third class; the families she watched on holiday, romping on the beach in careless freedom; the poor children in crowded homes, whom she saw when she delivered Christmas parcels with her mother. Though her curiosity about them had to go unsatisfied, she observed them all, and wove them into her day-dreams – mysterious, magical children, blissfully outside the stuffy Vicarage orbit.

The social life which the Streatfeild girls were allowed, was regulated by formal invitations. There was no casual dropping in at the houses of even approved friends, and other children were not encouraged to drop in at the Vicarage. If any children of lesser social status happened to be at the Vicarage at meal times – waiting to deliver a message, or helping with some parish chore – they ate in the kitchen with the servants.

Such treatment was not thought degrading or rude; it was the natural order of things. Indeed politeness, as she saw it, was something Janet insisted upon. But all too often good manners seemed to mean no more than an uninspiring set of taboos. 'Don't interrupt. Don't talk with your mouth full. Don't make a noise and disturb your father while he's writing his sermon.'

While Janet regulated the social side of life, William took charge of the religious side; and here the Streatfeild children found themselves faced with another problem. It never seems to have occurred to William that his children might not share his fervour, might not feel with him that Sunday was the happiest day of the week, might not rejoice as they sacrificed cake and jam and sweets in Lent. There was no discussion, and the children were quite unable to express their real feelings. They were obliged to acquiesce silently while their father created for himself an image of a devotedly Christian family, which was never entirely correct, and which, as they grew older, deviated further and further from the truth.

In a talk she gave, Noel described those childhood Sundays. 'They were a sad mistake, for it took years for any of us to outgrow the bad effects of them. We were called and given our prayer books, and before breakfast we had to learn the collect for the day by heart. Then of course came Bible reading. Then, after breakfast, we all had to say our catechism. My mother, who was I think sorry for us, used to make this a little more amusing than it might have been, by turning it into a competition. We all moved up or down a place, according to whether we got the answer right or not. I alone started at the bottom and remained there, because I could not be persuaded to answer the first question correctly. *What is your name? N or M?* My name happens to be Mary Noel, so for many years I stubbornly answered "Both!" At about half past ten we were dismissed from catechism in order to get dressed for Matins. From a very early age we attended the whole of this, including the sermon. After lunch we were read out loud to, not the books which were read aloud during the week; the Sunday book was always different. For some reason our Sunday books frequently seemed to be Sir Walter Scott. I have never been able to be fair to him since. The reading over, we were sent to get tidy for afternoon church. This was an enchanting children's service. My father was a most gifted story-teller, and year after year told a different story every Sunday afternoon. I don't think we really minded the afternoon service, but it was of course rather a lot of sitting still for children who had already been to Matins. Tea over there was sometimes a little more Sir Walter Scott, but usually we gathered round the piano and sang hymns till it was time to go to bed. Before getting into bed there was more Bible reading.'[3]

Into this carefully structured life Noel had, willy-nilly, to fit. The Streatfeilds were not unique. Plenty of other children, at that time, were being brought up on the same lines, guarded and fenced by similar barriers, their Sundays as strictly observed.

Those who conformed were happy, but conforming did not come easily to Noel.

The unspoken aim of such an upbringing was to instil a sense of quiet self-possession. A lady, Noel was made aware, should keep herself and her emotions in check. She should be conscientious and courteous, but cool, scrupulously self-denying though gracious to others, knowing that any unrestricted display of feelings flouted the rules of good taste. Slowly and painfully, through childhood and adolescence, Noel was forced into the mould. She learned reserve against the grain of her nature, but she learned it thoroughly. She grew eventually into the sort of woman who talked amusingly, but seldom scattered rash confidences around; and whose books were full of characters behaving as she had been trained to behave, concealing their worries, biting back their tears, keeping a stiff upper lip.

That was in the future, the end product of many a Vicarage argument; for while guiding Ruth and Barbara into the paths of righteousness was comparatively easy, and while Bill, at the age of eight, accepted his banishment to boarding school with approved stoicism, Noel found endless causes for rebellion.

Clothes, like the Sunday catechism, provided one of Noel's earliest and most long-standing grievances. She was to make numerous claims, in books and lectures, that as a child she had been very badly dressed. Photographs of this time give a rather different impression. William's unmarried sister, Aunt Sylvia, made most of the girls' clothes, and they were practical, hard-wearing, and rather ugly; but when Noel's imagination took over, the simplest garments could be nightmarishly transformed. For school there were blouses made of a striped cotton called galatea, with big collars and braid trimmings, worn with navy skirts. Sunday dresses were of white cambric, a fine linen, tied at the waist with broad satin sashes. They had scalloped hems, rows of minute tucks, and lace collars which pricked dreadfully when they had been starched. For playing in the nursery, the girls slipped into yoked pinafores which Janet had made and embroidered; and she also made them straw hats trimmed with butter muslin for summer. A horse once bit a piece out of Noel's.

She had, perhaps, one genuine cause for resentment. Everything was handed down from Ruth. Nobody, it seemed, really cared whether the clothes fitted or suited her; and, argue as she might, she just had to make do with them. Some had already been passed to Ruth by a wealthier cousin, Joan Streatfeild, so that by the time Noel wore them they were third hand. Complaints were of no avail, for to be clean and tidy was all that mattered. 'Hygiene,' Noel remembered bitterly, 'was miles ahead of charm.'[4]

When she was eleven, an American family came to St Leonard's for a year, and made the acquaintance of the Streatfeilds. They had a daughter called Roberta, about Noel's age, whose clothes filled Noel with envious longings. Roberta's mother remarked one day that 'she thought you couldn't take too much trouble to make a girl look cute.'[5] Noel was dumbfounded. That mothers might say such things was a revelation.

Her sense of being badly dressed contributed to the inferiority complex which weighed upon Noel during those years at St Leonard's. Circumstances made it almost inevitable. Because she knew that Ruth and Barbara were admired for their prettiness, she became convinced that she was plain. Once again photographs show that she was mistaken. Her wide forehead, and well-spaced, vividly blue eyes were striking, though the disconsolate droop of her mouth – 'Noel's dog's mouth', as her family called it – did not help her appearance. By the time she had reached her teens, belief in her own plainness was deeply ingrained, an intrinsic part of her ever-increasing certainty that she was the odd one out in the family.

She was the naughty child – that had been established in the kindergarten, and her reputation did not improve as she moved up the school. Partly she enjoyed her notoriety – 'What pride (I felt) in making the whole class laugh, what joy in doing something a little odd'[6] – but her bad reports blighted the end of every term, especially when Ruth's and Barbara's were always good. 'Term after term,' Noel recalled, 'I would loiter by every drain, longing to post my report down it, but I was always prevented by one of my sisters saying: "It will do no good for if you haven't got it Daddy will suppose it's worse than it is." Which was not true for no one could imagine my report worse than it was.'[7] She had, her father told her, as he sorrowfully lectured her on the grief she caused God and her family, a difficult nature.

But although she had the miserable conviction that she was plain and badly dressed, and although she knew she was troublesome and stupid at school, she maintained the odd certainty that she was special. It counterbalanced the inferiority complex. So instead of meekly acknowledging her failings, she tried to compensate for them by a cocky argumentativeness, which wore everyone down. 'I grew more difficult to get on with every day. My brother and my sisters put up with me, and for peace and a quiet life gave in to me more often than they should. "For goodness sake don't argue with her, it only makes her worse." Their friends did not like me much, and hoped I would be out when they came to the house. Most of the parties we gave were spoiled by me. I was sure nobody would like anything I suggested, and neither should they have, for my ideas were usually silly, and too grand; but I argued and argued about what we ought to do and ought to eat, until, exhausted, the family said, "Oh, all right." '[8]

Sadly, her mother seemed unable to help and guide her through these turbulent years. Unalike in character and temperament, they totally failed to understand each other. Noel, the extrovert, the show-off, horrified Janet, while to Noel her gentle mother seemed hopelessly vague and ineffectual. With Ruth and Barbara, Janet was patient and loving, but Noel's vagaries were beyond her comprehension. She never realized how much this difficult daughter craved love and admiration. And then, indifferent as she was to her own looks and clothes, she honestly could not see why Noel minded these things so much. Relations between them were sometimes strained almost to breaking point.

Ruth kept the peace whenever she could, but Barbara stirred things up. Without precisely meaning to be spiteful, she would tactlessly blurt out remarks like, 'Look, Mother. Noel's spilled the ink!' which were intensely provocative. She and Noel quarrelled and fought daily.

Apart from Ruth, the person Noel loved best was her father.

Stern he might sometimes be, but his unswerving commitment to his vocation seemed to her deeply enviable. She longed for the importance which would be hers if she too devoted herself to some great calling. But what could it be? She had no idea, and her ambitions swung wildly from nurse to tennis champion, from singer to prison reformer, like her great-great-grandmother, Elizabeth Fry.

(Some interesting similarities between Noel and her great-great-grandmother can be discovered in Elizabeth Fry's diaries. One entry from her teens reads – 'I must not mump when my sisters are admired, and I am not'; and later, recalling herself as a girl, she wrote – 'I was considered and called very stupid and obstinate . . . I think having the name of stupid really tended to make me so' – words which might have been written by Noel.)

Noel certainly felt a kinship for the Streatfeild side of the family which she never felt for the Venns. The Streatfeild grandparents, who had been so kind to Ruth, were favourites of Noel's too. When their grandfather had retired, he and their grandmother had settled down at Chart's Edge, a large, comfortable house, a mile outside Westerham in Kent. Here they carried on a relaxed way of life, very appealing to Noel after the tensions of the Vicarage.

'My father was the eldest of a family of eight boys and two girls,' Ruth wrote. 'I can still remember the general atmosphere of their home, which, I feel, represented the best of the late Victorian age. With all these young people growing up and going out into the world it was a very lively household; they had great affection for one another, and were amused by the different quirks of one another's character. They all sang, and were helpful in the parish in a very free and easy way. They sang minstrel songs at "penny readings", and on Sunday evenings hymn after hymn, not from goodness, but because they liked lifting up their voices. There were good-tempered maids, and dear Grand-Nannie who looked after me, and plenty of gardeners, and flowers everywhere. The food and drink were enjoyed, and although it was a proper clerical household, with family prayers and grace before meals, there was a feeling for gracious living, and an enjoyment of God's blessings, that I never met again in my austere Vicarage life.'⁹

Grand-Nannie had looked after William and his brothers and sisters when they were children. By the time Noel knew her, she was semi-retired, with her own private domain on the top floor of Chart's Edge; but she still kept a strict eye on the family, dosing anyone who looked poorly with her special brand of beef tea, which she called Golden Sovereigns, and always ready to tell again the stories of family life, which Noel loved. She could describe the beautiful pair of hand-sewn French boots which had once been given to the little Streatfeilds. 'They fitted none of the children, but Nannie treasured them, and whenever any of the children stayed with richer relations, the boots were taken, and put out to clean daily, to fox the servants that her children wore hand-sewn boots. With the boots went a dressing gown of great beauty, which, since all the children used it when they were away visiting, she christened "brotherly love" . . . . Whenever she was packing for one of the children, she was heard to murmur, "and on the top goes brotherly love." '¹⁰ How reassuring it was, Noel thought, to meet someone else who knew that appearances mattered. All the loyal, kind-hearted old nurses she put into her stories, were a tribute to Grand-Nannie.

Visits to Chart's Edge were full of fun and adventure. If some of the uncles were there, they could usually be persuaded into the family game of funerals. The garden would be searched for dead creatures, and, if none could be found, a crow was shot. Then all the family would dress up in black, with black bows on the dogs' collars, and, led by an uncle in a surplice, they would process up and down, carrying the box which served as a coffin, ringing a bell, and chanting Juliana Ewing's poem *The Burial of a Linnet*. The game could be endlessly prolonged, before the box was buried with solemnly hilarious rites.

One visit to Chart's Edge took place just after Janet had read *The Pilgrim's Progress* to her children; and, for no particular reason, they decided that Bunyan's City Beautiful must lie on the far side of Westerham Hill. Such quaint notions were perfectly permissible at Chart's Edge. The carriage was ordered, the gardener climbed onto the box, and off they drove to Westerham

Hill. 'At the top we got out,' Noel recalled. 'Below us, miles away, lay London. It had been an overcast morning, but as we gazed the sun came out, and was reflected from the far away roof of the Crystal Palace. "Look!" we cried. "The City Beautiful!" '[11]

Compared with the delights of Chart's Edge, the ordinary family holidays were usually wretched failures. Neither William nor Janet seemed to know how to plan a holiday sensibly. They would rent a house for a month, as families often did, taking their own servants to look after them, so there was no change in the menu. The houses too frequently proved to be primitive cottages, with no running water, in remote corners of Wales, or East Anglia, or Derbyshire. There was never enough to do. The rain seemed to lash down incessantly, except when it was unbearably hot; and such books and games as the children had brought were quickly exhausted. If they were at the seaside William insisted on a daily bathe, but he was the only person who even pretended to enjoy it. For Ruth and Noel the one great pleasure was watching other families, although they could never speak to them. Miles from home they might be, but the same insurmountable barriers existed.

In the black moments of childhood and adolescence it sometimes seemed to Noel that few things ever went right. And yet, unrecognized, there was a silver lining to the black clouds. Noel's miseries were nourishing her imagination. The best escape from reality lay in day-dreams. They provided a sure refuge when she felt lonely and misunderstood, the odd one out in the family. Her imaginative life flourished, and her books offer a clue to at least one of her favourite fantasies. It was the dream of being chosen when all seemed stacked against her; of being hailed – plain, stupid and tiresome though people thought her – as the special person she knew herself to be.

She used this dream in *The Painted Garden*. 'Jane was the difficult one. Jane was the inartistic one. Jane was the plain one.' Yet Jane is surprisingly chosen for the chief part in a film of *The Secret Garden*. Noel used the same theme in *Tennis Shoes* when awkward, bumptious Nicky (Noel's most brilliant self-portrait) is picked to receive the coveted course of tennis lessons that people expected would go to her talented and charming sister, Susan. She used it in *White Boots*, where the prospect of being a world champion skater opens before frail, skinny Harriet, and not the universally admired Lalla; and she used it in *Curtain Up* and *Wintle's Wonders*.

She dreamed of getting away from Vicarage life. Sometimes she pretended she was an only child, for only children seemed to have everything they wanted. 'They were always exquisitely dressed; not for them passed-down clothes. When there was a fancy dress party, not for them mother's efforts with butter muslin and paper. A dressmaker was called in, and the dress was made of taffeta and silk.'[12] There was the perennial dream of boarding school. The threat of being sent, as a punishment, to a school for the daughters of poor clergy was sometimes held over Noel's head – unavailingly. It sounded to her like heaven.

Amongst all her unhappiness there was a strangely detached strand. She had the ability to stand outside herself, and analyse the very troubles which were making her miserable. Later she was to be very good at describing children who felt misunderstood, because she had been so clearly aware of the feeling within herself. She was often to claim that she had a 'blotting paper memory' for childhood, a gift of total recall that she deliberately fostered from an early age. As each new injustice enveloped her, she vowed to herself that she would always remember, as long as she lived, just how she had felt.

School was a problem that seemed to have no solution. She frankly detested it. Lessons at the Hastings and St Leonard's Ladies' College were dull and uninspired. There was very little art, and no drama, music, games or dancing. Poetry was confined to a few drawing room pieces, selected by the teachers for the girls to learn by heart. Because of her early struggles with reading, Noel had been branded as backward, and she never made much effort to shake off this reputation; indeed she enhanced it, sometimes, with spectacularly bad marks. She perfected the technique of sitting through lessons without hearing a word, lost in a dream; and the only incentive to work was the fear that Barbara might be moved from the class below, and catch her up.

The cleverness of her sisters was just one of the depressing aspects of school life. At the annual prize-givings she sat scowling in the background, while the successes of Ruth and Barbara were applauded. On one awful occasion Ruth was kept at home with asthma, and Noel was asked to collect her prizes. She never forgot the humiliation of being congratulated by the chief guest in front of a hall full of girls who knew she was a dunce.

'What I think a high-spirited girl, who may not be good at her books, needs above everything is to have individual attention, so that somebody finds out something at which she can shine . . . The day a talent is found and fostered is the day when a girl starts to grow up gracefully.'[13] This was Noel's conclusion years later, but nobody at the Ladies' College gave her any individual attention, and she was left to foster her own talents, with disastrous results.

One thing she enjoyed, and was good at, was writing, and when she was fourteen she had the idea of starting a class magazine. Other girls contributed, but most of the writing was done by Noel. Wildly exciting romantic serials, poems, and mild snippets of school gossip poured from her pen; she even invented competitions. The magazine was successful, for, in a curious way, Noel was popular. Amongst all the dozens of well-behaved young ladies, she was unique, and everyone knew it. So for six months the magazine prospered, until, by some fatal mischance, it came into the hands of Miss Bishop, the headmistress.

Why Miss Bishop reacted so savagely is a mystery. A magazine sounds a harmless outlet for a difficult teenager. But Noel was marked out as a girl who never did anything right, and for her to have started a class magazine without permission must be a gross impertinence. She was summoned to the headmistress's study, where Miss Bishop tore the precious magazine to shreds, and forbade her to write another issue. This searing injustice provoked Noel to her worst act of defiance. She invented the Little Grey Bows Society.

The aim of the society was to be rude to the teachers. Every girl who joined got a little grey bow as a membership badge, and was awarded a hundred marks, one of which was docked each time she was polite in class. It was intended that the person left with the most marks at the end of term should win a prize. Unfortunately one of the members lost her nerve, and reported the society to Miss Bishop. It was the last straw. Miss Bishop wrote to William and Janet, requesting them to remove their middle daughter from the school at the end of term.

4

A Thoroughly Theatrical Child

If William and Janet had, at this point, looked back over Noel's troubled life, one trait would have stood out clearly. It could be seen when she acted Circe in the Amberley nursery, when she flicked ink pellets and mimicked Miss Bishop in the kindergarten, when she pestered her sisters and brother into adopting her absurdly grand schemes for their parties, and when she launched her magazine and the Little Grey Bows Society. She burned with a desire to make life more dramatic. She was, as she recalled in old age, 'a thoroughly theatrical child', and if no one else would provide a show in which she could play the star part, she would provide it herself.

There was an attractively honest side to her nature. She craved attention, but she needed to earn it fairly by her own efforts, good or bad. She could not enjoy the drama of collecting Ruth's prizes, since it put her in a false position.

Now she was the heroine of a new drama – the girl who was to be expelled from school. She could not help swaggering a little in front of her classmates. None of them would ever be expelled; they were so depressingly well-behaved. Secretly she hoped she might be sent to that school for the daughters of poor clergy. An air of mystery seemed to be hanging over the Vicarage, with discussions going on behind closed doors. Naturally the girls were told nothing – they never were – but Noel was sure that letters were being written about her, arranging some momentous change in her life.

But when at last the mystery was explained, she discovered, to her surprise, that it was not specifically to do with her. William had been appointed Vicar of Eastbourne, and they were leaving St Leonard's almost at once. There was to be a new parish, a new home, and a new school for Ruth and Barbara as well as Noel.

The move took place in February 1911. Eastbourne lay fifteen miles westward along the coast from St Leonard's. It was a large, important resort, planned, with its squares, wide roads, and opulent hotels, for stylish living. Anything vulgar was excluded. There were no shops along the seafront, fairs and funfairs were banned, dogs were even forbidden to bark on the beach. Male and female bathers were carefully segregated in different parts of the sea, and all dressing and undressing had to be done in the privacy of bathing machines. Most of the visitors, and a good proportion of the residents, were consciously and conventionally middle class. Their speech was primly emasculated, for anyone who used dialect words or mispronounced their vowels was despised. One of the reasons why Noel was later to enjoy Cockney speech so much was for its contrast with the over-refined, impoverished speech she had heard in her youth.

Although the church of St Mary the Virgin, where William was instituted, was the parish church of Eastbourne, it was not in the fashionable centre of the town. Both church and Vicarage were in the picturesque 'Old Town', inland from the sea, and under the downs. The church was part Norman, part medieval, and its grassy churchyard was surrounded by a cluster of pretty cottages. The Vicarage was a few minutes walk away, and a pleasant contrast from the spiky grandiosity of St Peter's Vicarage, for it was a rambling white house, ivyclad, with a large garden and delightful views.

Janet was pleased with the garden, and Ruth with the small room given to her for a studio, but Noel, as usual, was dissatisfied. A charming exterior could not hide the fact that it was a Vicarage, and she loathed Vicarages. She sniffed as she made her first exploration, and recognized its unmistakable 'beeswaxish, hassocks-cum-parcels-for-the-jumble-sale odour.'[1] The inevitable linoleum was laid on the hall floor, ready for the shuffling feet of the callers who would crowd the benches set out for them. Life in Eastbourne, Noel guessed, would be just like life in St Leonard's – dull, spartan and churchy.

In her novel *Myra Carroll*, one of the characters accurately reflects teenage Noel's feelings. 'I hate rush and flap and tear.

Vicarages are full of it. Bishops dashing in for Confirmations and losing buttons off their gaiters. Men's Societies meeting at the same time as Communicants' Guilds, and only one room free. A never ending roar for buns for school treats . . . Urgent notes to be dropped, parish magazines to be dropped, rows of desiccated females sitting with their feet on oilcloth in a roaring draught in the Vicarage hall. No peace, no elegance of living.'[2]

The rush and tear that the Streatfeilds had known in St Leonard's was intensified. William's ability and hard work had been noticed by the ecclesiastical hierarchy, and the move was an important promotion. Besides being Vicar of Eastbourne, he was a Rural Dean, with pastoral responsibility for all the clergy living in the Eastbourne area. Services, meetings, and duties of every kind multiplied. He had never cared for entertaining, but now he thought it right to invite his fellow clergy to dinner parties – a mixed blessing for them, as the food was poor, and the wine often undrinkable. William never touched alcohol, and whenever any was left in the bottle after dinner, he added it to the remains from other bottles, preserved in the cellar, and innocently offered the resulting brew to the next party of clergy.

It was William who chose the girls' school, one very different from the Hastings and St Leonard's Ladies' College. His reasons for selecting it were simple. He wanted a school within easy walking distance for the sake of delicate Ruth, where the girls did not wear uniform. William disapproved of girls in school uniform. From Noel's point of view Laleham was a good choice. It was a much smaller school than the Ladies' College, and so the discipline was more relaxed. There was a civilized atmosphere, with no clanging bells to marshal milling hordes of pupils, and the classrooms opened off a carpeted hall instead of long, bare passages. The approach to education was more enlightened too. Girls were expected to take an interest in the arts, and to be knowledgeable about painting and music as well as maths and grammar.

Nevertheless there were disadvantages, and Noel, being Noel, was quick to spot them. She found she was still considered very backward. The years of time-wasting could not readily be made up, and once again she was placed firmly at the bottom of the class. Like her great-great-grandmother, Elizabeth Fry, being labelled stupid tended to make her so; and as there were, in those days, no exams to pass, she drifted heedlessly along, unable to spell or punctuate properly, and hopeless at maths.

The headmistress, Miss Wilson, was a cultured woman. She prided herself on her appreciation of the arts, and she read poetry aloud beautifully. But, like Miss Bishop, she was a formidable personality. She wore *pince-nez* on a gold chain, and had an alarming habit of flicking them off sharply when she was annoyed. She did not fly into rages, as Miss Bishop had done, but she could be coolly cutting. A fellow pupil of Noel's once innocently asked her the identity of a bird they had seen on the daily school walk, and received the devastating reply – 'My dear child, if you don't know what a hedgesparrow is, I'm sorry for you.' It was Noel's misfortune that neither of her headmistresses had the sympathy, or the perception, to find and foster her talents. Miss Wilson, who was an ardent churchwoman, quickly came to have a high regard for William, and invited him to hold weekly services at Laleham; and it was said that, because of him, she smiled on all the Vicarage girls. Certainly Ruth had the privilege of using the school studio whenever she liked, but backward Noel never felt that any particular favours went her way.

The worst disadvantage was that the Streatfeilds were day-girls in what was mainly a boarding school, and so they suffered from a constant, frustrating sense of being slightly out of things. So many of the school's most interesting activities took place in the evenings, or at week-ends, when the day-girls were not there. They were second-class citizens; they could not hope for popularity among the more numerous boarders; and Noel's inferiority complex deepened.

Her worries about being plain and badly dressed reached their peak at this point in her middle teens. Looking back, she spoke of herself as pallid and spotty, her hair 'hanks of dullish green stuff that looked like string'.[3] On coming to Eastbourne, Janet had at once immersed herself in the garden, and took even less interest in her daughters' clothes. Over a childish liberty bodice, and the flannel knickers and black woollen stockings that never quite met, Noel had to squeeze herself into dresses made for Ruth's slimmer figure. She bulged, and she was horribly aware of it.

Eastbourne was not the best setting for a self-conscious girl of fifteen. It was much more fashionable than St Leonard's. On Sunday mornings in summer, people gathered along the Esplanade between twelve and one for the so-called church parade, when visitors strolled up and down in all the contemporary glories of satin and lace dresses, feathered hats and fringed parasols. They carried their prayer books as a badge of respectability, but everyone knew their chief object was to show off their clothes. Noel knew all about the parade, and chafed inwardly for the day when she could for ever abandon passed-down dresses and homemade straw hats, and shine with the most stylish.

In fact her proneness to self-dramatization led to quite unnecessary fears and anxieties. To her friends she was neither the fright nor the dunce she thought herself. ' "Stupid?" No,' one school contemporary wrote. 'She always had brains, but she wasn't interested much, I think, in school. I remember vividly doing her sums for her while she wrote pages and pages of essays. She was interested in writing. "Plain"? She had lovely eyes, full pouting lips, rosy cheeks, and was lots of fun. "Badly dressed"? Well, yes, because there was always the perpetual shortage of money. I don't remember her being naughty, but I think she was a bit of a handful, except in the things she was really interested in.'[4]

And here Laleham unexpectedly offered an exciting opportunity. Noel had not been there long when she heard some surprising news. The school was to put on a production of Euripides' *Alcestis*, in translation, at the end of the summer term, under the direction of Miss Hoste, who taught Greek mythology. Noel's hopes soared. Though she had often been made painfully aware of her lack of accomplishments, for she could not paint like Ruth, or play the piano like Barbara, and on the violin, which she reluctantly learned, she could hardly do more than scrape out a mournful hymn tune, 'Art thou weary, art thou languid', she knew that she could act.

One shining strand had run through the dreariness of parish life at St Leonard's. Amateur theatricals were popular, and from time to time Noel and her sisters had helped with entertainments for church social evenings or Mothers' Union parties; and Noel, with her dramatic talents, had excelled. She knew the intoxication of waiting on the stage, or in the half light of the wings, for the moment when the curtains creaked slowly open, and she could throw aside all her everyday trials, and live only in her part.

So far nothing too difficult had been asked of Noel and her sisters. When they were very young they performed action songs which Janet taught them, and they progressed to little sketches. In one, Noel played a waxwork slowly brought to life by a magician. But her greatest success was an imitation of her father. A box was carried onto the stage, its lid was removed, and Noel emerged, dressed as a gollywog in a blue tailcoat, with a blackened face and a woolly wig. Someone pretended to wind her up, and she began at once to imitate all William's best known actions and mannerisms, finally running off the stage exactly as he always ran to church, which brought the curtains together in a storm of applause. Hot and excited, Noel took her bow, savouring the glory of the moment.

William did not mind the imitation. He, with his brothers and sisters, had done just such things when they were children, and anything which his congregation enjoyed was welcome. The girls had the satisfaction of knowing they had done something to help their father – their contributions to parish life were usually minimal – and Noel in particular learned a surprising amount from these unsophisticated entertainments. She knew that she must pick up her cues quickly, so that the audience's attention did not wander, and she knew that it was fatal to speak through a laugh. She might be backward at school, but she had no difficulty in memorizing a part. Altogether she was very much at home on the stage.

These experiences fuelled her day-dreams. She began to imagine herself as a great actress, sweeping onto a brilliantly-lit stage, holding a vast audience spellbound, gracefully acknowledging their applause. She heard the news about the Laleham Greek play with a surge of excitement. Surely at last her talents would be recognized, and she would be offered a leading role.

As so often, she was doomed to disappointment. Because the rehearsals were to be held in the evening, all the chief parts went to the boarders, and Noel had to be satisfied with a place in the chorus. How successfully the girls tackled their classical tragedy on the Laleham lawn one hot July afternoon, Noel did not remember afterwards. The memory was clouded by her own humiliation. A hairdresser arrived at school on the morning of the play to contrive Grecian hairstyles for all the cast; but in spite of pins and curling-tongs, Noel's lank straight hair defeated him. The day-girls were sent home for lunch, and her walks to and from the Vicarage completed the wreck of Noel's chignon. She appeared on the lawn in her Grecian costume, with hair half up and half down, shedding pins, and scarlet with embarrassment.

The experience did not destroy her confidence. Parish entertainments were needed at Eastbourne as they had been at St Leonard's, and Noel began to spread her wings. When a new roof was needed for the parish hall, the idea of putting on a children's play to raise money was suggested, and the Streatfeild girls took charge. That was the first of several such ventures. Because many published playlets were very feeble, Noel began to write some herself, for the children from the church school to perform. Afterwards the scripts were lost, but Noel enjoyed writing them immensely, and she soon took on responsibility for whole productions. The children loved taking part in them, and Noel discovered what was, for her, the rare pleasure of pleasing other people.

So far she had only been to the theatre twice. A prejudice against it, the legacy of their puritan ancestry, lingered on among the Venns. They felt instinctively that playhouses were hotbeds of temptation, and acting an incentive to deceit. An elderly cousin of Janet's told Noel fervently, if irrationally – 'I should never care to go inside a theatre. How terrible if you died there!'[5] William had neither the time nor the inclination for theatregoing, so the two plays Noel had seen had been uncommon treats. Janet had taken Ruth and Noel to see *Alice in Wonderland* after Ruth had had a particularly painful time at the dentist's; and some Streatfeild relations had once given the girls a marvellous evening, with supper, and chocolates, and seats at a musical comedy called *The Country Girl*. Both occasions were indelibly printed on Noel's memory. She used *Alice in Wonderland* for Pauline's first play in *Ballet Shoes*, while the glamour of *The Country Girl* fed her imagination for months. In the tradition of the time, it was lavishly staged, with a huge cast, and spectacular costumes and effects. Noel was to describe how she sat 'in a kind of glazed, uncritical blur, so I could swear that at one moment, holding arches of flowers, one set of girls danced on the heads of another.'[6]

But besides these two plays there was an annual treat, which had begun while the family lived in St Leonard's, and continued after the move to Eastbourne. Every summer the children were taken to a theatre on the pier, to see a performance by Lila Field's Little Wonders.

Lila Field, a German by origin, though she had spent most of her life in England, ran a stage and dancing academy for children in London. Besides training them to act and dance, she found engagements for them in London productions, sometimes in plays she had written herself – young Noel Coward appeared in a play of hers called *The Goldfish* in 1910 – and every summer she took a troupe of about twenty of her best pupils, the Little Wonders, on a tour of seaside resorts, where they played twice a night, and often at matinées too, before enthusiastic audiences. Hastings and Eastbourne were always on their itinerary.

Their programmes were a hotch-potch of singing, dancing, and revue sketches, performed against the crudest of backcloths, with little scenery, and accompanied by an upright piano, two violins and a cello; but for Ruth and Noel they were occasions of pure ecstasy. They sat through the shows in a trance of happiness, their eyes glued to the stage, and for weeks afterwards they talked and dreamed about those marvellous children. Ruth filled her drawing book with ballet dancers, and Noel 'wove endless stories round that fabulous dancing troupe, sometimes including herself among them. Those lucky, lucky children, so miraculously free from the boring life led by other girls, especially girls whose home was a Vicarage.'[7]

Drawing and day-dreaming were not really enough. Noel and Ruth longed to know more about the children. Who were they?

How had they become Little Wonders? Who looked after them? Were they paid? Nobody they knew could answer these urgent questions; and the feeling was clearly conveyed that the child performers were in any case, like so many other children, on the wrong side of the class barrier. They were not the sort of children whom Ruth and Noel could ever know.

William's and Janet's views about dancing followed the rather strange logic of the time. Ballet did not meet with their approval. Ballerinas revealed far too much leg, something no Christian woman could ever wish to do. But some kinds of dancing were permitted, as long as they did not degenerate into showing off. Girls should be taught to move gracefully, and to be at ease in a ballroom; and with this aim in mind, Noel and her sisters had attended a dancing class in St Leonard's.

The class was held in the drawing room of a private house. The pupils began with a few loosening exercises, and went on to ballroom dancing, national dancing – which meant Irish jigs and Scottish reels – and Greek dancing, when they took off their shoes, and swayed about in graceful attitudes. The Streatfeild girls were not natural dancers, and being tall they were usually relegated to the back row of the class. Before long there was the customary humiliation over clothes to endure as well. A sudden craze for 'skirt dancing' swept the class, and the other girls all appeared in immensely full, accordion-pleated dresses, which still decorously covered their legs when the hems were lifted shoulder high. Noel and her sisters, in their white Sunday frocks, were obliged to sit out and watch. When they finally persuaded Janet that they must have accordion pleats, the craze was over. The other girls were now in brightly-coloured Spanish skirts, dancing with castanets.

An incident which took place at the class one day illuminated the gulf between the dancing which Noel was allowed, and the dancing of the Little Wonders. Another child brought her cousin, who happened to be a professional dancer. The nannies and parents, who sat round the room, tut-tutted disapprovingly, and the other children stared doubtfully at the newcomer. Presently she was invited to dance, and, rising onto her pointes, she began to spin and pirouette, kicking up her legs. Talented she

may have been, but the applause which followed her performance was lukewarm. It seemed vulgar in a private drawing room.
Nice, well brought up children did not dance like that.

The sense that they were beyond the social pale increased the
allure of the child dancers for renegade Noel. The more she saw
of the Little Wonders, the more avidly interested in them and
their dancing she became. When she and her sisters went to
Laleham, they found that the only dancing classes were held for
boarders on Saturday mornings, so Noel's lessons ceased. It did
not matter. In her vivid imagination she could enjoy dancing
even more, undistracted by her own incompetence.

Miss Wilson, the headmistress, was interested in ballet, and so
were several of the girls. They collected the picture postcards of
Anna Pavlova, the famous ballerina, which in those days were
sold as 'pin-ups'. Noel pored over them whenever she had a
chance. 'I can see (those postcards) still in my mind's eye,' she
wrote more than sixty years later; 'that magic and beauty of
movement, caught for ever in a piece of cardboard.'[8]

Anna Pavlova was considered by English audiences to be
unrivalled in the world of dancing. In 1911, when Noel first saw
her picture, she was already thirty, but her dancing was as
exquisite as ever; while her deceptively frail, romantic appearance, and the airy grace of every movement, combined with her
strong personality, made her quite unforgettable. In 1910 she had
danced a London season at the Palace Theatre. Some of the
Laleham girls had seen her, and talked eagerly about her. Noel
treasured every scrap of information, building it into her dream
world.

Then, in the autumn of 1911, the great impresario, Serge
Diaghileff, brought his Russian ballet to London. English audiences were used to individual ballerinas, like Pavlova, but they
had never seen a big ballet company before, and the impact was
shattering. Everyone who possibly could, thronged to the performances, and talked of Diaghileff's magic. It was not just the
perfect dancing of his principals – Anna Pavlova, Vaslav Nij-
insky, Tamara Karsavina, and others – thrilling though this was;
the productions themselves were exciting and spectacular
beyond anything yet seen on the London stage. Diaghileff was a

patron of musicians, painters and choreographers, as well as dancers, and he brought them all together in a sensational riot of colour, sound and movement.

Miss Wilson had already seen the Russian ballet in Paris, and knew that it was something her girls must not miss. Notes were sent to the parents, explaining that she would take a party of pupils up to London for a matinée. Poor Noel knew at once that she would not be able to go. Even if it were financially possible, William would not have approved. She tried to resign herself to the misery of being left behind, and learning as much as she could afterwards, at second hand.

Probably she made a nuisance of herself by pestering the lucky ones who had been to London with endless questions. Nobody could guess just how passionately she yearned to hear every detail. Her stream of questions, fired across the school luncheon table, annoyed Miss Wilson. Enthusiasm must be tempered with discipline, and Noel was altogether too vehement. Flicking off her *pince-nez*, she silenced Noel with a cutting reprimand.

Scarlet, biting back the tears, Noel tried now to close her ears to the siren talk. The injustice seared her. Everyone else could see the Russian ballet; but she, who would have appreciated it most, was denied the chance, and snubbed for merely asking questions. Under her turmoil of inferiority and resentment, real desperation was growing. Would she ever see the wonderful dancing she longed for?

She had two years to wait; and then, in 1913, Lila Field's Little Wonders came as usual to Eastbourne Pier, bringing a new star. She had been born Edris Stannus; and, although Ruth and Noel knew nothing about her, she was from a background which the Streatfeilds would have found quite socially acceptable, for she was the daughter of an army officer, with a background of Irish landed gentry. Like Ruth and Noel, she had begun dancing in a decorous private class, but she had not been satisfied. In spite of the opposition of her teacher, who had the inevitable horror of professional dancers, she had insisted on going to Lila Field's academy for a proper training. Later she was to be known to the world as Ninette de Valois.

The Little Wonders had a new act, a series of precocious

imitations of the contemporary stars of stage and ballet. Ninette de Valois danced Pavlova's famous solo, the Dying Swan. Although the dance was not technically difficult, the interpretation was breath-taking. Encored night after night, it held Noel and Ruth spellbound, as nothing before had ever done.

Ninette de Valois was, Noel recorded, 'an aristocratic-looking child, with long hair, which, in my memory, curled at the ends . . . She looked about twelve, but what a twelve year old! How infinitely removed from our gym-tunicked, bulging selves . . . Perhaps some might say that the Dying Swan was far too ambitious an effort for a child, that all too many children were styling themselves little Pavlovas; but I doubt if such things matter. What does matter is that Ninette de Valois was given the gift to open another child's eyes to the beauty of movement allied to wonderful music. Her dancing of the swan was to me perfection, and when you have the good fortune to see perfection, it changes your life.'[9]

It started Noel on the path to *Ballet Shoes*, and fame.

5

Emancipation

When she described the impact Ninette de Valois' dancing had on her, Noel spoke of her seventeen-year-old self as if she were still a child. This was characteristic of the time. As long as they were at school most middle class teenagers were considered children. They were sheltered and protected, hearing and learning only what those in authority chose for them. 'Strange though it may seem today,' Noel wrote in 1956, 'when children are expected to know not only what is going on at home, but all over the world, in schoolrooms before the First World War there was abysmal ignorance. Obviously there were enlightened homes where the topics of the day were discussed with the children, but it was more usual to keep serious talk out of the schoolrooms, and it was certainly kept out of ours.'[1] 'Children were supposed to be children,' she wrote elsewhere, 'shut off from grown-up cares and grown-up chores.'[2]

The Streatfeild girls neither helped with the housework nor read the newspapers. In their family circle certain attitudes were simply not open to question. Normal people, as far as they knew, always voted Conservative, belonged to the Church of England, believed in the British Empire, and supported the Cavaliers against the Roundheads. William, a typical late Victorian, disapproved of women holding political views, and he particularly detested the Suffragettes. Mrs Pankhurst, the Suffragette leader, was once invited to speak at Eastbourne, and someone rashly suggested that Noel and Barbara might present flowers to her. Only over his dead body, was William's horrified response; and Noel was left disappointed, not because Mrs Pankhurst meant anything to her, but because the fleeting hope of a new dress for the occasion had been dashed.

In the conventional society of Eastbourne there was no one to direct the girls' eyes towards wider horizons. Their parents were engrossed in their own concerns, and opportunities to spend time with their daughters were missed.

Looking back, Noel was inclined to blame her mother for neglect. She thought her too detached and casual, and not the guide and helper that a mother ought to be. Her sisters, who were closer to Janet in temperament, viewed her more sympathetically. They realized, as undomesticated Noel never did, what hours were consumed by the tiresome chores of an impoverished household, like altering clothes, turning sheets sides to middles, and balancing a tight budget. They appreciated too, as Noel did not, the sense of duty which drove their mother out to visit poor homes, the hospital and the workhouse.

Though she often felt alienated from her mother, Noel was much more ready to understand how her father's vocation separated him from the family. Already he was becoming what people were still calling him years after his death, 'the best Vicar Eastbourne ever had.' The claims of his parishioners were paramount, and instances of his kindness to them were innumerable. He was out helping them, talking to them, praying with and for them, from early in the morning until late at night, pausing only for hastily snatched meals. A neighbour recalled how 'he seldom passed my house, going out from the Vicarage, except he was running, but never failing to recognize everyone.'[3]

An endearing glimpse of him was given by someone who remembered his children's services. 'One afternoon he said he was very concerned about the bits of paper and rubbish left along the paths in the churchyard, and he also told us gently that we were getting noisy when coming into church. To remedy all this, he suggested we helped to keep the paths tidy by picking up any rubbish and putting it into the dustbin; and that if anyone was noisy, we quietly said "Ssh!", reminding them they were in God's house. Listening intently, we waited for the questions which ended the service. We had our answers ready. "Now children, what do you do if you see pieces of paper lying on the ground as you come into church?" "Say 'Ssh!' " we all burst out. Unperturbed he went on, "and what do you do if people are noisy in God's house?" "Throw them in the dustbin!" we answered triumphantly.'[4]

Although she loved and admired her father, Noel did not, as she grew up, find his churchmanship any more congenial. All the young Streatfeilds were bored by the endless round of services, and the long, metaphysical sermons that William preached. Noel and Ruth perfected a technique of fitting their own words into a hymn or psalm tune, so that they could talk to each other under cover of the music. Bill made the time pass by counting his father's split infinitives; just as, in her novel *Saplings*, Noel was to make a boy endure his clerical uncle's lectures by surreptitiously transferring dried peas from one pocket to another.

The rite of Confirmation, which took place in her middle teens, was dreaded by Noel. For one thing it marked the end of Christmas stockings. Instead of opening stockings, children who were confirmed went to Communion before breakfast on Christmas Day, another deprivation to add to the other deprivations she suffered with her Christmas Eve birthday. But her reaction against Confirmation went deeper. Ruth, after she was confirmed, had for a brief spell become very devout, decorating her own little altar with candles and flowers, and that sort of ostentatious piety made Noel cringe. Most of all, she detested being forced into the position of pretending that the ceremony meant anything much to her. She knew what it meant to her father, and she knew the gulf that divided them. There was William, glowing with joy that she would now be able to receive Holy Communion; there were all the relations and parishioners, praying for her, and proffering little books of devotion in limp leather covers; and there was she, repelled by all the fuss and emotion, the heroine of a drama in which, for once, she simply did not wish to take part. She tried to explain herself to her father, but he completely misunderstood her. 'I know just how you feel, darling, unworthy, and it's quite right you should. But none of us are perfect, that's why the Holy Ghost is sent to us . . . Shall we say a little prayer about it?'[5] Her mother, more sympathetic for once, tried to improve matters by letting Noel choose her own Confirmation dress; but, in a gesture of angry rebellion, Noel deliberately bought the ugliest she could find.

The Confirmation was the last big revolt of her childhood. When she was seventeen, Noel left Laleham, and suddenly grown-up life stretched ahead, enticingly blank and empty. Such a state of affairs suited her far better than the restricted life of nursery and school. How she was going to fill up the blankness, she had as yet no idea. Oxford and Cambridge now provided colleges for women students, with clergymen's daughters taking a high percentage of the places. They could enjoy three carefree years of study, and hockey, and cocoa parties, before they moved on to the teaching posts they were usually destined for. But candidates for Oxford and Cambridge needed Latin and Greek, and a high standard of mathematics, and Noel had no such qualifications. Later she regretted that she had not been to university; but even if she had been clever enough, William would probably not have wished her to go. Academic careers were, in his view, unsuitable for women.

There was no suggestion, at this point, that Noel's interest in theatre and ballet might lead anywhere. They were, of course, useful hobbies for a Vicarage girl. Noel had plenty of time now to put on parish entertainments, and, with the fervour of late adolescence she began to aim higher, trying out serious allegorical and religious plays with the local children. Ruth designed costumes, and together they tackled a miracle play, *Eagerheart*, with Noel in the title role; and *The Mirror of Souls*, in which the characters looked into a mystical glass, and saw themselves as they would appear to God. Sometimes the plays needed music. Noel had a pure, tuneful voice, and people remembered the intense stillness which fell upon the hall when she sang a carol, backstage, during a nativity play. As for her love of ballet, she had to satisfy it as best she could with books and magazine articles.

Meanwhile, Noel enrolled for a course in Domestic Science at the Eastbourne School of Domestic Economy. Whose idea this was is uncertain. Janet cared very little about whether her daughters were domesticated or not. They had never been encouraged to help in the kitchen, or attempt the simplest household tasks – making beds, or dusting. If the course tried to teach Noel such things, it failed, for she remained hopelessly undomesticated all her life, barely able to boil herself an egg. She did, however, keep on good terms with the Principal, Miss Randall, which suggests that her work was at least no worse than the other students'. Probably not much was expected of them, for no one as yet envisaged a future without plenty of servants.

Attendance at the School did not interfere with Noel's social life, which now, for the first time, began to flourish. The greatest advantage of leaving Laleham was that she could claim some independence, and establish her own circle of friends. She began, conventionally enough, with a formal Coming Out at the East Sussex Hunt Ball; not because the Streatfeilds hunted, but because the Hunt Ball and the Hospital Ball were the two great Eastbourne occasions for launching debutantes. The Hunt Ball of Christmas 1913, when Noel was just eighteen, was held at the Queen's Hotel, and Noel duly appeared, feeling unprecedentedly modern and fashionable. Her godmother had bought her a dress of white satin, with a draped hobble skirt, split up the side. She wore long white gloves, and had osprey feathers in her hair.

Some of the Eastbourne girls went on to be presented at Court in London, but Noel had to be content with society nearer home. Rather to her surprise she found herself very popular, and much in demand at parties and dances. From her ugly duckling adolescence, she had emerged tall, slim and pretty, with auburn lights in her thick brown hair, and a face illumined by the vivid blue eyes that had always been noticed. Photographs of the time suggest a girl of strong character, the result of her long years of rebellion. In contrast to her more ordinary and insipid contemporaries, she was interesting and unusual; and as her sense of humour developed rapidly with her freedom, she was always 'lots of fun'.

William and Janet were aghast at some of the new friends she produced. They were not at all the sort of people her parents would have invited to the Vicarage. Ardent and adventurous, but with no one to guide her taste, Noel was immediately attracted to anyone with a veneer of sophistication. Her friends were probably harmless enough, but their clothes and their manners shocked the Streatfeilds. Noel did not care, and on the £20 a year, which William allowed her for clothes, she tried to copy the wildest, most exotic fashions. 'Belts, bows and beads, in the wrong colours and the wrong places,'[6] she was to lament, looking back on her youthful self; but at the time, like any teenager, she loved dabbling in cheap, up-to-date accessories. She wanted to show the older generation that their stuffy ways needed shaking up!

She was, Ruth recalled, 'a honeypot for men'. This did not mean that she plunged into any particular love affairs. The rules governing relationships between the sexes were very strict, and no girl was ever allowed to go out alone with a young man. But at dances admirers clustered round Noel. One, perhaps, outshone the rest, Noel's cousin Derek Baumer. He was the son of Janet's elder sister, who had married an artist called Lewis Baumer. Derek was a year older than Noel, and clever and charming enough to make her eighteen-year-old heart flutter.

Emancipation was in the air, and it was not just discernible in the bows and beads and dances. More significantly, the girls' church attendance began to slip. They began to have better things to do on Sundays than sit through Matins, a long sermon, and the Litany. Tongues wagged at St Mary's, as the curates and parish pussies gathered in critical huddles, pitying the poor Vicar, and censuring his daughters. But neither William nor Janet ever referred to the situation. Janet did not greatly mind; William seemed not to notice. Overworked as he was, he relied on the comforting myth that he was totally supported by his wife and family.

Suddenly, in August 1914, Noel's easy life was shattered. An Austrian Archduke was murdered, treaties were invoked, and Europe was at war. At first, intense excitement swept over Britain. People did not expect very lengthy fighting, and they were prepared to enjoy the glory and drama. But before long it was apparent that the war would be a good deal more serious, even for civilians, than anyone had anticipated. In the southeast of England, where the Streatfeilds lived, there were fears of a German invasion. Secret leaflets of instructions, to be followed if the enemy landed, were issued, and William, as a community leader, knew what was to be done. Under the direction of special constables, people were to move northwestwards, over the Downs, taking food, money and blankets. Means of transport, livestock, fuel and tools were to be kept from the enemy, even if this meant destroying them. When, in December 1914, the Germans shelled the east coast towns of Scarborough and Whitby, the inhabitants of Eastbourne waited in trepidation for their turn to come. Already they could hear the guns thundering across the Channel, in the battles of Mons and Ypres.

Tension mounted high enough for even theatrical Noel, and she longed to do something positive. 'I was bursting to help my King and country in a big way,'[7] she wrote. She soon had the chance. With men enlisting in the forces, job opportunities for women multiplied rapidly.

A vast hospital of huts for wounded soldiers was set up on empty ground near the Vicarage, and, with a recommendation from Miss Randall of the Eastbourne School of Domestic Economy, Noel began voluntary work in the kitchen, preparing vegetables. The job was tedious, but with patriotic fervour Noel was ready to endure anything, and there was one special compensation. She was allowed to wear an apron with a Red Cross on the bib, a considerable status symbol in the early days of the war. She could not resist the temptation of going back to Laleham, to show herself off. Everyone must know that the once despised Noel Streatfeild was now engaged on important war work.

Such brighter moments were rare. The casualty lists from the fighting grew longer and longer, and William had the harrowing task of visiting the bereaved families, trying to find some words of hope and comfort for them. Early in 1915 there was especially bad news for the Streatfeilds. Derek Baumer, who had joined the army, was killed.

Evidence about exactly how Noel felt for him can only be speculative, but indirect proof can be drawn from her writing. She was always an intensely economical writer, making full use of every possible shred of her own experience; and, with this in mind, hints about her feelings for Derek may be inferred from her books.

The earliest evidence comes in her second novel, *Parson's Nine*, published in 1932. Noel sets her heroine, Susanna, to work, as she had done, in a hospital kitchen, and describes the anguish Susanna suffers over her twin brother's death, as she stands at the sink with curls of carrot peel bobbing against her fingers. Just so, equally stunned and griefstricken, Noel may well have stood, peeling carrots, while the distant roar of gunfire sent its incessant reminder across the Channel.

More importantly, in her fictionalized autobiography, *A Vicarage Family*, she re-created Derek as 'John', the cousin who alone understands and sympathizes with the heroine 'Vicky', who is Noel herself. Artistically 'John' has a valid role in the book, but the warmth with which Noel portrays him suggests that he is very much more than just a useful literary device. Perhaps she was bringing to life a once treasured day-dream, which revolved round the attractive figure of Derek. It seems unlikely that the feeling was mutual; Derek was in love with another girl. But Noel might well not have known this; or she might have been content, as a romantic teenager, to adore without hope of return.

For *A Vicarage Family* also suggests that Noel's ardour was firmly controlled, as her parents would have expected, and as the conventions of the time demanded. In her account of their relationship, though 'John' is a romantic figure, sexual overtones are minimal. For most of the book he is seen as a brother, very close and affectionate to 'Vicky' certainly, but as a boy might be to a favourite sister. Only at the end of the book does the feeling between them deepen, and even then the emotions remain unspoken.

A hundred years earlier another teenage Vicarage girl, Charlotte Bronte, was absorbed in erotic fantasies, woven round her Byronic hero, Zamorna. There seems to have been nothing of this in Noel's feeling for Derek. Her aspirations were far humbler, far less clearly defined. When 'John', industriously punting down a river, remarks that 'Vicky' is 'looking pretty', this is the climax of their relationship. Nothing more seems to be needed. When she learns of his death, 'Vicky' is heartbroken, but she shows no regret for never having received the words and kisses which would have made love more explicit.

Fiction for girls in the early twentieth century indicates that a profound chastity of imagination was common. Decades had to pass before Victorian taboos could be forgotten. Popular writers of the 1920s, like Elsie J. Oxenham, presented in their novels sedate little brides who, on their wedding night, kissed their bridegrooms, and then, snugly pyjama-ed, hopped into their single beds. Noel's dreams of Derek appear to have fitted this pattern. Years of training in self-restraint had had their effect, and sexuality was tightly battened down.

Fortunately new events brought their own diversions. In April 1915 something most unexpected took place. Janet had a baby daughter, Richenda. Noel described her reaction to this in *Away from the Vicarage*. 'Back in 1915 the girls' mother had given her two elder daughters a shock. She had told them she was having a baby. The girls had been horribly embarrassed by the news, and had never discussed it. They knew – but how dimly – how babies were conceived, and of course they must have been conceived themselves. But that was long ago, your father and mother didn't go on doing it – not when the rest of the family were nearly grown-up. But facts were facts, and (Richenda) was born.'

Janet had been horrified too. She was to say later that if she could have had an abortion, she would have done so. But the birth had the surprising consequence of improving her health. The internal damage, caused sixteen years earlier by the birth of Joyce, was somehow put right by this last pregnancy, and Janet felt better than she had for years. In considering her attitude to Noel, it has to be remembered that some at least of her apparent indifference was caused by her often feeling vaguely unwell. Unfortunately such things could not be talked about, and Noel had little idea that there might be anything wrong with her mother.

Noel did not get very much involved with the baby. For most of 1915 her attention was absorbed in the production of two ambitious plays. On 8 April, four days before Richenda's arrival, she produced *Vingt-et-Un*, a two-act fairy tale by Lucy and Virginia Wintle, in aid of the Red Cross; and on 13 January 1916 she followed this with *When Daydreams End*, described on the programme as 'A Phantasy in Three Acts by Noel Streatfeild'.

These plays were serious undertakings, put on to help the war effort. They were staged, not in the parish hall, but in Eastbourne's Winter Gardens Theatre; and they gave Noel her strongest, most intoxicating experience of what real theatrical life might be like. She played leading parts, and she involved herself minutely, with Ruth, in every detail of the presentation.

The girls began by visiting the church school, to pick children for the cast. This was difficult, for the headmistress, Miss Sutcliffe, wanted her say, and she considered respectability quite as important as talent. 'There's Mary,' she would begin. 'She has a nice voice, and she comes from a clean home. You can have her. You can have Grace. She's a pretty child, and has a good home too. Don't have that one. She's not the right sort of child at all.' Finally, between the three of them, an adequate cast would be selected.

'We used thoroughly to enjoy the rehearsals,' one of the little actresses recalled, 'and we were quite happy to do whatever Noel and her sister Ruth told us. Noel was always the leader, and was very dynamic at all times, with her vivid personality. She had a marvellous presence when playing her part which we all found quite thrilling.'[8]

The programmes indicate the scale of the plays. In *Vingt-et-Un* there were at least a dozen speaking parts, a solo dancer (remembered as 'exquisite' by a member of the cast), two dozen assorted spirits and court attendants, and an orchestra of three violins, two cellos and a piano. Noel played Zingara, the sorceress, an intensely dramatic character, who causes havoc among the inhabitants of a fairy kingdom, before she repents, and falls at the feet of the princess-heroine, begging forgiveness in an emotional finale. In the course of the play she also managed to sing a highly popular song of the time, 'Where my caravan has rested', which was received with loud applause. Ruth took two minor parts, a Spirit of Night, and 'Lighthearted Joy'. Her main attention was given to designing the costumes, which were made by the mothers, and a programme decorated with a whimsical, finger-in-mouth fairy.

As soon as *Vingt-et-Un* had been performed, Noel, flying higher, began to write *When Daydreams End*. This too demanded a huge cast of actors, singers and dancers, and had an augmented orchestra under a proper conductor. Noel played a kind of principal boy, a fantasy figure called Romance, who, assisted by a band of Daydreams, competes for the love of a human girl, Phylidda, with her earthly lover. Ruth played Love, the character who finally saves Phylidda from Romance's courtship, thus securing another dramatic, broken-hearted curtain scene for Noel.

To the programme of *Vingt-et-Un* a shy note had been appended. 'The audience is requested to be very generous in their criticisms.' It was unnecessary, for the play was an immense success; so much so that a different note was printed in the programme of *When Daydreams End* – 'It is specially requested that no Flowers or Chocolates are handed up onto the stage.' The players in *Vingt-et-Un* had been quite overwhelmed by the tributes from the audience, and Noel had been careful to see that all her little actresses had their share of the rewards. 'We were not forgotten at the end of the shows,' one of them wrote, 'and while bouquets were presented to the principals, we were each given a daintily wrapped bag of sweets.'[9]

'We had great fun with Miss Noel,' another child of those days remembered. 'I think as children everyone loved her. We had such happy times with her.'[10]

When Daydreams End was also the end of those happy times. Noel was no longer satisfied with just peeling potatoes and producing plays. Ruth, who had already done a little nursing, now took a permanent post as an art teacher. Barbara was in London, working in a Civil Service office. Bill had joined the army, although with his poor eyesight he could justifiably have been excused military service. Noel, the dynamic one, could not bear to be left behind. Characteristically she chose to astonish her family. She volunteered for a job as a munitions worker at Woolwich Arsenal.

The war, costing hundreds of thousands of lives, was not going well for Britain. Supplies of all kinds were disastrously inadequate, and in May 1915 Lloyd George had become Minister for Munitions, with a mandate to galvanize the production of arms. One result of this had been an enormous expansion in the numbers of munitions workers. Old restrictions on women and unskilled workers were relaxed; and by 1916 troops of girls, rich and poor, educated and illiterate, were pouring into factories to make the weapons and shells the army so desperately needed.

Noel was caught up in a tide of enthusiasm. Spurning the suggestion that she might volunteer at a newly created munitions factory in Eastbourne, she set off for London and the Woolwich Arsenal, the hub of British arms manufacture.

The Arsenal was a gigantic place, a town within a town. All round the original complex of buildings, new work-sheds had been hastily constructed along networks of muddy, unmade roads. Grim and gaunt, the sheds stretched away for as far as the eye could see, each one shuddering with the continual thump of heavy machinery. Bars of metal were stacked in toppling piles, ready to be made into guns, while in distant corners, behind huge walls, stood the 'danger buildings', where high explosives were made. Squalid and jerry-built, but pulsating with life, it could hardly have been more unlike decorous Eastbourne.

Half of all the workers at the Arsenal were now women, drawn from every walk of life; but society girl or charwoman's daughter, in the factory they were all treated alike. That in itself was a useful education for Noel. They all worked twelve-hour shifts, with a fortnight on the day shift and a fortnight on the night shift; and they all earned one pound a week, raised in 1917 to one pound, four shillings (£1.20). The only division was in the sleeping accommodation. There were hostels for working girls, and hostels for ladies, and Noel was given a room in one of the latter. But during the day the sheltered, chaperoned Vicarage girl was thrown among crowds of rough, loud-voiced Cockneys, and it demanded every scrap of her tolerance and humour.

'It was very brave of you to go and work there,' Ruth remarked to Noel after the war.

'My dear Ruth, it was not bravery,' Noel replied. 'It was ignorance. I had no idea what I was doing.'

Noel's job was making metal bands on a lathe. Only three movements, endlessly repeated, were needed; but if, as the shift dragged by, she lost concentration and faltered, her hands could be quite badly cut by the moving lathe. It helped, she decided, to sing. Even if the thudding machinery partly drowned her voice, the rhythm of the song kept her movements rhythmical too, and therefore safe.

She described her experiences in her first novel, *The Whicharts*, where one of the characters becomes a munitions worker. 'She struggled daily, with thousands of other workers, through a police-guarded gate. She had a numbered disc which checked her time-keeping. She wore a dreary khaki apron and cap. She became with the passing months almost an automaton . . . There were pleasant little pauses in the work. The ten minutes that was, on day shift, breakfast and on night shift tea. The hour for dinner. The half hour for tea on day shift and breakfast at night. There were curious long nights when her eyelids seemed to weigh a ton . . . There was the roar, roar, roar of the thousand lathes. The curious smell of hot brass.'

Only in one detail does that account differ from Noel's actual experience. She rebelled against the dreary khaki uniform. A fellow worker was able to describe Noel at Woolwich. 'I met Miss Streatfeild during my time in the fuse factory, where she also worked. She was absolutely charming, and I remember that I wore the universal cap and apron, but that she wore a charming flowered scarf round her head, and I believe a different overall. The work was very hard indeed, standing at our lathes; and if an air raid warning sounded the machinery stopped, and we all had to take cover . . . She was always great fun, and all the fitters and workers respected and loved her.'[11]

'Life would be much easier making shells,' Noel was to write gloomily in her diary, in the depths of the Second World War; but at the time it was far from easy. The period at Woolwich Arsenal was one she rarely referred to, although she wrote so compulsively about other periods of her life. Perhaps she hardly remembered it. Fatigue blotted out the long, monotonous succession of wearisome shifts; and to know that she could have been 'charming' and 'great fun', amongst the lathes and the straps, would perhaps have surprised her.

Historians have commented on the Arsenal's gay social life, with clubs and activities organized for the girls by their lady superintendant, Dame Lilian Barker; but there is no evidence that Noel enjoyed it. Certainly she never mentioned a lighter side of Woolwich life. Nevertheless she stuck to her work, with her stubbornness of character, and the sense of duty instilled at the Vicarage. She was not a person to give up.

In the end, it was physically too much for her. She began to suffer from colitis, and presently she was too weak and ill to work any longer. She was invalided home to Eastbourne, and before she had properly recovered, the war had come to an end. Ten years later she wrote in her diary – 'I always want to feel more than I do on Armistice Days.' In 1918 she was just thankful that the hard slog was over.

6

A Start in the Theatre

After the experience of living away from home, Noel had no wish to settle down quietly at the Vicarage again. Besides, the old family mould had been broken. Ruth was determined to concentrate on her career as an art teacher; Bill who, although badly wounded, had survived the war, was going up to Cambridge; Barbara was getting married. Three-year-old Richenda was a charming child, but Noel could not stay at home for the sake of her baby sister.

Some time between 1916 and 1918 Noel had made up her mind about what she really wanted to do. She was going to be an actress. Already she saw herself fulfilling those childhood daydreams of stage success. She had been a star actress in Eastbourne. Why should it not be just as easy in London?

The difficulty lay in breaking the news to her parents. She knew that Janet was unlikely to raise many obstacles. Like other mothers of the time, faced with alarmingly liberated daughters, she washed her hands of the responsibility of giving advice. There were more important things on her mind. The garden needed urgent attention. During the war most of it had been used for growing vegetables, for William had thought it wrong to waste time and energy on growing flowers, except a few as gifts for the wounded, or for funerals. Now all the beds needed re-stocking. Then there was Richenda, even though Nannie undertook much of the daily care of her. Noel's problems were, as always, a low priority. When she broached the subject of acting, her mother only said, 'Ask your father.'

One consequence of the war was to be an unexpected help to Noel. The theatre had come to be accepted as completely respectable. In a frantic search for amusement to divert the thousands of

67

soldiers on leave from the front, the theatre with its gaiety, romance and colour, had boomed. Families like the Venns, who had once shunned play-going, lost their scruples when their sons dragged them to popular shows like *Chu Chin Chow*. The Streatfeilds had taken Bill to a musical comedy, *The Maid of the Mountains*, the night before he was sent out to France. With no competition yet from films or radio, the theatre had never stood higher in public esteem than it did while Noel was nerving herself to speak to her parents.

It seemed, Noel recalled, an endless walk along the linoleum-floored hall, from the drawing room where she had been talking to her mother, to the study where William sat writing. How could she urge what might well seem to him a desperately self-centred ambition? Once inside the study, she could only manage the bluntest words. 'Daddy, I want to be an actress.'

Evidently William turned pale, but the rejection Noel had feared did not come. Like everyone else, William had had to move with the times. He knew that modern girls were embarking on careers, and looking at Noel, with her dashingly bobbed hair, and cheap, fashionable clothes, he could not doubt that she was thoroughly modern. Financially he was worse off than ever. Prices were rising, and war charities were a constant drain on his bank balance. It would be impossible to support his daughters until they married, however much he might wish to. There was, in any case, the chilling fact that they might not all marry. After the slaughter of the war, the newspapers were proclaiming that there were three million surplus marriageable women in Britain alone. William must have remembered too Noel's successes in parish entertainments. If she had to earn her living, acting might be a good way of doing it. To Noel's surprise he at once took a constructive line. He offered to find out the best place for her to train.

All the advice he received pointed to the Academy of Dramatic Art in London. (It was not yet the Royal Academy.) Noel was summoned for an audition in front of the Principal, Kenneth Barnes, and accepted as a student for the term beginning January 1919.

Noel was now twenty-three, quite old to begin training, but, with the disruption of war, the Academy was a ragbag of students of every age and type. Noel found herself in a very large class consisting almost entirely of women; serious students like herself mingling with war widows trying to rebuild their broken lives on a new career, and society debutantes whose mothers hoped that a stage training would give their daughters enough extra polish to attract one of the scarce young men. For reasons of economy, the Academy accepted nearly everyone who applied, and there was a constant battle for good parts. In acting classes there was no hope of getting more than an odd scene to study. *As You Like It*, for example, was chopped up, and all the tall girls, like Noel, were given a snippet of Rosalind to play in turn with the same Orlando; but during most of the classes she sat amongst rows of other girls, staring at the lucky few who were actually on stage.

Besides acting, Noel, for the first time in her life, took ballet lessons. From books and articles she already knew a good deal of ballet terminology, and something about posture and turn-out, how to breathe and how to count the beats of music. While many students regarded their exercises at the barre as a tiresome chore, Noel's keenness attracted the interest of Louis d'Egville, the dancing master. He told her that if she had come to him ten years earlier, he would have made her into a dancer; and although she knew that, with her height, this would hardly have been possible, she was gratified. She worked hard, until she could move with something like a ballerina's grace.

In the Academy curriculum there were also fencing classes; elocution lessons when the students recited Shakespeare, and practised breath control; voice classes which concentrated on correct diction; and movement classes in which the students learned mime, and useful techniques like how to fall, how to rise elegantly from a chair, and which knee to kneel on. The days were fully occupied, and the highest standards expected. The casual, slapdash way in which Noel had scraped along at school was not good enough for the Academy, where every word of a speech had to be memorized accurately, and every movement perfectly executed. She was fortunate to have the discipline of the

Arsenal behind her, for without that she might never have coped with the course.

The Academy was not residential. Once again Noel had a room in a hostel, which provided breakfast and dinner, and all meals at the weekend. She was the only drama student, and it was lonely slaving over her lines in the evening while the other girls rushed out to enjoy themselves. She did not find it easy, either, adjusting to her fellow students at the Academy. Eastbourne standards of behaviour, of self-control and carefully restricted conversation, simply did not apply. It was not just that many of the serious students were not from the same social class as the Streatfeilds. After Woolwich that did not worry Noel, and temperamentally she felt herself akin. These fledgling actors were as self-centred, assertive and emotional as she had ever been, tending to show off, and regard each other as rivals. The two things she found difficult about them were that they were so much more knowledgeable than she was, with years of devoted theatre-going behind them; and that they were hyper-critical, quick to point out the faults in each other's performances.

It was a shock to discover that she, the star of *Vingt-et-Un* and *When Daydreams End*, was far from being considered a star at the Academy. No one gazed at her in wonder; no one even praised her. The student who won the most applause was Audrey Carten, a brilliant and beautiful girl, a few years younger than Noel, and the most gifted member of her class. She was to have a brief, sensational successs with Sir Gerald du Maurier in a play called *The Dancers*, before she abandoned the stage for ever. At the Academy Noel made friends with her, but she also watched her with awe. She was honest enough to admit to herself that, compared with Audrey, she was second rate. As she struggled through her first term, the inferiority complex which had haunted her school days was never far away.

Back in Eastbourne for the vacation she hid her disappointments, and revelled in playing the part of the drama student to her unenlightened, stay-at-home family. Flaunting her daring, modern clothes, from which William averted his eyes, she held forth about her roles and her triumphs, demonstrated the new London dance steps, and swept groups of friends to the piano to try out the latest popular songs – 'K-K-K-Katy', and 'I'm forever blowing bubbles'. Being dashing and modern was really much more to her taste than battling with the character of Rosalind; and she could be a great actress at the Vicarage in a way she never could be at the Academy.

She was beginning to discover that acquiring the craft of acting, with all its specialized techniques, could be difficult, and even dull. Just as in writing she was, until the end of her life, blind to certain principles of punctuation and sentence construction; so, in acting, small but vital points of expertise always escaped her. For her, the key to acting lay in imaginative identification with a part. If she could think herself into the character, then she believed she could play it successfully.

She summed up what she tried to do in *Ballet Shoes*, where Pauline plays the young Edward V in Shakespeare's *Richard III*.

'The rehearsals slipped by Pauline like a dream; for the first time she was not acting – she was feeling a part. The child who was playing little "York" was a great talker, and liked to gossip with Pauline at rehearsals. Pauline knew it would sound silly to say, "Don't talk to me before I go on, I want to feel like a king;" but she managed to hide before her entrances, and she would shut her eyes, and imagine that the theatre had gone, and instead was a street in the old London of 1483. Down it she walked, a King, but a King who was on his guard, who knew himself a defenceless boy. She bowed to the imaginary curtsying crowd, she drew herself up with dignity hidden by courtesy, to meet the Lord Mayor and his train, remembering always that the greedy eyes of Uncle Gloucester were upon her, and he must not see she was afraid. In this spirit she managed to be so right at even the earlier rehearsals, that it did not seem strange to the nobles and the people to bow and curtsy to her. So strong was her own belief that she was a King, that they all felt it . . . At the dress rehearsal, after "York" had gone onto the stage, she stood a minute staring at herself in the long glass, and she did not see herself, but "Edward the Fifth" '.

There were no student grants in 1919, and living in London on £50 a year, which was all that her father could afford, was a struggle. Out of it she had to provide her own lunch and tea, pay her fares, buy her clothes, and hope to have a little over for seats in theatre galleries at a shilling a time. Her slimness fined down to a bony thinness as she skimped meals to save money, but she was determined not to have the other students chattering about plays she had not seen.

Theatre-going was an unfailing thrill. Plays did not begin until eight or nine in the evening, so, after a quick meal at the hostel, she would join her friends in a gallery queue. When the doors opened, they would hurry up the long flights of stairs to the vertiginous seats, from which they could look down on the richer members of the audience, taking their places in the stalls, dress circle and boxes, the men in white ties and tail coats, the ladies in elaborate gowns with furs and jewels. There was a buzz of gossip as people were recognized and pointed out, and occasionally applause would greet the arrival of some special celebrity. A little orchestra in the pit would add to the gaiety with a selection of popular tunes. Noel adored all the accessories of the theatre – the posters; the photographs of the stars hanging in the foyer; the tiers of red plush seats; the vast, draped curtain, silent focus of everyone's attention. At last it would rise, and the play would begin.

The mood of the theatre, in Noel's student days, was consciously bright. It was a time for driving away memories of muddy trenches and barbed wire with melodramas, spectacular musicals, and, above all, light drawing room comedies, in which pretty girls, with armfuls of flowers, tripped lightly onto the stage through French windows, escorted by young men in white flannels carrying tennis racquets. The best known stars were Gladys Cooper, Talullah Bankhead, Owen Nares, and Gerald du Maurier – Noel's particular favourite, with his cool, spontaneous manner which, as a drama student, she knew had been 'planned and worked at and worked at.'[1]

Noel dreamed of the day when her photograph too would smile down from the walls of theatre foyers, when her name would be emblazoned on buses, and when crowds would wait at the stage door for her autograph. Such things were a great incentive to hard work; and, as the terms went by, things began to happen at the Academy which encouraged her.

One of the directors, Miss Elsie Chester, awarded an annual prize for what she called Good Studentship. This was rather more an award for dedication and professionalism than for talented performances, but at the Academy all prizes conferred status on the winners. Elsie Chester, an alarming old actress, taught modern drama. Her stage career had ended when she was involved in an accident, and had to have her leg amputated. When Noel knew her, she walked with a crutch, which she was reputed to hurl at anyone who annoyed her. For other students her classes were a terrifying ordeal, but Noel was never frightened. She loved modern drama, and felt much more in tune with it than she did with Shakespeare. Her enthusiasm and diligence caught Elsie Chester's eye, and the Good Studentship prize for 1919 was her reward.

As she approached the end of her course, other students began to talk of her as someone with a promising future. Flora Robson, Noel's junior at the Academy, has recorded how, among the older students, she particularly admired Noel. Pretty, graceful, and a prize-winner, she seemed destined for success. Then came the dreadful disappointment of the Public Show, when all the students who were leaving performed before an audience of theatrical managers, agents and critics, gathered to pick out the most promising, and perhaps offer them contracts. The allocation of parts for the Public Show was vital, and, to her dismay, Noel was only given minor characters in two undistinguished plays. There was no chance at all for her to shine. She received a certificate of merit for her performances, but the important honours went to other students. Noel left the Academy in April 1920, with no job or contract.

The situation was close to disaster. Her father had paid her fees and her allowance in the innocent belief that, as soon as her training was over, she would start to earn her own living. She could not face her family, and confess that she was unemployed, especially after she had claimed to be so successful. She rushed to a theatrical agency, and because she was tall and slim, and could sing and dance a little, she was offered a five weeks' job as a chorus girl in a touring musical comedy. Thankfully she accepted it.

'We thought her very brave,'[2] Flora Robson recalled, unconsciously echoing Ruth's words about Noel at Woolwich Arsenal; and in some ways the two episodes were exact parallels. Noel snatched at the job without any idea of what it would involve. She would be earning money, and that was what mattered. Clearly, working as a chorus girl when she had trained as a serious actress, was something of a humiliation, but she decided she need not explain to her family just what she was doing. During her last term at the Academy she had chosen herself a stage name – Noelle Sonning; for she had become very conscious of a heavy weight of prejudice amongst many of her relations. Classbound, and Victorian in outlook, they had made it plain that, as far as they were concerned, actors ranked with tradesmen, and they did not want the distinguished name of Streatfeild to be 'dragged in the mud', as they were inclined to put it. How they would regard chorus girls Noel dared not even guess, and she congratulated herself on her foresight in appropriating a stage name behind which she could now hide.

In blithe ignorance, she set off on her tour. She knew that, in the hierarchy of the theatre, a musical comedy girl, though below a straight actress, was considerably above, for instance, a member of a pantomime chorus. The girls in the big, pre-war musical shows had enjoyed extraordinary prestige. 'That was the date when so many chorus and show girls married peers,' Noel wrote. 'That was the date when men queued at stage doors carrying bouquets . . . The whole country was searched to find beauties . . . Never since have girls held quite the position those girls had.'[3]

As a schoolgirl Noel had enviously studied the picture postcards of them which sold by the thousand, and for her the aura of their glamour still lingered on. The first week of the tour disillusioned her with cruel completeness. She had not realized how different chorus girls would be from Academy students, and how alien. Their chief preoccupation, on and off the stage, was how best to exploit their sex appeal to win themselves money and men. Noel liked money and men herself, but not enough to shake off twenty-four years of Vicarage training in blatant pursuit of them. As her dreams rapidly dissolved, she

74

began to see the other girls as mercenary, competitive and spiteful. Some were dishonest; a few drank too much.

She had no escape from them. They travelled in a troupe on the Sunday theatrical trains. They crowded together in dressing rooms which were usually the most distant from the stage, and so cramped that Noel had to keep her elbows glued to her sides as she applied her make-up in front of the communal mirror. Worst of all, they shared lodgings; and the combination of gossiping, quarrelling room-mates, with seedy, squalid rooms, was almost unbearable. For theatrical digs were as appalling a revelation to Noel as the chorus girls were. By the end of her stage career, she had gathered a fund of amusing stories about digs and landladies she had known; but in those first five weeks it seemed the very opposite of funny to be squashed into one of the back street houses with ouside lavatories, to which the chorus girls were directed.

On her blotting paper memory, which had recorded the miseries of her childhood, the horrors of digs were lastingly imprinted. 'The aspidistras, the enlargements of the landlady's family, the curious smell of old food and dirty carpets, the shiny horsehair sofa with the stuffing coming out and all the springs broken, the unspeakable bathroom, the bedrooms with wall-paper hanging in shreds, the sheets and blankets that needed a nervous examination before you dared get between them';[4] even hostels and draughty Vicarages had been no preparation for this.

It was hard work too. In the morning and afternoon they rehearsed on stage, and in the evening they performed. Total precision was vital. Every gesture, every high kick, had to be exactly synchronized. 'It's no fun, you can take it from me,' a chorus girl grumbles in Noel's novel *Tops and Bottoms.* 'Work, work, work. No real dancing – nothing matters but keeping time. We might be a lot of soldiers.'

From her five weeks' experience Noel was to draw valuable material for her books, but she had no idea of this at the time. She only knew how deeply thankful she was when her contract expired, and she was free to return to London. Kenneth Barnes, the Academy Principal to whom she went for advice, scolded her for her foolhardiness in taking so unsuitable a job, until Noel explained about the financial necessity. Providentially he had a good suggestion to make. She should audition for a place in a new Shakespearean touring company, which had just been started by an Irish actor called Charles Doran.

This was a marvellous chance for a beginner, though Noel did not at once appreciate it. She still thought of Shakespeare as too difficult, and longed to try modern comedy. But any job was better than none. She auditioned, and was engaged for £3 a week, to play Audrey in *As You Like It*, Titania in *A Midsummer Night's Dream*, Maria in *Twelfth Night*, a witch in *Macbeth*, and the boy and the French maid in *Henry V*. She added Katherine of Aragon in *Henry VIII* to her repertoire later.

With such a rich selection of parts, Noel's volatile spirits soared. She hurried home to the Vicarage with the news, ostentatiously hugging her copy of Shakespeare's plays. Even the most hidebound relations could not reasonably object to this. Throwing herself into the part of the great actress, she ordered an extravagantly large, waterproof-lined, theatrical basket, with her name painted on the lid, and stocked it with a selection of tights and shoes, and a box of brand-new make-up. 'Leading actors and actresses who have worked their way up, usually have only a few sticks of greasepaint, and a few pots of cream, and so on,' she wrote later. 'Beginners have immense make-up boxes . . . crammed with every conceivable shade of paint, suitable for making up anyone from an archangel to a demon king . . . It's a gorgeous feeling to have all that at the beginning, but it's a nuisance to keep tidy, and sticks of greasepaint soon get lost.'[5]

Noel joined the company for a period of intensive rehearsals before the tour started. Charles Doran, the actor-manager, was only eight years older than she was, and had gathered a band of keen, intelligent young actors, many of whom were to become famous. There were Ralph Richardson, Norman Shelley, Donald Wolfit, and Cecil Parker, with Edith Sharpe as the leading lady. Doran himself had been a member of Sir Frank Benson's celebrated Shakespearean touring company, though he had never achieved any leading roles, partly because he was short and stocky, and partly because he was not quite as good an actor as he thought he was. Unkind gossip hinted that he had started his own company because it was the only way he was ever likely to play Hamlet or Macbeth, but this was not entirely fair. He was, in fact, a competent actor, and he was a splendid organizer, with the gift of cementing the members of his company into a happy and enthusiastic team.

He was also an exacting producer who, from the first rehearsals, expected his actors to know perfectly every word and cue. This was no mere Academy rehearsing, but literally working for the company's bread and butter, for bad productions would earn little money. So he was relentless, and at times Noel despaired, certain that he would tear up her contract if she made one more mistake. Gradually she realized how constructive his volleys of criticism were, and how essential the disciplines of stage life. She learned that a professional actress had to be absolutely punctual for rehearsals and performances, and, once in the theatre, had to forget all personal worries and preoccupations. As she once said – 'Your entire family can fall down dead, but if you appear on the stage there must be no sign of it.'[6] That was the standard set in the Doran company.

When the period of rehearsing was over, the company began two years of travelling all over the British Isles, with a tour of the south coast. Charles Doran's was only one of numerous theatrical companies moving about the country in the early 1920s. Every town had at least one theatre, booking travelling productions to fill up their programmes. Usually the Doran company would give seven or eight performances in a week, including all the plays in the repertory. Then on Saturday nights, after the final curtain, no matter how exhausted they might be, all the cast helped to pack up the costumes and properties, so that they would be ready to travel to their next destination on Sunday. The Sunday trains were always full of actors, whiling away their tedious journeys with cards, cigarettes and reminiscences.

On arrival at the new town they would hurry to inspect the theatre, comment on the facilities, and allocate the dressing rooms. Then came the hunt for digs, and here Noel was lucky for, at the outset, Edith Sharpe suggested that they might share. The digs were still horrible, but having Edith to laugh with was some mitigation.

As she settled down, Noel found the company very congenial. She loved the security of belonging to a group, joining in its gossip and its practical jokes, taking an interest in the cricket and hockey teams the men somehow found time to organize. She enjoyed the gatherings in pubs and cheap cafés, when the company sat round discussing the current state of the theatre, or the interpretation of particular plays. She relished the fireside suppers when she and Edith at last got back to their digs. Unlike the chorus girls, the Doran players were very much her sort of people; and when the tour reached Eastbourne, she summoned up the courage to take them all to tea at the Vicarage.

Her feelings about Shakespeare changed. Exploring the plays through rehearsals and performances, listening to the discussions, she began to love and understand them with an unexpected passion. Scenes and characters sharpened, and became vivid. She was able really to imagine herself living in the Forest of Arden, or the fairy wood outside Athens. Later, in her stories, she used her own interpretations of the plays – a modernistic, balletic *Midsummer Night's Dream* in *Ballet Shoes*, *The Tempest* with a child for Ariel in *Curtain Up*; and through her accounts shines such authentic awe and excitement, that even her youngest readers can glimpse something of the thrilling quality of the plays.

Whether she was a success in her parts is uncertain, though 'the best Audrey I ever saw' was the verdict of a perhaps prejudiced friend. Noel kept no cuttings from her stage days, and, not being an introspective writer, never attempted to analyse or comment on her own performances. Looking back, in *Away from the Vicarage*, she remembered chiefly the hilarious moments of the tour – the time when she had a bad attack of hay fever while she was playing Titania out of doors, and sneezed more than a hundred times as she lay, supposedly sleeping, on her flowery bank; the time when the cue light failed at the beginning of *Macbeth*, and the curtain rose on three witches drinking a birthday toast from a bottle of port which they had hastily to conceal in the cauldron. Most of all, she watched and listened, letting theatre life sink into her blotting paper memory, with all its atmosphere, its personalities and its sayings. 'Overture and beginners, please.'[7] 'Put in your ambers, Bill.'[8] 'I want pace, and, of course, full value to the prose.'[9]

Yet even though she was learning and developing, she remained underneath the same reckless, impulsive girl, who rushed into things without foreseeing the consequences; and towards the end of 1922 she ran headlong into a confrontation with Charles Doran.

Like other managers, Doran frequently used drama students to fill small parts in his productions. Traditionally they were not given any wages; the useful experience was supposed to be payment enough. But by 1922 the actors' union, Equity, was beginning to raise objections to what it called unfair exploitation; and when Doran engaged a fifteen-year-old girl student to play Puck, the union demanded that she should be paid properly. Charles Doran, Noel wrote, 'was that type of Irishman who gets truculent when others interfere with his business'.[10] He refused to pay, and Noel suddenly found herself burning with all the crusading ardour of the Frys and the Venns. As a union member, she declared that she would call the company out on strike if the girl were not treated justly.

In the end the dispute was settled without a strike, and wages were paid to the unlucky student, who had never wished to be a cause of contention, but the unity of the company was broken. Noel might believe that she had fought a disinterested campaign for right to prevail, but to Doran she was a traitor, bent on destroying him when he had helped to promote her career. With most of the actors divided into two camps, the atmosphere in the company became so poisonous that, at the end of the tour, several members, including Noel, would not ask for a renewal of their contracts. Charles Doran, furious at the situation, let them go; and Noel was again without a job.

7

A Time to have Fun

Noel's stage career was at its highest point during her two years with Charles Doran. For the next seven years it gradually ran downhill, and although there were occasional upturns, she never again had the challenging range of parts or the intellectual stimulus that the Doran company had given her.

There was still plenty of work about for a young actress. Noel did a short season of melodrama in Portsmouth, and was then offered her first part in a London production, as a butterfly in *The Insect Play* by a Czech writer, Karel Capek, which opened in May 1923. The play was a satire on modern society, and all the characters were insects, dressed in strange, attenuated costumes of chiffon and gauze. Noel, Ruth recalled, looked charming – much more so than John Gielgud, playing opposite her in his first professional appearance, and hampered by a laurel wreath and a golden battledore and shuttlecock. As the first act began, the two burst into what was supposed to be a parody of bright, cocktail party chatter; but since all the ribaldry which gave life to the original text had been cut, the lines fell very flat indeed, and neither Noel nor John Gielgud had the skill to salvage them. Many hopes and much money had been invested in the play, which was intended to break new ground in the English theatre; but the critics damned it, and it ran for only six weeks. The producer, Nigal Playfair, was so furious at this disaster, that when the curtain rose for the last time on Noel's limping cocktail chat, he turned his chair round in his box, and sat with his back to the stage.

The failure of *The Insect Play* left Noel free for what was to be an infinitely more enjoyable venture. She was engaged by Donald Calthrop, the manager of the Kingsway Theatre in

London, to play Hermia in *A Midsummer Night's Dream*; a production which was quickly replaced by an undistinguished operetta called *Kate, or Love will find a Way*; equally rapidly replaced, in its turn, by *Yoicks*, a light revue, which pleased popular taste, and ran for a year.

Inconsequential though it was, *Yoicks* was to have a decisive effect on Noel's career as an actress, and so on the whole course of her life. Until it opened, late in 1923, she had thought of herself as a serious actress with unlimited possibilities lying ahead. She had worked hard; she was ambitious. She believed she would one day see the name Noelle Sonning in lights outside some big London theatre. *Yoicks*, and the friends she made at the Kingsway, turned her mind to other things, and blunted the sharp edge of her ambition.

The revue consisted of a brisk series of sketches, and song and dance acts, all fairly amusing, but too trivial to make real demands on the players. As a newcomer to revue, Noel had only a random selection of bits and pieces, since all the best female parts went to the leading lady, Marjorie Gordon, who was well-known in musical comedy, and the Gilbert and Sullivan operas. 'Never forget that an actress can always learn until her last hour,' declares Madame Moulin, a teacher of French drama in *Ballet Shoes*; but in *Yoicks* there was nothing much for Noel to learn. There was no need for the company to sit round in those long discussions which had engrossed the Doran players. Now, when the curtain fell, Noel tore off her costume, wiped away her greasepaint, and rushed out, in a cluster of friends, to a hectic round of parties and night clubs.

Sharing the top dressing room at the Kingsway Theatre with Noel were Selene Moxon and Sunday Wilshin, two actresses with whom she was to remain friends for the rest of her life. Selene, who used Cyllene Moxon as her stage name, and was called Moxie by her friends, was several years older than Noel. She was a Scot who, with no theatre training, and not much of a singing voice, had been stage-struck enough to apply for a part in the chorus of a famous pre-war musical, *The Arcadians*, and good-looking enough to be engaged. She was, in fact, one of the celebrated postcard beauties, tall, slim and dashing, a favourite with theatre managers since her admirers could be guaranteed to book seats in the stalls, night after night, for the sheer pleasure of looking at her.

Sunday Wilshin was ten years younger than Noel, only eighteen when the run of *Yoicks* began, but already she had a long theatrical career behind her. As a pupil of the Italia Conti Stage School she had played a wide range of children's parts, including a Lost Boy in *Peter Pan*, when she also understudied Gladys Cooper in the title role; Rosamund, the leading girl in *Where the Rainbow Ends*, a patriotic fantasy, the particular property of Italia Conti, who staged it in London every Christmas; and Puck in *A Midsummer Night's Dream*. She was small and sprightly, and knowledgeable and sophisticated beyond her years.

Moxie and Sunday had one important thing in common; neither was much interested in acting as an art. Perhaps because success had come easily to them, they were devoid of the ambition which had so far driven Noel. For Moxie the glamour of the stage had faded; Sunday had never really felt it. Their parts were no more than jobs to them; the theatre just the place where they happened to earn their living. Fascinating reminiscences would slip out in the course of their dressing room conversations, to be recorded on Noel's blotting paper memory. Moxie would describe how she had longed for the status symbols of the pre-war show girl – a gold chain handbag, a matching ermine muff and stole, and a rich admirer to take her on the river at Henley on 'Ascot Sunday'. Sunday dropped remarks about the techniques of flying in *Peter Pan*, which Noel used in *Ballet Shoes*. But they never thought of dissecting their parts, or analysing the state of the English theatre. They liked to go out and have fun, and, under their cheerful influence, Noel let her seriousness of purpose slide.

In their company she was discovering the sort of glittering world she had dreamed of as a teenager. The reputations of Moxie and Marjorie Gordon brought to the Kingsway Theatre an audience of well-heeled young men, eager to take the girls out after the show. The finale of *Yoicks* was a hunting scene, with the cast in pink coats, white stocks, and top hats, submerged in hobby horses from the waist down. As soon as they had cavorted onto the stage, a small band of accredited visitors would be discreetly admitted through the stage door – guardsmen, sportsmen, aristocrats; sometimes, Sunday claimed, 'a younger princeling from Buck House'. When the curtain had fallen, and the girls had made themselves reasonably presentable, their towering Cockney dresser, Ida, would summon the gentlemen to the top dressing room, and the evening's entertainment would be planned. If the escorts were wealthy enough they might all go to supper at the Savoy or the Carlton, and on to dance at the Embassy Club. For a less extravagant evening they might go to the Bucket of Blood, a night club run by Charles Laughton and his wife, Elsa Lanchester, which was a favourite with theatre people.

Noel felt like a butterfly that had suddenly burst from its cocoon. Exhilarated by the bright life of London, she threw herself into every new craze. She tried the latest dance steps, and sang the latest songs. She smoked, she drank cocktails, she played bridge, she learned words that would have horrified her parents. She wore filmy, revealing dresses over her fashionable silk stockings and cami-knickers. And she achieved considerable popularity, being pretty and vivacious, with an endearing readiness to laugh at herself when she was teased. Laughter was the vital ingredient in that frenetic society, still haunted by memories of the war. 1924, Noel wrote in *Myra Carroll*, was 'the period for loudly laughing about everything, whether it was funny or not.'

A glimpse of Noel in 1924 came from the writer Storm Jameson, who was Noel's near contemporary, and who rented the first floor of a house in Sloane Street where Noel already had rooms. 'My first sight of Noel was of a very young woman, a quite beautiful creature, leaning over the bannisters watching the arrival of my furniture, and throwing mocking comments over her shoulder to her friends. She was, I learned, an actress, with a small, obscure part in some not at all important play. Indeed I am inclined to believe it was not a play at all in any ordinary meaning of the term, but something less distinguished. Noel mocked it herself. We became friends very quickly, and she borrowed a handsome evening coat, to which she clung . . . She had many friends apart from the girls she shared her floor with, young men for the most part. She really was enchantingly lovely, and recklessly amusing.'

Keeping up with rich friends on her small salary from *Yoicks* was impossible. She needed a constant supply of new clothes, and if they could not be borrowed, like the evening coat, they might have to be begged. She cultivated a charmingly wistful look; a way of murmuring, when asked out, that she was afraid she had nothing to wear, which not infrequently led to the offer of a new dress, or the friendly gift of an envelope full of banknotes. Deep down inside herself she knew it was wrong to take them, but she could always find excuses for herself. She had had such a hard life – all those cast-off clothes and Lenten fasts in her childhood, the sweated labour of Woolwich Arsenal, the long hours and hard work at the Academy and with Charles Doran. Surely she had earned herself a little bit of fun.

Nevertheless it was a relief when Sunday suggested a way of improving her finances. She could easily get work as a model. In 1924 there were very few professional models – or mannequins, as they were called – and actresses were often employed to show clothes. Noel was graceful, and had a perfect model's figure, being tall and flat-chested, and so slim that, for a fancy dress party, Moxie and Sunday once dressed her in rags to represent a contemporary poster of starving Belgium.

Modelling was quite close to acting. The model had to know how to walk properly, and here the Academy's movement classes proved their value. Noel showed clothes in theatres and restaurants, and at the dress shows of famous couturiers, where wealthy customers sat round a large room at little gilt tables supplied with cigarettes and cocktails, and chose outfits for the next season. The lighting would be carefully planned, dim round the sides of the room, with a soft, flattering glow concentrated in the centre where the girls paraded. As each one entered between draped curtains, a spotlight would flood down on her, and appropriate music might be played. If the costume were spectacular enough there might be applause. The model would move forward with slow, gliding steps, pivoting in a quick turn to show the way a skirt was flared, or making a studied gesture to display the cut of a sleeve. Pockets, belts, linings – the model must remember to demonstrate them all. At the end of every show a group of girls appeared in Court dress, complete with veils, feathers and long gloves. They formed a line, curtsied, and, to a burst of clapping, slowly withdrew through the curtains to the fitting room, where, the tension over, they stood laughing and gossiping on white dustsheets, while the workroom hands carefully removed their clothes for them.

To equip herself a model only needed silk stockings, satin court shoes, and a minimum of underwear; and besides earning reasonable wages, she often had the chance to buy unwanted clothes at a discount. Or if a rich customer did not wish to be seen twice in the same outfit, she might pass it back to the original model for a nominal sum, or even for nothing at all. For the first time in her life Noel began to have cupboards full of lovely clothes, and wearing them was a pleasure that never failed.

Through her modelling Noel made friends with a designer, Christabel Russell, who was involved in lengthy, much publicized, divorce proceedings, brought against her by her husband, the Honourable John Russell, eldest son of Lord Ampthill. Divorce was rare in the 1920s, and this was a particularly sensational case, as it hinged on the paternity of Mrs Russell's little boy, and whether he could be heir to the Ampthill title. Christabel Russell insisted that her husband was the boy's father; John Russell denied it. Two men were cited as co-respondents in the divorce, but the cases against both were dismissed, and speculation about a mysterious, unknown lover of Christabel's filled the popular newspapers. The case dragged on through divorce courts, the Appeal Court, and finally the House of Lords, for Christabel refused to relinquish her son's claims. Noel was warmly on the side of her friend, and when journalists, in search of evidence, besieged Christabel's house, she volunteered to act as a decoy. The two women were very similar in height and build, and Noel enjoyed slipping out of Christabel's house, a cloche hat pulled well down over her face, drawing the excited pressmen after her.

Christabel Russell finally lost her case, and the divorce went through. Being so close to it must have made Noel wonder about marriage for herself. With plenty of admiring men friends, she had her chances to marry, but she let them all go.

Several reasons for this readily presented themselves to Noel. To begin with, she still considered herself absolutely committed to the stage, and she did not think that marriage and a career could be combined. This was, at the time, a popular belief amongst women. Noel expressed it through Dr Margaret Caldwell, a character of common sense and sound principles in her novel *Mothering Sunday*, who observes – 'I don't believe a woman can make a good job of a career, and a home and children. You've got to do one or the other.' As far as Noel could see, she still had a long climb ahead to the fame she hoped for. She did not want anything to jeopardize her chance of stardom.

Then, inevitably, her parents' marriage had had a strong influence on her. With so much in its favour, with their love for each other, and with William's unswerving belief that Janet was the most wonderful woman in the world, it had still had its clear limitations. Now that she was away from home, looking at her family from a distance, Noel was able to realize that William's very virtues had bedevilled it. He had idealized his wife, just as he had idealized his children, and this meant that he had failed to perceive their true individuality. He was so certain that Janet must be the perfect Vicar's wife, that he had never asked himself whether this was the role she might, at a more mature age, have chosen. Janet had not voiced her complaints, had not – perhaps – even formulated them, but Noel had seen her mother made tired and irritable by the pressures of poverty, and the duties piled onto a clergyman's wife. It must have seemed to Noel that marriage, even with the most loving husband, could well mean drudgery, and the loss of precious freedom.

She explored just such a marriage in detail in the opening chapters of her second novel, *Parson's Nine*. Her hero, David Churston, is a parson very like William Streatfeild, lovable, self sacrificing, devoted – and almost impossible to live with, since he keeps his gaze fixed steadily on heaven, while his wife, Catherine, only longs to enjoy a few of the pleasures of earth. Catherine is not a portrait of Janet. She is a whimsical, spirited woman, with more than a dash of Noel in her impetuous determination to have her own way. But she fails her husband, and he fails her. With good will and many admirable qualities on both sides, they are unable to achieve any real communication. Noel loved her father dearly, but in *Parson's Nine* she seems to examine and reject the idea of marrying a man of his type. She had no intention of being crushed under even an adoring husband's insensitivity.

Naturally too she was influenced by what she saw around her. Christabel Russell's divorce might be a rarity, but unhappy marriages were not uncommon. 'Look at our friends who married during the war. Would you be in their shoes?' she once asked Ruth; and it was a surprise to Noel that Ruth herself married happily. She had a sharp eye for marital difficulties, pinpointing many in her novels. As if to reassure herself, she often showed how a woman's career could drive a wedge between herself and her husband. 'He can't expect me to dash in circles round him when I'm in the middle of a book,' protests the authoress Elizabeth, in *Caroline England*. Sometimes in her novels couples drift apart because the repressions of their childhood, or an acquired veneer of sophistication, have made them shy away from deep feelings. One heroine, Myra Carroll, believes she loves her husband, 'only she did not want him looking sensitive and hurt every time she said something he did not like.' Such women, and she portrayed several, cannot confide in their husbands; but by refusing confidence, they are ultimately refusing love.

Both her belief in the importance of her career, and the very obvious difficulties of the married state, provided Noel with easy excuses for not being drawn into marriage herself. But beneath them lurked another. Noel was sexually cold. This was not something to be admitted in theatrical circles, where it was assumed that everyone spent their time falling in and out of love, so Noel kept it to herself, and outwardly enjoyed the company of large numbers of admirers. But none of them really attracted her.

Her family merely thought that she was unlucky in the men she met. 'The young men who fell for her were entirely unsuitable,' Ruth wrote, 'mostly rich young Guardees, who were always saying – "Oh Noel, how clever you are!" or – "Oh Noel, you are wonderful!" when what she needed was a clever, humorous man, who would simply say – "Noel, talk sense!" She would have needed a very special man.' And yet, pretty and charming as she was, 'a honeypot' from the time she left school, it seems unlikely that she never met such a man. On the contrary, she may well have met many, but she was unable to fall in love with them.

Plenty of evidence for this can be deduced from her novels, where romantic scenes are conspicuously absent. Noel was inclined to turn each scrap of her own experience into material for her books. She had a blotting paper memory for everything that happened to her, and the reader can share her enthusiasms and excitements, her moments of anger and despair. But never once does she portray the authentic sense of falling in love. No Streatfeild heroine feels her heart turn over at a distant glimpse of the beloved; none lies awake at night in agony over an unrequited passion. Instead, love seems awkward, something to be held at arm's length. Sarah, falling in love in *Shepherdess of Sheep*, chides herself for being 'sloppy'. In *Tops and Bottoms* Bobby snatches a kiss from a girl who attracts him, and then, straightening his tie, remarks with embarrassment – 'My word, think of us getting all soppy like this.'

It was an embarrassment that Noel shared, whether she acknowledged it to herself or not. She had no wish to be involved in a grand passion. Back in her teenage days it had been enough to dream of friendly companionship with Derek. She had never longed to touch him, or craved his embraces. An intimate conversation, or a passing compliment, was all she needed.

Perhaps the fault lay in her upbringing. Those incessant lectures on restraining one's impulses, which had come from her parents, and from Miss Wilson of Laleham, may have fatally damaged some emotional spring. She had learned to curb herself too well. Nor had her emotional development been helped by the injustices – real or imagined – which she felt she had suffered. They had taught her not to trust people. Her mother had disappointed her constantly; even her father had often failed to understand her feelings. Noel had become wary of close relationships. She saw them as a more likely source of bitterness than of joy. It was better not to give your heart away, than to have it handed back, pinched and battered.

Outwardly none of this was apparent. She learned to throw herself into the easy embraces and 'darlings!' of the theatre world. She revelled in fun and flirtations. But underneath it all was a coldness, a tragic hollowness where love might have been.

Family affections still tugged at her, but returning home from the gaieties of London was such an odd experience that she did not repeat it very often. The worlds of the Kingsway Theatre and Eastbourne Vicarage were separated by an almost impassable gulf, for the people Noel knew, the clothes she wore, and the beliefs she had acquired about the importance of money and the pursuit of pleasure, could not have been more alien to her parents. She coped with the situation by playing her role as an actress for all it was worth. She made herself look pretty and decorative, she fell into graceful poses, she pronounced on things in her clear, theatrical voice, banishing with her laughter and chatter the ghost of the shabby, resentful teenager she had once been. She exuded glamour to her small sister Richenda, who eyed in astonishment Noel's exotic dresses, her long strings of beads, her bandeaux, and the retinue of admirers following in her wake, offering flowers and chocolates. Richenda, rationed to two sweets a day, remembered the extravagance with which Noel dipped into a lavish, beribboned box, tried a chocolate, and, disliking the filling, flung it into the fire.

The staider parishioners at St Mary's Church were scandalized by her. 'So far as I can remember,' a contemporary wrote to her, 'your name used to be mentioned (quite unjustly) with raised eyebrows and lowered voices.' 'I well remember,' wrote another correspondent, 'how, when the Vicarage or its family were mentioned, it was in hushed and sympathetic tones, because the Vicar's daughter had gone on the stage.'[1] Noel did not care. Perhaps she might have appeased her critics by going to church, but she had by now lost the habit. Faith in God she never lost, and, many years later, she was to admit that, amongst all her pleasures, she was always dimly aware of a more meaningful life from which she had excluded herself. But, like so many other things, it could wait. Present enjoyment was what mattered.

William was, as ever, too immersed in his work, and Janet too detached, to take much interest in Noel's stage career. There had been a minor crisis when William had seen a newspaper photo-graph of *The Insect Play*, and been appalled by the diaphanous costumes, but it had been smoothed over. Noel was amazed, every time she went home, to discover how little interest her family took in the London theatre. They preferred to talk about Kitty, the wife of William's cousin, Eric Streatfeild, who was producing wonderful musical pageants in Eastbourne, with large casts of children.

Kitty Streatfeild, who was to become famous under her maiden name of Kitty Barne, was some years older than Noel, married but childless. A tragedy shadowed her life. She was a brilliant natural musician, who had studied the piano at the Royal College of Music; but her hearing had been badly damaged in what should have been a minor operation on her ear, and her hopes of a career as a professional musician were shattered. She enjoyed amateur music-making with her husband, who was a church organist and choirmaster; and she conducted small choirs and produced plays for the Girl Guide Association. Gradually her involvement in music and drama for Guides increased, and in 1923 she staged in Eastbourne an immensely successful pageant called *The Amber Gate*, which was so popular that it was fre-quently repeated.

The pageant presented, in a series of brief scenes, a galaxy of children who had been willing to sacrifice themselves for others, from the Old Testament boy David, to a child hero of the 1914–18 war. At the end of each scene, the particular child walked through an amber gate at the back of the stage, pushing it a little wider open, and the pageant concluded with hordes of Guides and Scouts rushing joyfully through the now fully opened gate. 'The idea of the play,' Kitty Barne wrote, 'is to point out to (children) that the way into their kingdom has been forced by a succession of wonderful boys and girls who have created and handed on a standard for children on which the Scout and Guide laws could be founded.'[2]

Noel saw *The Amber Gate*, and generously praised it as 'per-fectly lovely'.[3] She was impressed too by Kitty, whose quiet, gentle exterior hid such formidable talents. Not only was she overflowing with original ideas for her pageants, but she had a great gift for communicating with children. 'She was quite exceptional as a producer, getting children to respond with real enthusiasm very quickly,'[4] a friend wrote of her. Noel returned to London, but the idea of a large-scale children's pageant lingered in her memory, to be revived years later in her story *Party Frock*.

Another relation by marriage whom Noel saw frequently about this time was Lewis Baumer, the husband of Janet's elder sister, and father of Derek. He was an artist, and when the run of *Yoicks* finished, and Noel was temporarily 'resting', he began to paint the portrait of her which was finally exhibited in the Royal Academy Summer Exhibition of 1926, and willed by Noel to the National Portrait Gallery. Noel is shown in profile, her bobbed hair framing a beautiful face, whose wistful expression is counterbalanced by the very determined chin. She wears a sleeveless, yellow dress, and her fingers toy with a long string of beads. Boyishly flat-chested, half ethereal and half tough, she aptly characterized the mood of society in the mid 1920s.

8

Disenchantment

The end of the run of *Yoicks* meant that Noel had to start looking for work again. It was a disheartening business. After twelve months in her 'small, obscure part', agents and managers were hardly feuding for her services. The theatre itself was sinking from its former height of popularity, undermined by competition from all the novel entertainments of the mid-1920s – the dancing craze, with its latest sensation, the Charleston; the jazz cult; the big band concerts; the night club cabarets; the radio and the cinema. The demand for actresses, which had propelled Noel's early career, and filled the Academy in 1919, was now drying up, as managements lost money, and provincial theatres began to close.

For actresses of genius, or at least of outstanding talent, there was still plenty of work. Sybil Thorndike had recently electrified her audiences in Bernard Shaw's *Saint Joan*, and Edith Evans in a melodrama, *Tiger Cats*. But as Noel found herself obliged to struggle hard for even scrappy, temporary parts, and to feel thankful for every shilling she could earn by modelling, her fears grew that real stardom might be out of her reach. There were too many things against her. Pretty and vivacious though she was, she lacked the kind of forceful personality that could be easily projected across the footlights. She was nice to look at, but she was forgettable. Her height was a disadvantage when she auditioned for *ingénue* roles. The sweet young heroines of drawing room comedies could not be taller than their juvenile leads; and directors, noticing her inches, tended to fob her off with minor parts. She soon became aware too of how much ground she had lost during *Yoicks*. Certainly she had enjoyed a marvellous social life; but as a serious actress in the early stages of her career, she should have been making intelligent efforts to widen her experience, studying and observing and stretching herself, not frittering away so much time on pleasure. Perhaps if a substantial part had been offered to her, she might have risen to the challenge, and so remained tied to the theatre; but substantial parts were not offered to a little known actress, approaching thirty, with no particular achievements behind her.

The exact history of Noel's growing disillusionment with the theatre is impossible to chart. For five years after *Yoicks* she swung between confidence and disenchantment, but the latter feeling gradually came to predominate. Aspects of theatrical life, which she had hated during her brief spell as a chorus girl, returned to haunt her now as she searched for work. Beneath her carefully acquired, worldly shell, were the indelible marks of a Vicarage upbringing, with its reserve and scrupulous integrity; and she did not find it easy advertising herself to hard-boiled agents, posing for new sets of photographs to flourish hopefully, and being looked over coolly at auditions, her face and figure commented on by managers, who expected her to be grateful for any crumbs they might fling in her direction. In the agents' waiting rooms, and on audition stages, she noticed all the little subterfuges practised by other anxious women – the artificial brightness, the dyed hair, the clothes astutely chosen to make the wearer appear older or younger than her real age; and she was revolted by so much pretence. Later, in her novels, she was to portray several second rate actresses who, with varying degrees of insincerity and cynicism, exploited thin resources of talent and looks to their best advantage – Maimie in *The Whicharts*, Doris in *Tops and Bottoms*, Flossie in *It Pays to be Good*. Noel claimed that she 'really knew the Flossies of this world'[1], and it was in this period that she encountered them. Theirs, she was reluctantly forced to admit, was a possible way of making progress if one lacked that desirable attribute 'pull'. But it was not a way to which she could stoop herself.

After months of disappointment, Noel finally acknowledged that she was unlikely to be offered a part in another London production, at least in the foreseeable future, and she told her agencies that she would consider anything, anywhere. Moxie was staying in London, Sunday was setting out to tour the United States; but, in the late autumn of 1925, Noel packed her theatrical basket, and boarded the train for Newcastle upon Tyne, where she was to play Fairy Heartsease in the pantomime *Mother Goose*. It was a sad come-down from Shakespearean repertory and *The Insect Play*, and the sophisticated gaieties of London.

The company she found herself working with was quite different from any she had belonged to before. It included actors, singers, comedians, a speciality pair who played both a donkey and a horse, chorus girls, a principal ballerina, and – a troupe of child dancers. Noel had never quite forgotten Lila Field's Little Wonders, with their long-ago summer performances on Eastbourne Pier, but she had not worked with stage children, and her interest had lain dormant for eleven years. When the pantomime children appeared with – as far as Noel was concerned – total unexpectedness on the Newcastle stage, such a surge of excitement swept through her that she felt, she told Ruth, 'like a bottle with the cork blowing out of it'.[2] All at once she had been given an opening into the magic world of stage children, which she had so longed to penetrate.

Pantomime children, the stage school principal, Italia Conti, once declared, were 'absolutely of the gutter'. Italia Conti's own pupils were chosen and trained for the theatre classics beloved by middle and upper class parents – *Peter Pan*, *Where the Rainbow Ends*, and *Alice in Wonderland*, and the effect they made was carefully calculated. They were expected to speak with impeccable accents, and move with the grace acquired through expert ballet lessons. At auditions, 'if ringlets and black satin coats were the fashion among pert young stage children, a Conti child would appear in a simple, coloured coat, with hair smoothly brushed and braided, giving a demure air of distinction that did not fail to catch a jaded manager's eye.'[3] They were, in fact, the sort of stage children whom Noel was to choose for her characters; but part of the impulse which led to their creation came, paradoxically, from the working class pantomime dancers of Newcastle.

These children were lively, hard-working, determined ju-

venile troupers, dashing into the theatre for rehearsals, their
attaché cases bulging with ballet shoes, comics and packets
of sweets, always ready to tease their matrons and mimic the
rest of the cast, but never, by a second, missing their cues to go
on stage. Noel watched their sheer professionalism with fas-
cination. Behind the scenes she noticed that, unlike her own
teenage self, they were 'astonishingly self-reliant . . . shrewd
and businesslike beyond their years'.[4] When they were on stage,
she gazed in admiration at 'those neat legs raised so easily over
their heads, those nimble cartwheels and splits, those pretty
little professional gestures and hand-kissings, those bright
smiles.'[5] One routine, where the children were dressed as goslings and chanted – 'Gobble, gobble, gobble. Quack, quack,
quack', lingered inexplicably in her memory, so that thirty years
later she used it in a pantomime scene in her story *Wintle's
Wonders*.

But Noel did not just watch. She asked questions – all the
stored-up, practical questions she had longed to ask the Little
Wonders. 'There were two matrons in charge of the children . . .
and they replied to everything I had ever wanted to know. Where
did the children go to school? Who taught them their lessons?
Did their mothers travel with them? How much money did they
earn?'[6] The answers sank into Noel's retentive memory. She
learned about the licensing of child performers, and the strict
supervision of their education; about their earnings, and their
contractual obligation to bank a certain percentage as an invest-
ment for the future. She learned how, once they were engaged,
they were virtually taken out of their parents' hands, and looked
after better, probably, than ever before in their lives. Many came
from homes where there were no regular, nourishing meals or
fixed bedtimes; but under the care of the local authority, as
licensed performers, they ate properly, and had statutory periods
of rest and sleep, with the result that their health and physique
improved enormously. They acquired possessions such as they
had often never had, like dressing gowns and toothbrushes; and,
more subtly, they acquired a self-discipline, essential in the
theatre, which would be an asset for the rest of their lives. Far
from despising them as being 'of the gutter', Noel thought that,

compared with many of their contemporaries, they were greatly to be envied.

What use she would make of all this information, she did not yet know; but her passionate interest in the children carried her through what would otherwise have been the 'screaming bore'[7] of the pantomime. Apart from the perverse satisfaction of wearing a quite preposterous costume – silver trousers, a jewelled breastplate, and a silver helmet – and discovering curious points of pantomime lore – 'You hold your wand in your right hand to bless, and your left hand to curse'[8] – she was afraid that her two months as Fairy Heartsease would be absolutely profitless. But she was wrong. Someone who saw the pantomime by chance, mentioned her name to an actor-manager, Arthur Bourchier, and just before the run ended she received a telegram from him, inviting her to talk to him about her next engagement.

Noel's hopes, which had sunk so low the previous year, revived immediately. Arthur Bourchier was a well-known figure in the theatre, an actor of solid ability if not of real brilliance, the veteran of many heavyweight parts like Henry VIII, Bottom, and Long John Silver. Acting did not occupy all his attention, for he loved production and management. He had run the Garrick Theatre for many years at the beginning of the century, dominating his company by the force of his personality, charming them when he was in a good mood, terrifying them when he was not. By 1926 his style of tyrannical management had very much gone out of fashion, but he had no intention of capitulating to the more democratic trends of the times. He was a despot by nature. He summoned Noel peremptorily, as he had often summoned his players, and she hurried to London, flattered and excited.

She saw at once that there would be no problems about her height. Arthur Bourchier was a big, burly, rugged man, with a bass voice, and a background of Eton and Oxford which drew him to others, like Noel, from the upper middle classes. He intended, he told her, to tour with a revival of his successful 1920 production of A. E. W. Mason's thriller *At the Villa Rose*. He would play the central character, Inspector Hanaud, and he was considering Noel for the part of the enigmatic heroine, a girl who pretends to be a medium, and finds herself accused of involvement in a murder at the end of a disastrous *séance*. Noel studied the part, and then leaped at the chance with all her old impetuousity. It would bring her back into the serious theatre, and she had no fears about submitting to the rule of Arthur Bourchier.

The tour went well, for the play never failed to grip its audience, and Noel enjoyed herself. Bourchier singled her out for special attention, frequently inviting her to have supper with him after the performance, and listen – over oysters and champagne – to his fascinating reminiscences about the Edwardian theatre. That this apparent warmth might cover depths of coldness and malice simply did not occur to Noel. When he decided to take *At the Villa Rose*, with a number of other productions, to South Africa, and invited her to go too, Noel joyfully accepted.

She gained just one thing from the South African tour – a love of travel which lasted all her life. She had only left England once before, for a holiday in France, and South Africa overwhelmed her with its splendour. 'Table mountain with that cloud hanging over it like a tablecloth,' she wrote. 'The flower sellers selling those simply gorgeous heaths. The Cape Dutch houses. Stellenbosch with those miles of orange groves, and oranges glowing against those misty blue mountains. The wild flowers I saw from the train on the way to Port Elizabeth: arum lilies, delphiniums, geraniums. Almost it's too beautiful.'[9]

The scenery was the only pleasure, for life in the Bourchier company quickly became a nightmare. Arthur Bourchier's preference for her roused the jealousy of other actresses, and when Noel made a naive attempt to break away from his dominance, and turn to other male members of the cast, his favouritism changed swiftly to angry resentment. Soon Noel found herself cold-shouldered by everyone, and learned that a closely-knit group, which in the days of Charles Doran and *Yoicks* had seemed such a support, could equally well be a trap from which there was no escape. Day after day, week after week, she was obliged to work, travel, and share rooms with people who openly disliked her. Arthur Bourchier had none of Charles Doran's gift for welding his company into a team; it suited him quite well that Noel should be punished. There were moments when he seemed to relent, and smile on her again; but if, lulled by this, she tried to recapture something of her old status, he pounced on her with tigerish ferocity. Such cruelly capricious treatment was something she had never encountered, and she did not know how to deal with it. Enduring Bourchier's moods was even worse than displaying herself at auditions, and she grew utterly sickened by the whole theatre world.

The work of the tour was unrelenting. Even when she was ill with altitude sickness in Johannesburg, little mercy was shown to her. She was expected to get on with the job and not make a fuss. She still enjoyed *At the Villa Rose*. The author, A. E. W. Mason, who was staying in Capetown, saw it, and wrote to congratulate Noel on her 'admirable performance'; but she did not care for the rest of the repertory which, apart from *Treasure Island*, consisted of light comedies. 'I played young girls,' she recalled, 'and in those days they didn't have much to say. They would appear at French windows, and say "Who's for tennis?" and things like that.'[10] Such parts mainly demanded a carefree charm, which Noel was far from feeling.

Possibly Arthur Bourchier's moods were connected with ill health. The tour was physically taxing for him too. In Johannesburg he went down with pneumonia, rallied, sank, and was suddenly dead. The shock to the company was immense. Some of its members began to suggest that the rest of the tour should be cancelled; but Noel, with the stubborn determination which had made her fight Doran over the student Puck, insisted that their contracts should be honoured. The fact that, without Bourchier to draw audiences, the rest of the tour was a flop, did not increase Noel's popularity.

She came home at last, knowing that all the old magic of the theatre had gone. She had lost her ambitions, and was beginning to admit secretly to herself that she would be glad of an excuse to abandon her career. But what else could she do? There was no one she wanted to marry, and waves of depression swept over her as she contemplated the treadmill of theatrical agencies, provincial pantomimes, and overseas tours. In fact she quickly found new, though transient, engagements, one a tour with the famous matinée idol, Owen Nares, but her zest for acting had gone.

At this point, as if her unconscious mind were preparing her for an imminent change of direction, she became aware of small pressures turning her towards the idea of writing. One came during a Sunday train journey, as she moved with her new company 'from last week's flop to next week's landlady and her eternal kippers,'[11] as she ruefully put it. She began to review aloud 'all aspects of travelling by rail on a cold Sunday, the stage as a career, management, audiences, theatre-goers, and theatrical digs.'[12] The review was not complimentary, but as her fellow travellers roared with laughter, one elderly actress made a fateful remark. Noel was in the wrong job, she said. With such a talent for words, she ought to try writing.

The idea stuck so that when, not long afterwards, she was back at Eastbourne Vicarage, 'resting', she enrolled for a correspondence course in writing. Her feelings about her home had changed as much as her feelings about the theatre. The old need to dazzle her family had disappeared. Instead she was discovering new virtues in them, and their way of life. Her father's reputation, unlike hers, was growing. In 1925 he had organized a huge church conference in Eastbourne, addressed by bishops, archbishops, cabinet ministers and peers, on such diverse subjects as industrial problems, the League of Nations, and 'our Trusteeship for other races'. The Archbishop of Canterbury had preached at St Mary's, and William's arrangement of events had received high commendation. He was now marked out for promotion, but he never varied his intensive round of services and pastoral visits – the latter made harder now by the bitterness which the economic depression and the General Strike had caused. For the first time in her life, Noel tried to take an intelligent interest in what her father was doing, simultaneously discovering, with some surprise, how much less it mattered that her parents were not interested in the theatre. Imperceptibly the whole balance of her values was changing.

Ruth and Barbara were married, Bill was working abroad, but she had Richenda's companionship to amuse her. To Noel, recalling her own childhood, Richenda seemed unbelievably emancipated. As a solitary, if not exactly an only child, she had not been kept shut in the nursery, but had moved freely among the grown-ups. Rather than being told constantly what to do, she had been allowed to make her own choices, and she seemed far more mature and responsible at twelve than Ruth, Noel and Barbara had been. She was briskly confirmed at the age of eleven, before she was old enough to indulge in excessive piety like Ruth, or aggressive hostility like Noel; and now the enviable prospect of boarding school lay ahead of her. Noel loved talking to her, and speculating about what her life might have been like if she had been born in 1915 instead of 1895.

Meanwhile she was working at her correspondence course; and when she was asked for two short stories, she chose to try fairy tales. Disappointingly they were sent back, labelled too imaginative, and unlikely to sell. One of them, Noel had been particularly pleased with. It told the story of a conjuror who turned his daughter into a rabbit and then forgot the magic formula for turning her back, so that he was left with a rabbit to rear, while the daughter was brought up down a rabbit hole. On an impulse, Noel sent it to a children's magazine – one whose name she subsequently forgot, and which soon closed down. Back came not only an acceptance of the story with a cheque for two guineas, but also the suggestion that she might write a full length children's book.

Whimsical fantasy was popular with children's editors in the 1920s. It was the age of Pooh, Dr Doolittle, and a host of self-consciously light, artificial fairy tales. The conjuror story fitted the mood nicely, and later Noel wrote a few other stories in the same vein, notably *Dennis the Dragon* in 1939. But interesting and encouraging though the magazine's suggestion was, she had no time to pursue it, as she had been engaged for a tour of Australia in a play by Donald Calthrop called *The Wrecker*. All she could do was to pack pens and paper, and resolve to find time for writing on the long sea voyage.

Never had Noel set off as reluctantly as she did at the end of October 1928. She was sick of the theatre, bored by her feeble roles, and hardened against the glamour which had once allured and ensnared her. She could see, too, how black the future looked for ordinary actresses, now that the 'talkies', the first films with soundtracks, and almost universally American, were packing the cinemas and emptying the theatres. But she did not feel confident of escape. She knew now that she enjoyed writing, but the little fairy tale offered no more than the vaguest, most tentative promise of a new career.

As the boat for Australia, the SS *Ascania*, steamed southwards through the Atlantic, Noel decided to keep a diary. She unpacked one of her new notebooks, headed it 'Noelle Sonning', since she was travelling under her stage name, and in shaky writing, and even shakier spelling and punctuation, began on a record of her activities and her emotions.

Noel was not a self-analytical person. She had a straightforward, even childlike, approach to life – one of the reasons why she communicated so well with children. Describing her voyage to Australia in her second fictionalized autobiography, *Away from the Vicarage*, she claimed that she had devoted much time to thinking about herself and her future, but the diary contains no evidence of this. Instead it presents a simple, almost naive, account of much suffering and depression, shot through with occasional moments of ecstatic happiness, but more or less devoid of introspection. 'By a great determination under no circumstances to think at all, I am bearing life,' she wrote on 21 November. 'Sometimes the future looks so dreary that if I looked ahead at all I'd feel I couldn't go on.'

One theme of the diary is Noel's homesickness. For the first time in her life she was desolate at parting from her family. She had left them so easily in the past. Now it quite alarmed her to realize how much she had come to depend on them, since her experiences in South Africa had damaged her trust in other people. 'I felt very depressed last night,' she confided in her first diary entry, on 1st November. 'The moonlight shone on the water, and made a path like a white road over a purple moor. I nearly cried – fancy if one could walk down that path and find oneself at home.' When the *Ascania* stopped at her ports of call, Noel looked eagerly for cables, but her hopes were usually disappointed. 'Against all my instincts, which told me there could not be one,' she wrote in Las Palmas on 2 November, 'my unconscious self had promised me a cable – from home I suppose – why should they have cabled? God knows – anyway they haven't and I feel depressed.' Sometimes she was tempted to cable home herself, 'just to receive a friendly word,' but, besides the cost, 'they certainly won't answer' (20 November). Her parents had not caught up with the new Noel.

Dejection and homesickness pushed her into uncharacteristic self-pity. Usually she set a high value on courage; 'keep your chin up,' was one of her favourite mottoes. But now she let her standards slip. The weather was often poor, the ship was claustrophobic, and with only daily games of bridge for small stakes to relieve the monotony, she wallowed in gloom.

The diary does not record directly the moment when the darkness first lifted, and it reveals only gradually the passion which was to dominate her Australian tour. On 8 November she sprained her ankle playing deck tennis. ('Disgusted beyond bearing. No games and much liver will now be my portion for weeks.') As she rested with her foot up, she must have attracted the attention of two women about her own age, Daphne Ionides and Ruth Robinson. They came up and spoke to her – and life began again to shine for Noel.

In spite of her Greek name, Daphne was completely English. Her father was a wealthy art connoisseur, with houses in Hampstead and Hove, and Daphne herself was unmarried. She was tall, good-looking, elegant, and very good fun, equally ready to laugh at other people or herself. At home she dashed about in a Bentley or a Mercedes, amused herself on the racecourse, and went to parties and dress shows; but she also gave her time generously to help deprived families in south London. She was the sort of person Noel most admired, and before they had known each other more than a few days, she had capitulated utterly to Daphne's charm.

Now that Noel had realized how little men mattered to her, there was a vacuum in her heart, and Daphne filled it. The warmth Noel had initially felt for her blazed quickly into an ardent affection. Daphne's company was both a delight in itself, and an escape from the other members of the theatre party. But from its start, somewhere in the Atlantic, a threat hung over the new friendship, for Daphne and Ruth were travelling only as far as Capetown.

'Daphne and Ruth are packing – a most depressing sight,' Noel wrote on 15 November. 'God I hope loveth those whom he chaseneth (sic) – he certainly chaseneth me – he sends me to Australia with 9 people – 7 definately (sic) distasteful – 2 charming but not quite me – and these two, one of whom I like more than anyone I've met for years get off at Capetown.'

Soon the *Ascania* reached South Africa. Daphne and Ruth disembarked, and Noel was shattered. 'God but I'm lonely!!' she mourned in her diary on 18 November. 'The little bit I had of perfect understanding with D has left such a blank that I've had a lump the size of an ostrich egg in my throat all day – but thank the gods for the meeting. Such a lovely oasis of a friendship.'

Her attempts to be philosophical soon failed. She felt desperately lonely, hemmed in by an uncongenial crowd of fellow passengers. 'Today they formed a sports committee . . . (I) looked on with the courage born of despair while amusements were thought of – amusements ye Gods!!! Leave us alone' (19 November). Made aloof by her misery, she kept other people at arm's length. 'There was racing tonight – they asked me to dice for the first race. I agreed – for I know I look standoffish for I haven't yet spoken to one of the passengers who came on at Capetown. They are of that variety who considder (sic) a nice high-necked Taffetta (sic) frock with long sleeves – tastefully finished off with lace at the neck, and a string of pearls from Woolworths – adequate evening dress – and I'm sure they think me proud – the little man who asked me to do it treated me like the Squire's wife come to open the local flower show' (22 November).

The training of stage and Vicarage prevented Noel from quite giving way to her wretchedness. She even managed to find occasional diversions. She watched with interest two music hall acrobats who were travelling on the ship; she attended a church service, and won a bridge tournament. And inexorably the *Ascania* carried her onwards. They sailed along the south coast of Australia, stopping briefly at Albany and Adelaide, and docked in Melbourne on 8 December.

From now on the progress and success of the play should have been her chief concern, but she could not take any interest in it. It was a melodrama about the wrecking of a train, with Noel as the leading female villain – 'a dreary play' was her verdict on it. Everything conspired to depress her, quite apart from the absence of Daphne – the heat, the exhausting rehearsals, the photo calls. 'Really to stand in a blaze of electric light – dressed in a frock and coat of velvet, the latter fur trimmed – with the temperature at about 100 degrees – and the photographer obviously no good – is trying a girl rather high.' (13 December) Never, throughout the diary, does she make the smallest comment on her own, or anyone else's performance, on the audiences, the notices, or any other aspect of the play. Only once does she even mention its name. 'A day confined to the dentist and two performances of *The Wrecker* – could anything be more bloody' (20 March 1929); a comment which underscores Noel's total disenchantment with the theatre.

The approach of Christmas 1928 deepened her gloom. 'Christmas Eve – my birthday – never was anything less like Christmas – they keep it in this country as the lower orders keep August Bank Holiday at home – I've fought a very violent depression all day – which reached its climax when a band outside the theatre played "Hark the herald angels sing" – I feel so far from everyone I love.' Christmas Day simply had to be endured. 'Got a cable from Kitty and Eric – pleasant! but I would have liked one from the family – odd they haven't wired – and I would like one from Daphne.'

Then, miraculously, she heard that Daphne and Ruth were on their way to Australia. 'Felt superbly happy,' she recorded when they landed on 6 January. 'I had reached a kind of dead pitch of thinking nothing – wanting nothing – expecting nothing – and now they've arrived and I want too desperately all they or rather all Daphne means – companionship – real happiness – everything.'

Private and reserved as she was, Noel could not bring herself to be very explicit in her diary about her feelings for Daphne. Perhaps she could not even be explicit to herself. On their arrival in Australia, Daphne and Ruth came straight to Melbourne, where Noel was based. But, after a week, Ruth went on to

Sydney, and Noel and Daphne were left together at the Menzies Hotel, where Noel had extravagantly booked rooms for the visit. 'Daphne will move up next to me – it will be devine (sic) to have her so near,' she recorded briefly on 15 January, and, the next day, 'Daphne has moved up by me. Much was said between us – we now have the most perfect understanding.'

The exact nature of this perfect understanding remains unexplained, and there is no evidence that any physical relationship developed. In Noel's adolescent dreams about Derek, companionship and mutual sympathy had been enough, and this may have been the case with Daphne. But the companionship and mutual sympathy were clearly of a particularly deep and passionate kind, different in quality from anything Noel had experienced before. For the week that she was alone with Daphne, she tried to concentrate on present happiness, but, before the end, the dread of separation began to overshadow her.

'I bought myself a gramophone today. I've called it the Holy Ghost – for I shall certainly need a comforter,' she joked desperately on 22 January. (Even though Noel seldom went to church nowadays, words from the *Te Deum*, 'the Holy Ghost, the Comforter', were branded on her memory from years of repetition.) 'Daphne is packing today,' she wrote on 23 January. 'She leaves tomorrow – oh Hell!!' 24 January left her drowned in wretchedness. 'Daphne has gone . . . I feel so bleak – so unutterably lonely again – how delicious the last fortnight has been – especially this last week – I've got so low and depressed that if I stop doing things for a moment tears just run down my cheeks.' The next day's entry shows no lifting of the dark clouds. 'Feel very low tonight. I've missed Daphne terribly its (sic) become a sort of dull ache like toothache – but tonight I seem to have got it badly again and I feel all tears.' For some time afterwards, phrases like 'I *do* miss Daphne' recur in the diary.

Noel had not known such an excess of emotion before. Tentatively she circled its more alarming aspects. 'Lunch with Jean Martin and Miss Rutherford,' she wrote on 26 January, falling back on other acquaintances now that Daphne had gone. 'We discussed Lesbians all lunch – the waiter's ears flapped.' Unfortunately she made no note of what was said.

Lesbianism was a very topical subject. In 1928 a woman novelist, Radclyffe Hall, who openly flaunted her own Lesbianism, had published *The Well of Loneliness*, an immensely long and turgid novel about a tomboyish girl who falls in love with women. The book had been indicted for obscenity, and banned in England, but copies from foreign publishers were easily available, and, at this crisis, Noel was able to get hold of one. 'Am enthralled and terrified by *The Well of Loneliness*,' she wrote on 29 January. 'I can't put it down – it haunts me.' 'How confused and miserable my mind is,' she continued the next day. 'I wish I'd never started to read the W of L, it terrifies me to death.'

Radclyffe Hall and her lover, Una Troubridge, made no secret of their relationship. They were well-known figures in certain London circles, and the prosecution for obscenity had inevitably increased their notoriety. Noel shrank, appalled, from that kind of self-parading. Her deepest feelings were something to be hugged closely to herself. Now, both her upbringing, and the discipline of the stage, gave her the strength to hide her inner turmoil, and carry on. Quite possibly she never mentioned her despair to the other members of the theatre company. It was easier to let them believe that heat and exhaustion were responsible for any flagging of her spirits.

To admit, even to herself, that she was more attracted to women than men, would in any case have been fairly cataclysmic. By now she had probably decided that sexual union with a man was not what she wanted. But it was one thing to live, as many of her friends did, single but ready to consider marriage if the right man presented himself; and another to recognize candidly that her deepest passions were being aroused by a person of her own sex. All the assumptions of the worlds in which she had lived had seemed to direct her towards the common paths of heterosexual relationships. The Vicarage girls had been brought up expecting to marry. At the Academy of Dramatic Art, and in the theatre, it was taken for granted that a man in tow was a desirable status symbol. Noel was neither very introspective, nor unconventional, except in the most superficial way. For her to change the current of her thinking would have meant a great inner upheaval. Yet, looking back over her life, perhaps she could discern some indications of an innate preference for women. Before the voyage to Australia, the people who fascinated her most – apart from the conventionally romantic feeling about Derek – had been the dancer, Ninette de Valois, and the Academy actress, Audrey Carten. Daphne – beautiful, magnetic, and tantalizingly unattainable, for she seemed constantly to leave Noel behind – was their natural successor.

Noel may not have formulated all this clearly to herself. She continued to behave, outwardly at least, as a normally heterosexual woman. She liked men as friends; she enjoyed their company. But the relationship with Daphne remained on its own special plane, separate and infinitely precious, different in quality from ordinary friendships. Noel must have known this after their traumatic partings.

A new disaster was in store. Before Noel left England her father had told her in confidence that he had been asked to be the new Suffragan Bishop of Lewes, and the news was made official in December. 'How glad I am,' wrote Noel on 26 December. 'He will make a nice bishop – and love the work. Confirmations have always been very near his heart.' Her parents moved to their new house in Lewes, and within less than two months, the blow fell. On 17 February 1929 William died of a sudden heart attack in the train on his way back to Eastbourne for a dental appointment.

The shock of his death was never forgotten by many of his old parishioners at St Mary's. They could still remember it vividly more than fifty years later. 'There are many of us still who think of the day when the Old Town stood still, unable to realize what had occurred,' wrote one correspondent. 'Bob Hart, the Verger, was seen by some inhabitants, making his way to the church weeping; and those people, then unaware, questioning his distress, were answered, "I've got to toll the knell for Canon Streatfeild." '[13]

'Our Head came into the classroom about 11.30 a.m.,' wrote another. 'She was obviously very upset, and after a few words with our teacher, asked us all to stop and listen to the church bell tolling. The Bishop of Lewes had died. We hadn't got used to him leaving Eastbourne, but this was really good-bye.'[14]

Far away in Australia, Noel was paralysed. The shock was all the worse because, most unfortunately, she had picked up a newspaper and seen the headline ENGLISH BISHOP DIES IN TRAIN, before she had received the cables her family had directed to the theatre. There were no planes back to England in 1929, so she could not possibly attend the funeral. She had to stay where she was, get on with the play, and suffer her agonies of grief alone. She had bewailed the loss of Daphne in many diary entries; but the loss of William left her pages almost blank for weeks. She had sometimes gone against his wishes, frequently flouted his moral standards, and abandoned the religious practices he had taught her; but he was always the person she loved and respected most, ever since the days when he read *Tanglewood Tales* aloud to her in the dark dining room at Amberley. His unswerving faith had been to her a silent judgement on everyone else's tawdry and timid self-seeking – including her own. His dedication to his vocation had given her a standard for life, and ultimately a theme for her books. Now, at the age of only sixty-three, he had gone.

Bereft of William and Daphne, Noel completed her Australian tour 'like a zombie'.[15] All was weariness and heartache. After a gap of a month, the diary resumes for a week in the middle of March, and includes one striking entry for 18 March. 'Tried to write *Marge* all morning – the plot is write (sic) – but . . . it needs terribly light handling. I can see how it ought to be – but I can't get it. I think I shall finish it – in the rough – and then try re-writing it in a far lighter strain.'

Presumably *Marge* never was finished; certainly it was never published. But the entry shows that writing was something she was now prepared to work at hard and seriously. On board the *Ascania* some dreary hours had flown while she scribbled another story called *Bluebell Bloggs*. (Naming her characters was not Noel's strongest point, as her Fossils and Bottles and Onions and Elks show; and the names in her early books are rather prone to whimsical alliteration, with Tiny Timpson, Felicity Fortesque, and Leon Low, while her own chosen pen-name was Susan Scarlett.)

'My thoughts go so quickly that two hours passed without a pause,' she wrote of *Bluebell Bloggs*, 'but oh how bad most of it is – I shall re-write it of course when I can get a typist – its (sic) very

bad – very bad indeed but I must finish it I have so much to say.'
(26 November) She lent the manuscript to her fellow actress, Jo
Wilson, who was charmed with it. 'I really must do some
writing,' Noel noted on 29 November. 'Her enthusiasm has
spurred me on – but oh the labour – the brain is willing but the
wrist is weak.' Like *Marge, Bluebell Bloggs* was never published.

And as the tour came to an end, and she returned home
through Bangkok to visit Bill who was working there, her
decision was firmly taken. She was bored, overstrained, and
tired out, and, as she wryly remarked in her diary on 23 November,
her whole career had been 'marked by failures to triumph.'
She would give up the theatre, and try her luck as a novelist.

9

A New Career

Nothing perhaps better illustrates Noel's characteristic mixture of courage, impetuosity and innocence than her decision to become a writer. She knew as little about the literary world as she had about Woolwich Arsenal, or the life of a chorus girl. She simply recognized in herself a growing compulsion to write, and surrendered to it, with no more forethought or preparation than was needed to book herself a quiet room in a London hostel, borrow her father's old typewriter, and buy a few packets of paper. Her one slender insurance against the failure of this new venture was to leave her name with the usual theatrical agencies, in case the offer of some very attractive part presented itself. But there were no offers; indeed the agencies were already overburdened with 'resting' actresses. 'The slump was beginning,' Noel explained later, 'the hungry thirties were upon us, and all over the country theatres were closing down and showing talking pictures, which were cheaper and more profitable. It was ages since I had played in London, and there were precious few tours going out. I retired from the stage, and, sad though it may be, nobody seemed to notice that I had gone, nor have they ever asked me to go back.'[1]

But before Noel could start writing, there was the problem of her mother to be tackled. Noel had found her dressed in widow's black, desolate, impoverished, and homeless, since the houses she had lived in had always been church property. She had few friends, and even fewer interests or ideas about how to fill the empty years which stretched before her. Adrift in uncongenial lodgings, she showed an alarming inclination to cling to Noel, while abandoning fourteen-year-old Richenda to the care of school friends and their families.

Noel had already intervened on Richenda's behalf when, after their father's death, she had been removed from the boarding school where she was happy, and sent to a day school where she was miserable. Alone of all the family, Noel had understood how Richenda must be feeling, and she had cabled from Australia to insist that Richenda was returned to her boarding school. From now on she took a special interest in her teenage sister, helping her to choose her clothes, and taking her to the theatre.

With Janet, however, she tried to become as little involved as possible. The homesickness she had felt in Australia had been for the secure family which revolved round her father, not for a *ménage à deux* with her mother in some dismal boarding house. Unmarried daughters were still expected, as a matter of course, to sacrifice their lives to widowed or elderly mothers. Other women writers, contemporaries of Noel's whom she was later to know, Rose Macaulay and Phyllis Bentley, found themselves fettered and their writing hindered by mothers who, though not necessarily tyrannical, could not conceive that a single daughter might reasonably have higher priorities than a lonely parent. Novels of the period, like Winifred Holtby's *The Crowded Street* and Radclyffe Hall's *The Unlit Lamp*, analyse this predicament, painfully common when the 1914-18 war had left so many young women without the chance of marriage, and lingering Victorian prejudice prevented their taking jobs. Noel might have been driven into such a position if she had been less determined. As it was, she found rented accommodation and a paid companion for Janet, and retreated thankfully to her hostel at 11 Cromwell Road.

The hostel was necessary because Noel was so undomesticated. She never learned to cook, and she did not risk taking a flat until she was earning enough to pay someone to run it for her. But after the cheerless Vicarages and squalid digs she had known, a hostel was bearable, even a strictly run one with lists of rules pinned to the walls. She had a single room, and during the day, while the other inhabitants were working, she had total, uninterrupted silence, in which to write her novel, *The Whicharts*.

Or rather she should have had silence, but to begin with it was broken far too often. Old friends had discovered that Noel was back in London, and the idea that she was doing something as improbable as writing a book reduced them to near hysteria. They naturally assumed that she was free for long chats on the telephone, lunch dates and matinées. They badgered her shamelessly. But as *The Whicharts* progressed, and Noel became more and more engrossed in it, the interruptions grew intolerable, until suddenly she saw a way of ending them. She would not get up in the morning. She would simply stay in bed, writing by hand, and if anyone rang, or called for her, she would tell them bluntly that she was still in her pyjamas, and therefore unavailable.

The trick worked perfectly. The flood of visitors and telephone calls dried up, and Noel was left with a habit which lasted all her life. She would go down for breakfast, and then return to her bedroom and bed; and there she stayed, writing, until the early afternoon, when she would get up, type the next piece of her manuscript, and be free for an evening's enjoyment.

She was helped in sticking to this routine by the self-discipline she had learned as an actress. The theatre had taught her to be punctual, and to work however she might be feeling. Now she put these lessons to good effect. 'It's a very disciplined life, a writer's,' she once said. 'You must learn to work. You see, you sit by yourself and nobody's going to write for you; there's no excuse possible – you have got to finish your book . . . You must learn somehow to give up the hours each day (four hours, we'll say) to straight writing, no matter what temptations there are to go out and have a good time.'[2] Perhaps as she sat in bed, driving her pen over the blank sheets of paper, she remembered the example of self-discipline her father had set. She had certainly inherited from him an appetite for work. And presently the book began to flow, the drudgery lightened, and sheer pleasure predominated.

In spite of her success with the conjuror story, she could hardly have been more of a novice. She was strangely ignorant of the contemporary world of books, for in the hurly-burly of theatre life, her habit of reading had slipped. *The Well of Loneliness* is the only book mentioned in her Australian diary. The hours spent in childhood listening to Janet reading aloud had given her a good grounding, but she had scarcely widened her range. She had not been the sort of person who flew to books for escape or consolation, and she was more likely to fly to the bridge table for amusement. As a result she started her writing career untouched by current literary trends, free to choose a plot that was unique, and to work out a style that was entirely her own, witty and vivid as well as slangy and ungrammatical.

The Whicharts sprang from Noel's disenchantment with the theatre. Deftly, and with a sharpness underlying the surface brightness of the novel, she exposes all the facets of theatre life she had hated herself. She shows up the theatre as a trap from which there is no escape; as an arena where innocent girls are exploited, and corrupted; as a treadmill of monotonous, low-paid slavery; as the background for endless pretence, hypocrisy and deceit. It is a jungle where the hard, the greedy and the immoral fight and scheme for pitifully small rewards. Noel makes her readers laugh, but she makes them shiver as well.

Following *Bluebell Bloggs* and *Marge*, Noel chose the typically idiosyncratic name of Whichart for her three heroines. Maimie, Tania and Daisy are the illegitimate daughters of a brigadier, killed in the war while they are still tiny. Knowing he is dead, Mamie and Tania decide he must be referred to in the Lord's Prayer – 'Our Father Whichart in heaven'; and so they adopt the surname Whichart.

For lovers of *Ballet Shoes*, the opening lines of *The Whicharts* are a surprise.

'The Whichart children lived in the Cromwell Road. At that end of it which is furthest from the Brompton Road, and yet sufficiently near it to be taken to look at the dolls' houses in the Victoria and Albert every wet day, and if not too wet expected to "save the penny and walk".

'Saving the penny and walking was a great feature of their childhood.

' "Our Father," Maimie the eldest would say, "must have been a definitely taxi person; he couldn't have known about walking, or he'd never have bought a house at the far end of the longest road in London." '

Apart from the names, the opening of *Ballet Shoes* is identical, even to the vagaries of the punctuation; for, written six years earlier, *The Whicharts* is a more adult, more cynical version of the children's story which was to become known to millions. The Whicharts, like the Fossils of *Ballet Shoes*, are adopted sisters. They share a father, but have different mothers, who for various reasons have abandoned them. Golden-haired Maimie is born to the daughter of a Scottish minister, who dare not reveal her illicit affair to her parents. Thin, sallow Tania is the offspring of a carefree, promiscuous Russian who will not be tied down by a child. ' "I've had plenty of men before – how could I have been so careless – God knows! . . . positively boresome!" ' Red-haired Daisy's mother is a dancer from Balham who dies in childbirth. The gallant brigadier assumes responsibility for his daughters, and then dumps them on his first, discarded mistress, Rose. With the help of Nannie, Cook and the housemaid, Rose brings up the children in surroundings of impoverished gentility; and when the brigadier's death leaves her penniless, she takes in lodgers. It is one of these, a teacher in Madame Elise's Dancing Academy, who suggests that the children should earn their living on the stage. Maimie, with not enough talent to rise above the chorus line, uses her sex appeal to win the men and money who, in her eyes, stand for success. Sensitive, introverted Tania loathes the theatre, and endures misery as a reluctant juvenile trouper, though she enjoys a brief, happy spell in a Shakespearean company clearly based on Charles Doran's. Only hard-boiled Daisy elbows her way to a profitable career as a dancer.

In characterizing the three Whichart sisters and their relationships, Noel turned to memories of her own childhood. Maimie, the eldest, may at times be promiscuous and greedy, but with her fair prettiness, her aspirations, and the warmth of her affection for Tania, she embodies traits Noel loved in Ruth. Tania, directing her own love back to Maimie, and reacting against the sordidness of stage life, reflects Noel's own feelings; though, to establish her separate identity, Noel gives her the passion for machinery which was to be inherited by Petrova in *Ballet Shoes*. Daisy is drawn with scant sympathy, and although in personality she is not like Barbara, she was a peg on which Noel hung her exasperation with younger sisters who outshone their elders. Maimie and Tania are presented without condemnation, in spite of their acutely observed faults and weaknesses. They are the victims of a system; and it is the system, not the victims, which must be judged. And behind the overt picture of the theatre, an earlier memory perhaps stirs, of the Vicarage world, which also entrapped children, and made them its unwilling victims.

To grip her readers, and pull them into the story, Noel uses what, in 1930, were shock tactics. Mistresses and illegitimate children are introduced in the first chapter, swear words drop casually from the girls' lips, and fifteen-year-old Maimie has a scare over a possible pregnancy. The gossiping, breathless, exclamatory style perfectly fits these uninhibited, up-to-date heroines.

' "It's the money I want," ' teenage Maimie declares. ' "And the sooner I put myself in the way of getting some, the better. You know, it seems to me that having money is the only thing that really matters. If you've got money you can go where you like, do what you like. People always seem extra nice to the rich. If you're poor, people are kind to you. Who the hell wants kindness!"

' "Money can't buy happiness, you know," Rose said softly.

' "Oh, my God! Fancy handing that slop out to me. If ever people ought to know that money is happiness, it's us. Look at us! Taking in boarders. Too few servants. Too few clothes. Us children dancing to help things out. Then look at some of the girls at school. Everthing they want. Money poured on them. And they taking it as their right. Why not us? I swear to you, Howdy, I won't be poor. I don't care how I get money, but I'll get it somehow." '

The book was finished in the autumn of 1930, and Noel suddenly found herself at a loss. She had no idea which publisher to approach, and almost instinctively she turned to Daphne Ionides for help. For, while she had been writing, she had been re-establishing her relationship with Daphne; and the fact that this was proving to be as good as she had hoped, added zest to *The Whicharts*. Daphne was now to be seen in her true setting, as a wealthy, sophisticated woman, with a large circle of friends, but she was still brimming with kindness towards penniless, insignificant Noel. She took the precious typescript, and passed it on to an influential acquaintance, the writer Roland Pertwee.

Noel had never met him, although she knew his name. He had written novels, short stories, and plays including *Interference* which she had seen in Australia, with a famous silent scene in which the hero, afraid his wife has committed a murder, searches a cluttered stage for incriminating evidence. The typescript of *The Whicharts* disappeared into Roland's house, and there it seemed to remain for a very long time, while Noel curbed her impatience as best she could, and existed on the overdraft which Bill had arranged for her.

'I am a slow reader, who savours well, like the old claret drinkers, who are no more,' Roland told Noel. But, having read and savoured *The Whicharts*, with careful deliberation, his verdict was favourable, and he sent the book to his own publishers, Heinemann. Still Noel waited, pretending to be unconcerned, but with panic in her heart, silently echoing all Maimie's imperatives about earning money. At last the longed for letter came.

'March 18th 1931

'Dear Miss Streatfeild,

'I have to apologise for having kept you so long waiting for a decision concerning your book, *The Whicharts*. I had it read by two people and the reports were so encouraging that I took the manuscript with me to the south of France three weeks ago so that I might read it myself. The book has very great qualities; it is brilliant and unusual and I should most certainly like to publish it.'

The letter was signed by Charles Evans, the managing director of Heinemann who dealt with fiction. He invited Noel to visit him, and settle the contract, which offered her a fifty pound advance. Recalling the interview in *Beyond the Vicarage*, Noel wrote of herself – 'She came out of Heinemann's office walking on air, she almost danced down the street, she was rich, famous people had liked her book, soon – quite soon – everybody would see her book in shop windows. Oh glory! Glory! Glory!'

Charles Evans' words 'brilliant and unusual' were echoed in

many reviews when *The Whicharts* came out in September 1931. Pasted in overlapping layers, the notices filled fourteen pages of a big new cuttings book Noel bought. Half the papers in the country seemed to mention it, from the *Sunday Times* to the *Staffordshire Sentinel*. Foremost among them was the review in London's *Evening News*, by a leading critic, Frank Swinnerton. 'Those who like reality, with a strong dash of humour and improbability, should make a point of reading the most promising first novel I have read for months,' he began. 'It is full of faults . . . but it is high-spirited, witty and enjoyable, and has been written by one who is in touch with life.' A few reviews complained of 'the proprieties occasionally being lost',[3] or 'the overwhelmingly blunt and outspoken language',[4] or suggested that Noel needed a course in punctuation,[5] but the general consensus was remarkably satisfactory. After ten years in the theatre 'marked by failures to triumph', Noel had triumphed with her very first book.

In 1930 Rose Macaulay, one of the best-known novelists of the time, had opened her new novel, *Staying with Relations*, with the words – 'Catherine Grey, a young female, and, like so many young females, a novelist – '; and Noel indeed now found herself one of a large band of youngish women writers. In the seriousness of their work they ranged from Virginia Woolf to Barbara Cartland; they were often consciously feminine; they were usually prolific.

Several newspapers reviewed *The Whicharts* with the latest novels of two women writers who had already made names for themselves. They were *Julian Probert* by Susan Ertz, and *Finch's Fortune* by Mazo de la Roche. Each represented one of the main strands in contemporary women's fiction.

Julian Probert is the study of an eighteen-year-old boy. It follows in theme and style a whole series of novels which explore the predicament of young people in the uncertain post-war world, where the uprooting of old values had left a wilderness through which safe and easy paths were hard to find. Vera Brittain's *The Dark Tide* (1923), Winifred Holtby's *The Crowded Street* (1924), F. M. Mayor's *The Rector's Daughter* (1924) and Rosamond Lehmann's *Dusty Answer* (1927) were some of the books which had already appropriated this territory, and *Julian Probert* differed only in the sex of its central character. They were earnest, sometimes agonizing, psychological studies; novels which exposed their characters to the pain and bewilderment the writers themselves had felt, and which frequently left their problems unsolved.

Finch's Fortune represented a very different strand, that of romantic, escapist fiction. Unlike Vera Brittain, or Rosamond Lehmann, or Susan Ertz, the writers of these novels made no pretensions to deep psychological analysis or literary style. They told their stories to amuse the many idle, middle class women who had both the time and the taste for light novels. Among the better known were Barbara Cartland, Georgette Heyer, Berta Ruck and Denise Robins; and there were dozens more. To this category might be added the women crime writers, who were beginning to flourish. Agatha Christie, Dorothy Sayers and Margery Allingham had already established their reputations when Noel began to write.

Neither the grave delineation of personal problems, nor the romance of beautiful heroines and dashing heroes, appealed to Noel. She was not introspective and analytical; nor was she prone to falling in love. The novels to which hers are most closely allied are the lively, irreverent stories which Rose Macaulay was writing at about the same time – *Keeping up Appearances* (1928) and *Staying with Relations* (1930) – stories to be enjoyed for their sparkling wit, and their idiosyncrasies of plot and character.

Life for Noel bloomed and glowed as it had never done before. Her childhood day-dream had come true. She, the backward sister, the dunce of the class, was at last a success, a writer praised in the best papers. She had longed as a child to do something 'very grand and important'.[6] Suddenly she had achieved it – or so it seemed as she pored over the reviews, pasting them into her book.

Her success led excitingly on to new things. John Galsworthy, the celebrated novelist and dramatist, sent her a letter of congratulation, describing how he and his wife had read *The Whicharts* aloud, and laughed over it. He was in the habit of writing kindly to young novelists, but Noel did not know this. She basked in the pleasure of being praised by the author of *The Forsyte Saga*. She was even more flattered when Galsworthy proposed her for membership of the PEN club, a society of poets, playwrights, essayists, editors and novelists, which aimed to cultivate international friendship and understanding through literature. Members were expected to have published at least three books before they were admitted; but Galsworthy, as president, waived the rule for Noel, in an unprecedented tribute to a novice. Noel was elected in June 1932, and soon became a committee member, with a flair for running social events.

Clemence Dane, whose long, fascinating story of a theatrical dynasty, *Broome Stages*, had also just been published by Heinemann, sent congratulations. Noel resumed her friendship with Storm Jameson, and began to be invited to parties to meet other literary celebrities. In *Beyond the Vicarage* she described a mortifying blunder when, over cocktails, she was introduced to a 'small, interesting-looking woman', whose name she did not catch, and innocently asked if she were a writer. Only afterwards did she discover that the woman was Rose Macaulay.

The new literary friend whom she liked best was Roland Pertwee. He was a tall, handsome man, ten years older than Noel, coming from a not dissimilar south coast, professional background, as his father had been a Brighton architect. Roland had spent some time as an actor, even touring Australia, as Noel had done, though with a more distinguished company. She was interested, too, to hear that he had acted with Italia Conti's pupils in *Where the Rainbow Ends*, and had acquired a profound admiration for stage children. Later he had tried to earn his living as a painter, and – again like Noel – had only turned to writing when other means of supporting himself had failed. He was a warm-hearted, witty man, with a self-deprecating humour which appealed to Noel, and a vast knowledge of literature, which immensely impressed her. He became a loyal friend, a candid adviser, and even an occasional collaborator, writing the music hall lyrics for Noel's third book, *Tops and Bottoms*.

Roland and his wife Dorothy had a big Victorian house in Drayton Gardens, not far from the Cromwell Road, where they gave parties for literary and theatrical people, which Noel, always a keen party-goer, loved. Most of the guests were wealthier and more famous than she was, and, as in the days of *Yoicks*, she found keeping up with them a hard struggle, but she was used to living beyond her means. Not for anything would she have missed the gay evenings of gossip and charades at Drayton Gardens.

Before long, Roland invited Noel to stay at Highleigh, his Devonshire estate on the river Exe, near Dulverton; and here he introduced her to a new hobby, which she took up with characteristic enthusiasm. 'Roland Pertwee was a keen fisherman, and his family and guests were supposed to be the same,' she wrote. 'I was keen, and I wanted more than anything to learn. Roland Pertwee has many virtues, but patience is not one of them, or at least not the sort of patience you have to have with people who want to learn something they have no talent for. He himself is a wonderful fisherman, and he tried by example and rage to make a fly fisherman of me. I understood perfectly what was expected of me, and still do, but whatever it is that those who fish do with their wrists, which makes the fly flick onto the water and flick away again, my wrist never learned to do.'[7]

Noel accepted her clumsiness with a good grace, deciding that if she could not catch salmon, she could, and would, enjoy coarse fishing. It gave her a splendid opportunity for thinking. She had always found the bath an excellent place for having ideas, and the river bank was nearly as good. She would stare at her float, or watch the moorhens and dragonflies, while she brooded on her stories.

For, despite friendships and pleasures, writing was the most important thing in her life. Believing that a great future lay ahead of her, Charles Evans of Heinemann gave her very special treatment. Because of her precarious finances, he arranged for her to receive three pounds a week instead of the usual half-yearly royalties; and, partly to justify the payments, he employed her as a reader. He knew that, with her clear, uncluttered mind, she could make unusually objective comments on a manuscript. But he insisted that writing must be her main occupation, and in the next four years she completed four more novels.

As a beginner, Noel had one enormous advantage – a very

wide experience of life to draw upon. Her first five novels ranged over surprisingly different fields. In *Parson's Nine* (1932), forgetting the theatre, she returned to the Vicarages of her childhood, with the story of the Reverend David Churston, and his nine children, all named after characters in the Apocrypha. There was a theatre element in *Tops and Bottoms* (1933), but she also used some quite new material. Daphne had persuaded her to help with social work among the deprived families of Deptford, and all Noel's anger about poverty and degradation was poured into the book. *Shepherdess of Sheep* (1934) was set in an Edwardian country home, rather like her grandparents' house, Chart's Edge, its leisured life maintained by a bevy of servants. *It Pays to be Good* (1935) returned to the territory of *The Whicharts*, with the story of Flossie Elk, who begins, like Maimie, Tania and Daisy, in the squalor of Madame Elise's Dancing Academy, but rises to stardom, and marriage to wealthy Lord Menton.

Progressively, through these five books, Noel mastered the art of novel-writing. To begin with she made mistakes, but she seldom repeated them. Through inexperience she handicapped herself in *Parson's Nine* with far too many characters. She manages extraordinarily well to give the Vicar, his wife, and all the nine children at least a modicum of individuality but, as the book progresses, several recede into the background while others grow in prominence, until in the end Noel simply focuses on the youngest girl, Susanna, as she tries to stifle her grief for her dead twin, first in a flurry of dissipation, and then by writing a novel. The strength of *Parson's Nine* lies not in its construction, but in its analysis of the tensions inside a Vicarage family, which are presented with as much passion, and more subtlety than the theatrical tensions in *The Whicharts*. Being at least in part autobiographical, it also contains amusing memories from Noel's childhood. It is the first of several books to include Grand-Nannie with the French boots and 'brotherly love'.

In these first two novels Noel enjoyed shocking her readers with her themes and her use of language; but the shock was to some extent a literary tactic, an amusing ploy, like walking around her father's parish in outrageous clothes. In *Tops and Bottoms* she embarked on a subject by which she herself had been genuinely shocked – the life of the London slums. Beaty, her heroine, is born in a slum street called The Bracks. 'A hundred and ninety-eight squalid, grim-faced houses lolled up against each other down one side of it, and down the other was a high black wall belonging to a soap works, over which a smell of boiling fat was permanently wafted. The wall was used by The Bracks' tenants as a blackboard, on which to write foul insults about each other, lewd would-be witticisms, and, continually, for other unseemly purposes.' Beaty is temporarily rescued from this degradation, but association with a tribe of third rate music hall players drags her back into the gutter again. Over-emphasis on squalor was Noel's mistake in *Tops and Bottoms*. It is her darkest, most turgid novel; and though sharp flashes of wit bring the music hall scenes alive, the character of Beaty is too insipid to prevent the narrative from sagging in places.

Nevertheless the reviews, favourable enough for *The Whicharts* and *Parson's Nine*, reached new heights of praise. The novelist Compton Mackenzie enthused in *The Daily Mail*. 'The intense pleasure I enjoyed in reading (this) book induced me to cancel two reviews I had written of other books in order not to waste a week in bringing *Tops and Bottoms* to the notice of readers, and when a hard-worked reviewer voluntarily sacrifices two nights' reading he must be feeling that the book which calls for such a sacrifice is exceptionally worth while . . . The story is new, or as nearly new as anything can be, and it displays a wide knowledge of humanity mingled with an exquisite compassion that never approaches sentimentality.'[8]

In *Shepherdess of Sheep* Noel chose a theme which was to become very familiar in her later novels, the insecure family. Her heroine, the unfortunately named Sarah Onion, goes as governess to a country house, where she finds an invalid mother, a well-meaning but spineless father, a domineering grandmother, and a mentally disturbed child, Jane, as well as a delightfully portrayed collection of servants. *Shepherdess of Sheep* is an advance on the three previous novels. The construction is tauter, the characters – especially lively, impetuous, tactless Sarah – are well drawn, and a chilling atmosphere of pretence lurks beneath the bright surface. The pretence is that Jane is a normal child; and, when the mother dies, an undue sense of responsibility for Jane compels Sarah to refuse an attractive offer of marriage. A last twist of the knife comes when Jane too dies, and the self-sacrificing Sarah is left without home, occupation or prospects.

When the book was published Noel was, for the first time, bombarded with anguished letters from her readers, begging her to write a sequel, or to assure them that Sarah did in the end achieve a happy marriage. But Noel was greatly enjoying the exercise of power over her characters and readers, and had no intention of sinking into commonplace romantic conventions. To produce an ironic rather than a happy ending was an assertion of her independence, and perfectly justified by the sales and notices she received. Full of confidence, she plunged back into the theatre for *It Pays to be Good*.

The story of Flossie Elk was the most vivid and convincing one she had written yet. She laid bare the hypocrisy of Flossie, a ruthlessly self-centred musical comedy star, by contrasting it with the honesty of the other main characters – Flossie's touchingly humble parents; her dancing teacher who has lost an aristocratic lover because, unlike Flossie, she was not coldly and technically 'good'; and Mouse, Flossie's unwilling mentor in London society, who, with beauty and talent, once aimed at the same goals as Flossie, but was too inherently nice to achieve them.

Written with crackling energy, *It Pays to be Good* is witty, intelligent and subtle. Noel passes easily between the Elks' South London greengrocery and Mouse's elegant West End flat; from the homely devotion of Flossie's parents to the sophisticated triangular relationship between Mouse, her lover, and his wife who is Mouse's best friend. The reviews announced, more or less unanimously, that it was Noel's finest book so far.

The Noel who, at the beginning of 1936, sat in her new flat in Hertford Court, Shepherd's Market, reading the reviews of *It Pays to be Good*, was a rather different Noel from the one who had scribbled in bed in the Cromwell Road hostel. Success had given her confidence, maturity, and – for the first time in her life – money. Of course there was never quite enough money, for her standards had risen in proportion to her fame, but she supplemented her income with short stories for magazines, which she tossed off with the light, amusing touch which illumined her novels. At last she could afford her own home, with pretty furnishings, and the essential domestic help.

She was no longer painfully thin, now that she earned enough to eat properly. Her publicity photographs show a rounded face, exquisitely made up, framed by softly waved hair cut in a fringe across her forehead. She began to visit Elizabeth Arden's beauty salon for manicures and facials. With a gay round of parties and entertaining, theatres, cinemas and ballets, she liked to look her best.

But pleasure was only one strand in what was basically a hard-working and serious life. Another strand was her involvement in Deptford. The social work to which Daphne introduced her, brought Noel into contact with many very poor families. She had joined the Deptford voluntary Child Care Committee, whose members attended school medical and dental inspections, and afterwards visited the children's homes to persuade parents to have the prescribed treatments carried out. In theory it sounded simple: in practice it was extremely hard, a long battle against apathy and ignorance. Many fathers were unemployed and depressed; mothers were worn out by child-bearing, and the futile struggle against hunger, disease and dirt. Slum conditions in the 1930s were appalling. The tiny, overcrowded houses were infested with rats and bugs; sanitation was primitive; and sensible ideas about diet or health did not exist. Gap-toothed parents declared that it was kinder to let their children's teeth rot, and be pulled out, than have them painfully filled; while the mother of a child with a damaged ear assured Noel that a dose of Syrup of Figs would cure it.

Noel threw herself into this challenging work with all the zeal of her Venn and Fry ancestors. However absorbed she was in her writing, she began to make time every week for Deptford and its problems. Theatrical digs had partly accustomed her to squalor, and she had mixed too widely to worry about class divisions. Soon she was making genuine friendships with harassed mothers, charming them with her warmth and readiness to share a joke, and leading them on to talk about other difficulties besides their children's health. Noel could never completely identify with the Cockneys. Some of their ways remained incomprehensible – the ritual spoiling of the youngest child, the discipline of threats and bribes, the lack of daily planning. But she grew to have an enormous admiration for the courage with which they survived their terrible conditions. What made them so tough, so gallant, and so irrepressible, she wondered; and she began to read the history of South London, discovering with delight that Sir Walter Raleigh had spread his cloak for Queen Elizabeth to walk on in a Deptford street, and that Charles II, exiled in France, had promised his mother that they would eat cherries in Deptford again. After her reading, a glow of romance brightened Deptford for Noel.

Presently Daphne had another idea. All the Child Care Committees in London needed more support, and she suggested that Noel might go out to schools, colleges, and women's organizations in the suburbs, and appeal for help. Noel seized the chance eagerly. With her stage training, the prospect of public speaking did not daunt her, and a missionary ardour inspired her. She began to appear in a variety of assembly halls, pleading the cause of South London. 'I have come to ask if you have time to give,' she told an audience in Purley. 'It would reward you a thousand times with interest.' 'London has been combed through and through for Child Care workers,' she told listeners in Croydon. 'You are handy, and I do think it is your responsibility.'

Next day, with equal dedication, she would plunge back into her writing. Having committed herself to a literary career, she did everything with a thoroughness unknown in her stage days. She worked at grammar and punctuation, although she never completely mastered either, and she joined the London Library to widen her reading. She acquired a literary agent, and subscribed to a press cutting agency so that she would not miss any of her notices.

Her publisher, Charles Evans, helped and guided her to an unusual degree; indeed, in the judgement of Storm Jameson, who also published with Heinemann, he adopted a 'somewhat proprietorial attitude' towards her. This was understandable when critics were writing 'Miss Streatfeild is definitely one of our novelists that matter',[9] and 'she will not have to wait long before she is one of our best-selling novelists'.[10] Yet some of Noel's friends wondered if the relationship between her and Charles Evans was not exceptionally close for a writer and a publisher. Probably Noel, still unmarried, pretty and full of vitality, was an exceptionally attractive writer. At all events, Charles Evans visited her flat with unprecedented frequency.

In *Beyond the Vicarage* Noel refers to herself at this time as being in love with a married man. Her autobiographical books are by no means a reliable source of information, and are even less reliable on the affairs of Noel's heart than on most things. Occasional, carefully vague allusions in them to conventional love affairs fitted the image of herself she wished to produce, and truth was temporarily forgotten. Presumably, in *Beyond the Vicarage*, she is referring indirectly to the situation with Charles Evans; but whatever he felt, Noel herself was certainly not deeply in love. Apart from anything else, the fact that he was married would have been an insuperable barrier to her. She disapproved, as strongly as her father, of broken marriages and divorce. Indeed the only point of the reference in *Beyond the Vicarage* is to explain why she felt the need to get away from London. She did not intend to prolong or intensify the situation in any way.

Perhaps she was a little touched by it. She had never written men out of her life, even if she had decided that marriage was not for her. Being admired was always agreeable. Probably it was not a coincidence that at this point in her career, in *It Pays to be Good*, she drew her most skilful portrait of a woman in love – Mouse, who is hopelessly entangled with a married man.

But there is no reason to believe that Noel was deeply affected by Charles Evans' attentions, whatever they may have meant to him. Daphne was still the most important person in her emotional life. This was something she kept very much to herself. Though she was ready to flirt light-heartedly, and to be the life and soul of a party, it would have embarrassed her to display real love in public. To flaunt a love at which eyebrows might have been raised was utterly impossible. So she guarded assiduously her innermost feelings; and because she never discussed, or wrote

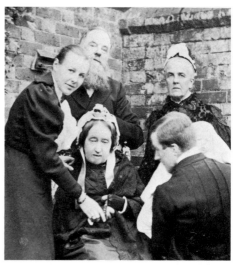

*Janet (on the left) with her sister, Edith,
and her stepmother, Louisa Venn.
(Above) 1894, Great-grandmother Hannah
Streatfield, a daughter of Elizabeth Fry, with
Grandfather and Grandmother Streatfield,
Janet and William, holding Ruth in his arms.*

*Janet and William in 1897 with their three daughters,
Noel, Ruth and Barbara.*

*Grandfather and Grandmother Streatfeild
with some of their grandchildren: Ruth,
Noel and Barbara (on Grandmother's lap)
and Peter and Joan (Uncle Harry's
children).*

*Noel and Ruth about 1898.
(Below) Noel giving Barbara a ride in the
garden at Amberley.*

The family at Joyce's christening.

(Below) Ruth and Noel in the garden at Chart's Edge with Bill in the background.

(Below) Janet with her children in the ~arage garden, Noel, Barbara, Bill on his ~her's lap, and Ruth.

(Left) Noel, Barbara and Ruth at the gate between the Vicarage and the Church at St Leonards on Sea.
(Above) Ruth and Noel with an unidentified child on holiday.

(Below) Family portrait taken about 1904.

Noel saying goodbye to a church outing in 1906, and
dressed as Mrs Varley for a parish entertainment.
(Below) Noel with her sisters, Christmas 1905.

v

(Left) Noel aged 10 in 1906 and
(right) aged 18 in 1914.

St Peter's Vicarage, St Leonards on Sea.

*The girls of Laleham School, Eastbourne. Noel is standing
wearing a tie on the far left. Ruth is next to her.*

The attractive Eastbourne Vicarage.

May Week 1919. Noel and Ruth visit Cambridge.
(Below) Noel as Zingara in 'Vingt-et-Un' in 1915 with Ruth
and another attendant.

War-workers. Janet is second from the left and Ruth second from the right in the front row. (Below) Girls of the Woolwich Munitions factory in 1916. Noel is second from the right in the back row.

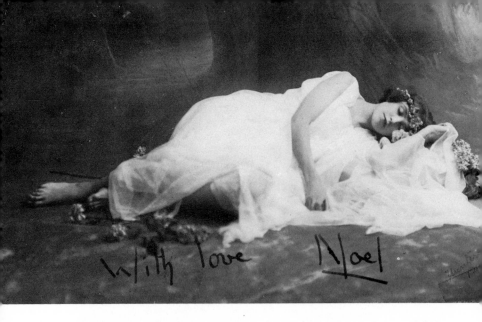

With love Noel

With the Doran Shakespeare Company. (Above) Noel as Titania, and (below)
the Company in the Vicarage garden. Noel is sitting cross-legged on the grass in
front of Richenda and her mother. Ralph Richardson is on the right with his arms
folded, and Donald Wolfit is up in the tree.

(Left) Noel aboard 'SS Ascania', 1926.
(Above) Noel Streatfeild, the author.
(Below) Richenda, surrounded by her
grown–up family in 1917.

(Above) Noel with Deptford children in 1942. (Left) WVS worker with her famous mobile canteen taking cups of tea to a hard pressed bomb clearance squad. (Below) Noel digging her bombsite garden in Elizabeth Street.

(Above) Noel with her publisher, Billy Collins, at a party at the Dorchester Hotel after the war. (Below) Noel with the producer, Josephine Plummer, and the cast of 'The Bell Family', the children's radio serial. (Right) Very Important Person signing autographs at a Puffin Exhibition.

Roger H

*A portrait taken to mark Noel's 70th birthday. She is standing
in front of the Lewis Baumer painting of 1926.*

about, love between women, probably very few of her friends knew how she felt.

Storm Jameson gave a revealing account of Noel at this time. 'She had acquired a certain assurance, a pleasant assurance, very pleasant, something more solid than the rippling high spirits of the young girl with her bevy of admirers . . . Why did she never marry, so attractive, so marvellously alive as she was in her youth and middle years? We discussed intimately many things, people, events, but never touched, even in the lightest way, on her seeming indifference to any thought of marriage. This was not deliberate on my part: I never gave it a thought. It was as if some room we were in together was always dark, or absolutely empty.'

That the room was kept dark was Noel's wish, but it had one serious consequence for her as a writer. Her children's books succeed marvellously, but her adult novels lack the emotional dimension that would make them not merely good, but great. She was observing human nature with, as it were, one partially blinded eye. Her lack of any genuine involvement in ordinary sexual passions left an area of darkness in her books as well as in her life.

Although love scenes were, on the whole, missing from her novels, reviewers were unanimous in pointing out the two particular fields in which she excelled. One inevitably was the theatre. 'What she doesn't know about dancing girls and the theatres they dance in isn't worth knowing,' remarked a critic in *The Star* of *It Pays to be Good*. The other was her portrayal of children.

Studies of children had been an important part of every book she had written. The Whichart girls, the Parsonage family, wretched Beaty of The Bracks, Sarah Onion's pupils, and Flossie Elk, were shown in detail, growing from babyhood to adolescence and beyond, so that the reader sees clearly how the adult is a natural development of the child. The cuttings in Noel's scrap book proclaim her mastery over and over again. 'Miss Streatfeild really knows the truth about the nursery'.[11] 'The child studies are, as one would expect from Miss Streatfeild, masterpieces.'[12]

Noel did not pause to consider the direction these reviews

were pointing in. After *It Pays to be Good* she wrote a play, *Wisdom Teeth*, which she sent to Ronald Adam at the Everyman Theatre, where it was produced, with some success, in March 1936. The only change in her career which she was contemplating was from novelist to dramatist. But someone else had been noticing the reviews, and pondering over them: Mabel Carey, the newly appointed children's editor for the publishing firm of Dent. Early in 1936 she invited Noel to visit her, and put forward a surprising proposal. She wanted Noel to write her a children's story about the theatre.

IO

'Ballet Shoes'

In *Beyond the Vicarage* Noel describes herself as stunned by Mabel Carey's suggestion, and replying that she had never thought of writing for children. If these were her words, they were not strictly true. The conjuror story had been published in a children's magazine, and quite recently Noel had written a set of short plays for children, collectively entitled *The Children's Matinee*.

These had been requested by an old Eastbourne friend, Mrs Bishop, who had decided to raise money for charity through a children's entertainment, and asked Noel if she could provide the script. She could offer Noel the use of an old billiard room in her house, now equipped as a theatre, with a proper stage, lighting and dressing rooms, and she promised to find as many child performers as were needed. She wanted the entertainment to fill a whole afternoon, but its exact form was left to Noel's devising.

Remembering perhaps her teenage plays, Noel agreed, although the request must have seemed rather inconvenient. She was writing, she was reading manuscripts for Charles Evans, and doing occasional book reviews for the press; while, to occupy any spare moments, there were her work in Deptford, her responsibility for Janet and Richenda, and all her social engagements. But she loved hard work, and relished a challenge. Probably she wrote *The Children's Matinee* between *Tops and Bottoms* and *Shepherdess of Sheep*, composing it very hastily, so that the resulting text is disappointing.

Mrs Bishop stipulated that the plays, though performed by children, should be intended for adults, and this created a dilemma. 'There are two sorts of plays for children,' Noel explained in an introductory chapter; 'first the sort (and these are much the best) written for children to act and children to see, and a second sort written for children to act and grown-ups to see. These, I am sorry to say, are the second kind, but I wrote them specially for a charity that badly wanted money, and though I admit children are much the nicest audience, grown-ups are much the best payers, so I had to write these kind of plays to make a lot of money.'

The eight plays which make up *The Children's Matinee* reflect Noel's difficulty. Their subjects were chosen to appeal to children – cats going into Noah's Ark, fairies at a christening, the princess and the pea – but the treatment is heavy-handed and wooden. Where there should be action, the plays are static, overburdened by dialogue; and rather than humour which children could enjoy, Noel offers the humour of adult remarks coyly spoken by children. That *The Children's Matinee* was remembered with affection by its performers, was due mainly to Noel's direction. She went down to Eastbourne to take charge, and the immensely long instructions and stage directions printed with the text, show what care she took over every detail. She saw to the scene painting, the efficiency of the curtain, the sound effects, and the make-up. She commandeered Richenda to be the stage manager, raised a small orchestra, and persuaded mothers and nannies to make costumes, though not to help the children with their lines. 'Do not allow the children to be taught their words by somebody at home,' she warned in her introduction, 'for by this method appalling and totally incorrect inflexions are acquired which can never be eradicated.'

Her energy and vitality made *The Children's Matinee* an unforgettable experience for the cast. 'I can only remember Miss Streatfeild as a marvellous person,' one performer recalled, 'inspiring one to do one's best, kind, full of fun, and obviously quite young, although naturally she seemed old to us little ones . . . (Her) idea was that children should have the opportunity to perform in as near professional an atmosphere as possible, and not be given second best. She treated us as people, not babies, and never talked down to us.'[1] Indeed the real value of *The Children's*

Matinee is that it shows Noel taking children's acting very seriously two years before Mabel Carey made her momentous suggestion about the theatre story.

For once Noel did not welcome a new idea. She consulted Charles Evans, who said rather grudgingly 'that I could do it if I wanted, but that (Heinemann's) would not want to publish it as there was not much money in children's books.'[2] Heinemann's indifference left Noel free to sign a contract with Dent's, but the prediction that she would not make much money was discouraging. Then too there was the distraction of her play *Wisdom Teeth* going into rehearsal at the Everyman Theatre, with an old friend from Doran days, Edith Sharpe, in the leading role. It was a serious play, designed, like her novels, to shock, with its dual themes of divorce and drugs. And she was longing to start work on her next novel, the life story of a woman born in 1870, which required careful research for the background. Altogether there did not at first seem enough elbow room for anything as unimportant as a children's book.

It was not in Mabel Carey's nature to push. She was an excellent judge of character, and she guessed that Noel would presently come round to the idea. Even if some factors influenced Noel against it, others, equally strong, would be pulling in the opposite direction.

One of the favourable factors was Noel's changed attitude to the theatre. When she had left it, she had left with absolute finality, for the stage world was exclusive. People were either inside the magic circle or outside it, Noel discovered, and she had chosen to be outside. Her theatrical friends had accepted, if incredulously, that she was now a novelist; they even admired her for it; but the barriers had gone up, and since her return from Australia, Noel had been no more than an uninvolved theatregoer. But somehow, during those five years of watching from the far side of the footlights, the old romance had begun imperceptibly to creep back over her. Of course she could never again be as starry-eyed as she had been in her youth, but the harsh judgements of *The Whicharts* were being softened. The same process was taking place as had taken place – if more rapidly – in her attitude to the Deptford slums. After a shock, imagination had set to work, and the dingy street, or the sordid theatre, were reinvested with a visionary glow.

At the beginning of 1936 she hoped that *Wisdom Teeth* might restore her old footing in the theatre, but she was disappointed. None of the actors understood her nostalgia for backstage gossip, and the smell of new scenery and greasepaint. She was 'the author', to be deferred to, and held at arm's length. How fortunate this was, Noel may not have realized, but from childhood the unattainable had always fired her imagination, and now it spurred her towards the new story.

No theatre experiences of the mid-1930s excited Noel more than the ballet. It had come to her almost as a new discovery. She had never forgotten Ninette de Valois dancing the Dying Swan on Eastbourne Pier, or the postcards of Pavlova which had filled her mind with images of beautiful movement; but during the war, and then during her stage days, other preoccupations had stifled her interest.

The early 1930s were a crucial time for ballet. Diaghileff's death in 1929, followed by Pavlova's in January 1931, seemed to leave the world of dancing without leaders or direction; but a number of great Russian teachers, exiled by the Communist revolution, had settled in London, and through their instruction kept the ballet alive in England. Amongst them were Nicholas Legat and Enrico Cecchetti, who both shared in the training of Ninette de Valois, and Serafina Astafieva, who taught Alicia Markova. When, in 1931, Ninette de Valois persuaded Lilian Baylis of the Old Vic Theatre to join her in founding the Sadler's Wells Ballet School and the Vic-Wells Ballet Company, there were just enough British dancers to make this frail new venture a success, and Markova was ready to dance the leading roles.

As soon as she heard of it, Noel became an enthusiast for this first British ballet company. 'I from stupidity missed some of the early stages at which I could have been present. When I woke up to what had been going on, and now was actually happening, the Vic-Wells Company was established at the Sadler's Wells Theatre . . . (After that) whenever I could possibly manage it, I was at Sadler's Wells.'[3]

Noel was one of a flood of new patrons. All over England

ballet was being talked and written about, and ballet schools were springing up, full of eager little girls who, in the rompers that preceded leotards, practised their *demie-pliés* and *battements* at the barre, and dreamed of dancing like Pavlova or Markova.

In 1933 another ballet company, the Ballets Russes de Monte Carlo, took London by storm. Founded by Colonel de Basil in an attempt to revive the Diaghileff ballet, it included among its stars Irina Baronova, Tamara Toumanova and Tatiana Riabouchinska, a trio of enchanting dancers, still in their early teens, and known as 'de Basil's Babes'. All three had acquired an amazing technique from teachers of the old Russian tradition, and were well able to interpret the taxing classical roles. Noel was utterly captivated by them, and squandered every shilling she could spare on seats for their performances.

'I think I must have been fated to be taught to love ballet by children,' she wrote. 'Of those three I think Baronova taught me most. For just as the child Ninette de Valois had left an indelible mark on my memory with her interpretation of the Dying Swan, so Baronova gave me something I shall never forget when she danced in a ballet called *Présages* to the music of Tchaikovsky's fifth symphony.

'All great dancers have moments of perfection when what makes them great seems to fuse together; their dancing, their technique, their musicality; and something so beautiful is arrived at that for a second you stop breathing. Baronova often gave me such moments. . . Two children, Ninette de Valois and Baronova, first showed me what classical dancing could mean, and so it was they who influenced my future life.'[4]

The Ballets Russes de Monte Carlo left London, but the memory of fair-haired Baronova in the scarlet tunic she wore for *Présages* haunted Noel. How extraordinary that this exquisite ballerina was just a little girl of fourteen, who came out of the stage door in white socks, under the careful wing of her mother. In *It Pays to be Good*, Noel took a cynical look at child dancers. Flossie Elk calculates exactly which curtsys and gestures will bring an audience to her feet, and fill her dressing room with flowers and chocolates. But Flossie's was not the only story. Through her frequent attendances at Sadler's Wells, Noel had met Arnold Haskell, a devoted writer on ballet, who had toured with the Ballets Russes. He knew the 'Babes', as Noel discovered, and for him Baronova was the ideal classical dancer. As he described her instinctive genius and singleness of purpose, the idea of writing about such a child took root in Noel's mind; and one day, thinking over Mabel Carey's suggestion, she had a sudden inspiration. 'I saw what such a book could mean to me. I would let one child in the book be an actress, but one should be a child dancer. A child of startling talent, such as I had seen in Ninette de Valois and Baronova.'[5]

Even with this idea, and with nostalgia for the theatre to sharpen her interest, Noel did not intend to waste much effort on her story. *The Whicharts* lay to hand; its simple outline still looked serviceable. As quickly as possible, Noel started to rehash it, turning it into a story for children.

Ballet Shoes, the name Noel gave her new book begins very much as a bowdlerized version of *The Whicharts*, tidied, and moved a few rungs up the social ladder. Like Maimie, Tania and Daisy, Pauline, Petrova and Posy Fossil are adopted sisters, though their descent is unblemished. Pauline is the only survivor of a shipwreck, Petrova is the orphan daughter of Russian aristocrats, and Posy the child of a widowed dancer. Great-uncle Matthew, who collects fossils, picks them up by chance, and leaves them with his great-niece Sylvia in her large house in the Cromwell Road. When he disappears on his travels, the money he left for the children runs short. Lodgers are taken in, as they were in *The Whicharts*, and once again one is a dancing teacher, who arranges the training by which the girls can earn their living.

At this point the divergence between the stories becomes more pronounced. Madame Fidolia's Academy of Dancing and Stage Training, to which the Fossils go, and which, with its grand premises and rules of etiquette, reminds their Nannie of Buckingham Palace, is a far cry from Madame Elise's shabby Academy, where soiled rompers dangle from pegs, and outworn ballet shoes litter the dusty floors. Madame Fidolia, like Italia Conti, trains her children to appear in the most prestigious London productions; Madame Elise is satisfied if she can turn out third rate juvenile troupers, who shout and stamp their way through choruses in obscure, downtown music halls. Physically Maimie and Pauline resemble each other, but where Maimie is stuck with inferior chorus work, Pauline is revealed as an actress of exceptional talent, progressing through *Alice* and Shakespeare to the desirable goal of a Hollywood contract. Daisy and Posy are both red-headed dancers, but Posy aspires far higher than Daisy's small successes in pantomime and revue. There is a mystique about Posy's dancing, conveyed not in descriptions but in tantalizing hints. 'She was the only child since the school started that Madame had picked out from the baby class to come entirely under her supervision;' and she wins the glittering prize of selection for the Manoff Company. Tania and Petrova are the most similar pair, both in their love of aeroplanes and cars, and in their being the most sensitive and perceptive of their particular trio of sisters; but Tania, although free of the theatre, is left to an uncertain future, and Petrova is given the solid satisfaction of a house near an aerodrome. The happiness awarded to the Fossils is total, and – in the terms of the book – deserved; that for the Whicharts is partial, and bittersweet. Noel is already demonstrating what was to be an important difference between her adult and her children's books. The former invariably settle for clear-eyed realism; the latter are allowed the comforts of romance.

Helped by her blotting paper memory, Noel set herself to recapture, in *Ballet Shoes*, something of the thrill with which she had watched Lila Field's Little Wonders. She presents the theatre as it was in her teenage day-dreams, not as it was in Newcastle upon Tyne or South Africa. The actors, producers and stage managers are kind and helpful, auditions are interesting experiences, talent is always recognized and never provokes jealousy, small rivalries are easily smoothed over. A haze of glamour is shed over everything, from Madame Fidolia with her cerise silk shawl and pink tights, to the spectacular production of *A Midsummer Night's Dream*. And beyond the Academy and theatre, the fantasy stretches outward, to include the house in the Cromwell Road, where the lodgers, like fairy godparents, give each Fossil sister the thing she most needs and wants – to Pauline an education in Shakespeare, to Petrova an introduction to machinery, to Posy a ballet training.

Just as in all the best fairy tales, romance is firmly anchored to reality. Pauline and Posy may be extraordinarily gifted, but they need food and clothes just as much as any other children; and with her own long experience of existing on a pittance, Noel makes their financial problems almost as absorbing as their careers. The girls' only valuable possessions – necklaces from Great-uncle Matthew – go in pawn to their sympathetic lodger, Mr Simpson, so that Pauline can buy an audition dress – a black velvet, distinguished in its simplicity; a reminder again of the Conti children, but also of other day-dreams of small Noel's, as she fretted over Ruth's cast-offs. Clothes are given their rightful importance in *Ballet Shoes*. And here, at last, Noel found a use for the information about earnings and working conditions she had gleaned during the run of *Mother Goose*, so that the stage careers of the Fossils are documented with complete technical accuracy.

Ballet Shoes was the warmest book Noel had written, full of fun, excitement and family affection; yet it was the book over which she had taken least trouble. 'The story poured off my pen, more or less telling itself,' she recalled. 'I distrusted what came easily, and so despised the book.'[6] She finished it in three months, handed it over to Mabel Carey, and turned thankfully to her panoramic novel, *Caroline England*.

Only one aspect of the preparation of *Ballet Shoes* interested her – the choice of an illustrator. With extraordinary intuition, Mabel Carey suggested that an artist living in Dorset might be the best person.

'Do you mean Ruth Gervis?' Noel exclaimed. 'She's my sister.'

Mabel Carey did mean Ruth, who was making a reputation as an illustrator of children's books. The two sisters had already fulfilled a childhood ambition of working on the same book when Ruth illustrated the text of *The Children's Matinee*. Their collaboration on *Ballet Shoes* was perfect, Ruth's drawings imprinting for ever on the readers' minds the definitive versions of pretty, blonde Pauline, dark-haired Petrova with her shy half-smiles, and lively little Posy. Much later, writing about E.

Nesbit's Bastable family, Noel invented the bus test. 'One way of gauging the aliveness of a family in a children's book is to ask yourself: "Would I know them if they sat opposite me in a bus?" The answer in the best children's books is invariably "yes". Who could fail to know the March girls, not individually, but as a group? . . . The Bastables would not have time to sit down before everyone who knew them would be whispering: "Look who's here!" '[7] Partly at least through Ruth's illustrations, the Fossils would seem as likely a family as any in fiction to pass the bus test successfully.

Ballet Shoes was published on 28 September 1936. Beautifully produced in a silvery dust jacket, 'it crept out quite quietly',[8] but it did not stay quiet for long. Although for most of the year children's books were not noticed in the press, space was made for reviews in the weeks before Christmas, and Noel read with astonishment a loud and universal chorus of praise. Her trifling little book was being called absorbing and enthralling, 'a sparkling story',[9] 'fascinating and accurate',[10] 'delightful and very original'.[11] Mary Stocks in the *Manchester Guardian* described how 'seven solid hours of educational conference were brightened by the thought of getting back to its closing chapters.'[12] Marie Scott-James in *The London Mercury* commented – 'Miss Streatfeild has done what many writers for adults have tried and failed – drawn a convincing picture of a dancer. Posy, one feels sure, will be with Colonel de Basil next year.'[13]

All the parents of the girls in the ballet schools must have rushed to buy copies, with thousands of other parents and relations as well. In December Noel passed Bumpus's bookshop in Oxford Street, and 'a sight met my eyes which astounded me. One entire window was given up to piles of my book and around the window like a frieze hung pink ballet shoes, with a pair of Karsavina's shoes as the centre-piece. I can see myself staring and staring, a whole window to my book – it couldn't be true.'[14] In another London bookshop, Hatchard's, the children's department could not cope with the demand, and a special downstairs counter was allocated to *Ballet Shoes*. Copies were rationed, and even Noel was only allowed to buy two. The first edition sold out; new editions followed as fast as Dents could manage. Child dancers from the Mayfair School of Dancing were photographed for publicity material, and Noel herself chose a ten-year-old redhead to represent Posy. She afterwards became famous as the ballerina Moira Shearer.

One of the words which occurred most frequently in reviews was 'original'. Afterwards, when theatre and ballet stories inspired by *Ballet Shoes* had multiplied beyond counting, its initial impact was forgotten, but in the context of 1936 it was extremely original.

In the mid 1930s the most acclaimed children's writer was Arthur Ransome. *Pigeon Post* was published the same autumn as *Ballet Shoes*, following *Swallows and Amazons, Swallowdale, Peter Duck, Winter Holiday* and *Coot Club*. Joanna Cannan with *A Pony for Jean*, and M. E. Atkinson with *August Adventure*, like Noel, began writing for children in 1936. Dr Doolittle, William Brown of the *Just William* series, and the Chalet School books were well established. Mary Poppins, Mumfie and Biggles were comparative newcomers. Winnie the Pooh was ten years old, and an acknowledged classic. Angela Brazil was nearing the end of her long career, with around forty novels to her credit. Enid Blyton had been publishing short stories, poems and books about nature since 1922, but none of her best-known characters had yet appeared. Rising above a mass of whimsical fairy tales, by far the most striking fantasies were John Masefield's *The Midnight Folk* and *The Box of Delights*, while Alison Uttley's tales of Little Grey Rabbit were already loved for their quiet charm. These were the exceptions. A mass of stereotyped school and adventure stories padded out the children's book lists.

Ballet Shoes was different in both its setting and its outlook. Not one among the hundreds of fictitious schools had been a stage school; and the Cromwell Road house, with boarders crammed into every spare room, was quite unlike the spacious manor houses and vicarages inhabited by the general run of child characters. A central London background was in itself unusual. That the country was infinitely superior to the town was an article of faith with most children's writers, who aligned themselves with the popular 1930s cult of outdoor life. Arthur Ransome pre-eminently, but many other writers too, presented an idealized picture of country holiday life, filling the reader's mind with images of cloudless skies, ruffled water, and hedges rich with meadowsweet and wild roses, of campsites with kettles slung over the fire and sausages sizzling, of swimming, boating and caravanning, and sleeping under the stars. Very occasionally, on holiday, the Fossils dip into this world, but for them reality is the London Underground, or the Earl's Court Road with its motor showrooms.

If the setting of *Ballet Shoes* was original enough, the ethos was startlingly so. Most characters in contemporary children's books were firmly placed in the middle or upper classes at a time when such people had both ample leisure, and the money to enjoy it. With servants in every household, these story-book children have no practical chores to curtail their freedom. Campsite cooking and washing up are rare adventures. The reader moves in a well-ordered world of bishops and baronets, writers and artists, and clergymen redeemed from any suspicion of undue piety by 'a particularly human twinkle in his eye', [15] or 'a humorous curly mouth with a grin not too far off'. [16] Boarding school education is taken for granted, and the names of Eton, Winchester and Harrow sprinkle the pages familiarly. To be sent to the village school is a disaster, [17] while a Commercial Academy is a humiliation almost beyond bearing. [18]

In such a society the question of earning one's living, as the Fossils are obliged to do, scarcely arises. This did not mean that hard work was in itself frowned upon; but children were expected to work only at certain permitted things, and in standard ways. Sport could be practised constantly, as long as it was amateur, not professional sport. Professionalism, carrying the taint of money, was no concern of young ladies and gentlemen. The mixture of uneasiness and scorn with which Noel's Edwardian dancing class had watched the child professional, lingered on. So the kind of rigorous training provided by Madame Fidolia and her staff was quite new in fiction. Children in books managed on their own, and developed self-reliance without always running to grown-ups for help. The Swallows and Amazons learn to handle boats with no advice from sailing school instructors, and without even life jackets to save them if they make some terrible mistake. 'Better drowned than duffers,' telegraphs Commander Walker, with the same breezy, let-them-stand-on-their-own-feet attitude, which allows his wife, later in *Swallows and Amazons*, to leave nine-year-old Titty alone on her island. Similarly when Joanna Cannan's heroine, Jean, declares that she has taught herself to ride 'by sad experience and out of books'[19] the reader knows she is to be applauded for showing the independence of spirit which was the convention of the time.

Within the limits of amateurism and self-sufficiency, children were allowed to excel, as long as it was clearly understood that prizes and rewards were quite unimportant. These were, of course, often won, but they were usually received with an approved offhandedness. Children who were too competitive in gymkhanas were condemned as pot-hunters. So both the pleasure with which Pauline and Posy naturally regard their successes, and the importance which they attach to them, were a daring departure from tradition. Professionalism was made, for the first time, respectable.

Equally original, though here Mabel Carey must take the credit, was the choice of the theatre as a subject, for long-standing puritan prejudice, and the exaltation of the amateur, had previously combined to make it unacceptable. Amateur theatricals and dancing had always been allowed in children's books. Back in the nineteenth century Juliana Ewing had used a children's drawing room play with charm and dramatic effect in *A Very Ill-Tempered Family*,[20] and somewhat later Elsie Oxenham, in her many 'Abbey Girls' books, had preached moral uplift and widened horizons through folk dancing.[21] But association with the professional theatre had always implied condemnation. When the Victorian moral classic *Jessica's First Prayer*,[22] revealed that Jessica's mother had been on the stage, it was explaining euphemistically that she was a prostitute. Its famous contemporary, *A Peep behind the Scenes*,[23] fiercely attacked the false glamour of the theatre, and it was certainly not the author's intention that, for most readers, the impression of the glamour far outweighed the solemn warnings. The book's heroine, Rosalie, who dances with pink roses in her hair, was the first, and – until the Fossils – the only child star in children's literature.

Noel did not at all realize what an innovation she had made. 'I don't think I knew what had come before me in the way of books,'[24] she said twenty years later. Even if she had wanted to know, it would have been difficult to have found out, except by very extensive reading. There was no body of critical work on children's literature, to provide a background against which she could place *Ballet Shoes*. Reviewing was sporadic. It was assumed that children's books, apart from a few recognized classics, were fundamentally unimportant, an assumption linked to the suspicion many parents had about their children reading at all. To be 'stuffing indoors with a book' was a sign of moral degeneracy in many middle class households of the 1930s; while battered school 'libraries' hidden in dark cupboards, or collections banished to the distant shelves of unwelcoming public libraries, spoke eloquently of the value most frequently attached to children's books.

When serious criticism did begin, it was often said that Noel had initiated a new *genre*, the career novel. Of course no such intention had crossed Noel's mind as she dashed off *Ballet Shoes*; and the career books which proliferated particularly in the 1950s, with their emphasis on information – case histories, rather than stories, of young vets or social workers or hairdressers – bear little resemblance to anything Noel wrote. The difference lies in a confusion between careers and vocations. Noel's books were not meant, as most career novels were, to help readers make a rational decision about their future. They were stories of children discovering in themselves some strong vocation, and working with disciplined enthusiasm to achieve it. Pauline, Petrova and Posy owe not a little to William Streatfeild.

What makes a children's classic? Something of the secret of *Ballet Shoes* can be discovered when it is compared with two books about children with vocations, written by friends of Noel's, which appeared soon after it, were hailed in their turn, and then forgotten.

Arnold Haskell's *Felicity Dances* (1937) has a similar story to *Ballet Shoes*, with two little girls who work and dream about their future as ballerinas. But while Noel, with her blotting paper memory, unerringly chose just the detail of training and performance which would most interest children, Arnold Haskell overloaded a slight narrative with long synopses of ballets, and moral reflections. With many good ingredients, the final result is too serious, too educational; while by contrast, in *Ballet Shoes*, sheer light-hearted fun and excitement sparkle on every page.

For Kitty Barne's *She shall have Music* (1938) Noel claimed direct responsibility. Worn out by the many plays she had produced since *The Amber Gate*, and with her work as music and drama adviser to the Girl Guide Association, Kitty Barne had collapsed, and was seriously ill when Noel went to visit her soon after *Ballet Shoes* was published. 'I sat on her bed,' Noel recalled, 'and said that amateur theatricals were killing her; they might be fun, they might be worthwhile, but it was time she turned her talents to something else. In a weary voice she asked: "What work?" and I said: "Instead of writing plays for children, write books for them, and let the first be about a musical child." She wrote that book, and in so far as a book is ever a classic in its author's lifetime, that one is.'[25]

This was generous praise, and not undeserved. *She shall have Music* tells, with considerable charm, the story of Karen, whose musical genius carries her over many daunting obstacles to the scholarship which finally secures her career. Noel placed it on every list of ideal children's books she ever composed, and for a time it enjoyed great popularity, only just missing the 1938 Carnegie Medal for children's books. But gradually, while *Ballet Shoes* was constantly reprinted, *She shall have Music* faded from view. It was not just that a musical career lacked the glamour of a theatrical one, or that plays and ballets are more likely to stimulate a child's imagination than concerts, though these factors clearly raise difficulties. As time passed the heroine, Karen, proved to be too much a stereotype of the 1930s. She is polite, modest, and uncompetitive, and these qualities went out of fashion. The Fossils seemed exceedingly modern in 1936, but their special traits – the enthusiasm, the toughness, and the self-centredness, so characteristic of children – proved to be timeless and universal. They could belong equally to any period. Nearly fifty years after its publication, when *Ballet Shoes* had sold ten million copies, Noel was receiving letters almost identical with her original fan mail.

'Dear Noel Streatfeild,' wrote a child in 1937, 'I do want to tell you how much I like your book *Ballet Shoes*. It is one of the best books I have ever read.' The sentiments were to be repeated over and over and over again.

II

Difficult Characters

The extraordinary success of *Ballet Shoes* was not wholly to Noel's liking. She felt, perversely, that she was being praised for the wrong thing. She was a writer for adults, and she half resented the lavishing of so much attention on a children's book. Nor was her resentment lessened by the difficulties she had with her next novel, *Caroline England*. It was planned on a larger time scale than any of her other novels, and the sheer amount of ground to be covered made it unwieldy and diffuse. After the easy writing of *Ballet Shoes* it was a hard grind, and, looking at it critically, Noel was disappointed.

The heroine, Caroline, born in 1870, has a life of almost unrelieved gloom. She suffers a miserable childhood at the hands of a sadistic nannie, a repressive aunt, and one of the domineering grandmothers who recur throughout Noel's books. Elopement with a husband who proves unfaithful, and several unsatisfactory children, add nothing to either Caroline's happiness or the reader's, and a lonely old age brings the book at last to its end. Caroline is Noel's most dreary heroine, and although some reviews praised particularly the scenes of childhood, the book's reception was tepid compared with the acclaim for *Ballet Shoes*.

Noel was tired. She had been working at top pressure for six years, with visits to Deptford, and perhaps the relationship with Charles Evans, to increase the stresses of her life. She had invested great hopes in *Wisdom Teeth*, which had been well received, and had even transferred briefly to the West End, but which ultimately failed to make any significant impact. She had begun to long desperately to get away from London, and let a change restore her exhausted vitality.

Meanwhile, and too quickly for comfort, she was being

prodded further into the world of children's books. No one had asked her to lecture about her adult novels, but after *Ballet Shoes* she started receiving invitations to speak on children's books from as far away as Manchester. The fees were tempting, and she enjoyed lecturing, but she was alarmingly ignorant about her subject. She hurried to the London Library, and renewed acquaintance with some of the books of her childhood, recalling her repugnance at the hero's long-drawn-out death in Juliana Ewing's *The Story of a Short Life*, which her father had once read aloud with tears pouring down his cheeks – 'I can never see the cover of a Mrs Ewing book now without feeling vaguely embarrassed,' she confessed[1] – and the dissatisfaction which tinged her love for the *Alice* books – 'I remember thinking as a small child that if Alice did not go to sleep we should hear more about her home.'[2] Having dealt with the Victorians in her lectures, she skipped rapidly on to *Ballet Shoes*. She still knew nothing of E. Nesbit whose books she was later to admire very much, or indeed any writers after Frances Hodgson Burnett and Kenneth Grahame.

Mabel Carey naturally wanted to follow up the success of *Ballet Shoes*. Noel tried at first to protest that her children's books were only a sideline, and that she wanted to go to America; but another suggestion, cleverly implanted by Mabel Carey, gave her new inspiration. If *Ballet Shoes* had sprung partly from Noel's envy of Lila Field's *Little Wonders*, were there other children whom Noel had envied?

That set Noel thinking, and looking back over her school days, she remembered clearly envying the girls who were good at games, especially tennis. Physically clumsy, and with no ball sense, she had been hopeless herself. 'I suppose no one could have less talent for sport than I have,' she wrote. 'The tennis sets I must have ruined . . . I can still see the expression on people's faces when a hostess said, "Oh, Noel, you haven't played yet. Now, who shall partner Noel?" '[3] Yet with the obstinacy characteristic of her adolescence she had refused to admit the truth to herself, and had day-dreamed of fame as a tennis star.

When she heard all this, Mabel Carey responded enthusiastically. She was planning a series called 'Tales of Sports and

Games', with other writers already preparing stories based on golf, cricket and sailing. A tennis story would fit the pattern perfectly. With her vitality renewed by the prospect, Noel threw herself into some thorough research. She watched children being coached in tennis, talked to them about training methods, and ransacked libraries for books about tennis champions.

The thinking time, before she actually started a book, was always important to Noel. She needed to be completely familiar with her background, and to know her characters intimately. Now, as she researched the story which she was to call *Tennis Shoes*, Noel thought deeply about what a junior tennis star would be like.

A starting point was Posy, a child who, seen from one angle, is ruthlessly self-centred, and a deplorable show-off, and, from another, so dedicated to her vocation that ordinary standards hardly apply to her. Such characteristics are also part of Nicky Heath, the heroine of *Tennis Shoes*. But Nicky is a more complex and interesting character than Posy, for, as Noel dug back into the past to revive memories of her tennis ambitions, she began also to remember attitudes and aspects of her own temperament which tallied remarkably with traits in Posy and Nicky. Always able to laugh at herself, she could now admit honestly that she must have been very tiresome, cocky and argumentative, but she could also understand why she had been so. The reason was that unshakeable conviction that she was special. It had taken years, and one long false trail, to discover where the specialness lay; but it had been there inside her, and no one had recognized it. Remembering it all so clearly, it now seemed right and appropriate to bestow just such a conviction on Nicky, giving her an arrogance which maddens her family, and for which the justification is only gradually revealed. Nicky is as close as Noel got to a self-portrait, drawn with subtlety and wit. She is difficult, assertive and conceited; she behaves as idiotically as Noel herself had sometimes done; but as a genius discovering herself she is totally convincing.

In choosing a heroine like Nicky, Noel took an enormous risk. Bumptious characters got short shrift in children's books, and Nicky does not even have Posy's romantic background to provide an excuse for her. She is no semi-orphan, clutching pink ballet shoes in the cradle, but a suburban doctor's daughter. In ninety-nine books out of a hundred Nicky would get her come-uppance, trounced in some dramatic competition like the pony book pot-hunters. Instead she is allowed the success she herself expects, and Noel's writing is so skilful that by the last tourna-ment the reader is eagerly cheering her on.

The book centres on the contrast between two sisters, Susan and Nicky. Susan is the ideal heroine of the 1930s, modest, good-mannered, sporting, a natural conformer. She works hard at her tennis, reaches the final in her first tournament, and is praised by a discerning tennis correspondent. A brilliant future seems within her grasp. Yet all along it is clear to an alert reader that Susan lacks one vital element – a match-winning tempera-ment. She is too self-conscious, too nice, and too unsure to have complete faith in herself.

While attention seems focused on Susan's high destiny, Noel is dropping tiny clues about her tiresome young sister, Nicky. Some apparently trivial juggling shows Nicky handling balls better than Susan. When Nicky begins to play tennis, 'it was odd how often, without any apparent effort on her part, her strokes came off'. Even her exasperating habit of arguing about every-thing shows an instinctive hunger for mastery, so deficient in Susan. Annie, the maid who understands Nicky, remarks – 'Funny kid, you are. You can do anything you put your mind to.' But what value is a maid's opinion, compared with a tennis correspondent's? Minor accidents prevent Nicky competing in tournaments, so that her progress goes unmeasured for a long time. Susan, who practises with her, is too immersed in her own game to notice Nicky's. When the crucial moment from Noel's childhood day-dreams arrives, and Nicky, not Susan, is picked for special coaching, the choice is both astonishing and absol-utely right.

Tennis Shoes moves at the leisurely pace of the 1930s, creating a comfortable family atmosphere with holidays, plays and visits to the circus, as well as tennis. Noel wrote best when she could write expansively. Characters are introduced who would even-tually become over-familiar in her stories, but who are now fresh and original – the ineffectual mother supported by her genteel dogsbody, Pinny; the tough, kind-hearted Cockney maid, Annie; the precocious small brother with a talent for singing; the adored family dog. D. L. Mays, a *Punch* cartoonist, captured them all in charmingly simple illustrations, full of period details of hats and deck chairs and penny slot machines. But leisurely days are only the background. The theme of the book is Noel's characteristic insistence on the highest professional standards, on Nicky working out her vocation, with toil and sweat and self-sacrifice. *Tennis Shoes* was always one of Noel's favourite books, and deserved to be. She handled her plot and characters with tremendous skill, and once again the reviews were warmly enthusiastic.

It was published in 1937, at the end of an extraordinarily crowded summer, which only a person with Noel's energy could have survived. As soon as she had sent the manuscript to Dent's, she set off to fulfill her dreams of visiting America. Ever since the gay days of the early 1920s, America had been a magnet to her. She had danced to American jazz bands, drunk American cocktails, and soaked herself in American films. The Hollywood contract, which she awarded Pauline at the end of *Ballet Shoes*, represented for her, as for almost everyone at that time, the pinnacle of theatrical success. America stood for all that was modern and dashing, the new world where anyone might hope to win fame and fortune.

Noel hoped that her fortune might come through writing film scripts. If she could get some really lucrative assignment, she might be able to give up all the tedious bits and pieces of reviews and magazine stories which were still essential to supplement her income. *Ballet Shoes* had done very well financially, but she wanted a larger flat with more elegant furnishings, and she wanted to travel, and somehow her royalties always melted away. So she crossed the Atlantic to New York, where the firm of Random House was publishing *Ballet Shoes*, and then hurried on to California.

But all her hopeful inquiries and contacts failed. No one wanted another English script writer; and if, indeed, anyone knew her work, they must have recognized that her gifts were hardly suited to contriving the lushly romantic films which were Hollywood's speciality. After a brief stay she returned to England, a little disappointed, but determined to go back again and try harder; for the warmth, beauty and luxury of California were entirely to her taste.

Back home an exciting new project awaited her. Mabel Carey wanted her to write a book about a circus, and had arranged for her to tour with the celebrated Bertram Mills circus to gather material.

Circus stories were nearly as rare as theatre stories, though one had been published in 1936, Howard Spring's *Sampson's Circus*, which gives a delightful picture of a carefree, amateurish company, where nobody practises much, where the 'ferocious man-eating tiger', and the 'wild Cossack horse' are docility personified; but where the performers are sustained by a strong sense of comradeship, a love of display, and unlimited quantities of sausages, liver and bacon. It is the old-fashioned, traditional kind of circus which had ambled through the English countryside since the beginning of the nineteenth century. There were still such circuses on the roads, but Bertram Mills circus, which Mabel Carey had contacted, was a very different affair.

It had been founded in 1920 when Bertram Mills, a former carriage builder and circus enthusiast, had been invited to revive the pre-war Christmas circus at Olympia. Having got a brilliant international show together, he was unwilling to disband it, so for most of the year he held it together with countrywide tours, returning to London for the Christmas season. By 1937 his circus was an enormous organization, with artistes recruited from all over the world, and standards of perfection which equalled or excelled anything Noel had seen in the theatre. Merely to watch the build-up, when the circus reached a new site, was breathtaking. Armies of tent-hands laced together the gigantic canvases of the big top, hauled them over two seventy-foot king poles, hammered in five hundred half poles and quarter poles, and dug and sawdusted the ring. Spacious animal lines were erected, and three miles of electric cables were rigged up. In 1937 this formidable build-up, with its complementary pull-down, took place in forty-seven towns – a record for the circus.

Noel plunged into circus life with typically whole-hearted enthusiasm. Usually she stayed in a hotel near the site, but occasionally she stayed in one of the caravans which were drawn up in an appointed order round the showground. She watched rehearsals and performances, she talked to artistes and stage hands, she got to know the animals, and she learned the circus jargon. Being an animal-lover, she was relieved to find that cruelty had no part in the animals' training. They were taught by 'gentling', which she described as 'praise, a pat and a present'.[4] Such a method kept the animals alert and happy, and a happy animal was safer to handle than an unhappy or sulky one. But although she adored the dogs and horses, she could not quite stifle her doubts about making genuinely wild animals perform.

The philosophy of the circus people interested her greatly. Living in self-sufficient isolation, they developed a team spirit which carried them through every crisis or emergency. Some of these emergencies made enthralling stories. Rainstorms caused floods, when everyone from lorry drivers to acrobats dug trenches to divert the water from the big top. There had been a fire, when everyone helped to lead frightened animals out of danger, and a scare when four tigers escaped and had to be recaptured. Most disastrous was the gale which ripped the twenty-five thousand square feet of the canvas big top to shreds in ten minutes. Noel did not actually witness any of these excitements, but she filled her notebooks with everything she heard.

When she had collected all her material, she set off again for California, travelling in a slow cargo boat. During a stop in Mexico she made a light-hearted visit to a fortune teller, and was intrigued to hear that although much gold would pass through her hands, only in 1939 would she touch it and keep it. She never thought of connecting the prophecy with her book, on which she was already hard at work. She always liked working on boats.

She stayed in America for seven months, but instead of scripts, she seemed only to have time for her book, which she had named *The Circus is Coming*. It was not easy to find the best way of using her material, and, in spite of the tour, she was aware of many gaps in her knowledge. Too many of her questions had been answered vaguely – 'Oh, it's just our way,' or 'It's always done that way.'⁵ Lacking the sense of sure-footed familiarity which she would have liked, she decided she would have to write the book from an outsider's viewpoint. She would have two central characters, as ignorant as she had been, who would gradually learn about the circus.

Cob's circus, the imaginary setting for the book, is based on Bertram Mills', with its troupes of tent-hands and dancing girls, and performers from many countries. She packed the story with the intimate details she had learned about animal behaviour and personality, and about teamwork and professional dedication. She spotlights a handful of families – the Russian Petoffs, the German Schmidts, and the French Moulins – and shows how they work continually to improve their acts. The Schmidt children take everything, from making their beds to training their sea-lions, with the same grave solemnity, while Fifi Moulin, chic and self-possessed, has Posy's impersonal certainty about her own ability. Unrelenting effort is natural to them all; no one wastes time fooling around.

Into this austere world Noel introduces an orphan brother and sister, Peter and Santa. It is their misfortune that their Aunt Rebecca has brought them up exactly as a duchess, whose maid the aunt was, brought up her children. Improbable though this seems, it had actually happened to the beloved Grand-Nannie of Noel's childhood. Her mother had been the nursery maid in a castle, and had brought up her own offspring like the castle children. For Grand-Nannie, most of whose life was spent looking after children in big country houses, this had not mattered, but Noel must have wondered how a young girl, with Grand-Nannie's upbringing, would have fared in a harsher, less well-ordered *milieu*. Such speculation gave her the starting point for *The Circus is Coming*. When Aunt Rebecca dies, and the threat of separate orphanages hangs over Peter and Santa, they run away to find their only other relation, Uncle Gus, who is a clown in Cob's circus. The rest of the story shows how they adapt themselves painfully to circus life, and how the experience changes them.

If Noel took a gamble with Nicky in *Tennis Shoes*, she took an even bigger one with Peter and Santa, and the triumphant success of the book was the reward for her courage. Peter in particular is a most subtly developed character. In the opening chapters he appears molly-coddled and cissy, with a condescending manner which disguises from everyone, including Peter himself, his cool, resourceful brain. Through the folly of Aunt Rebecca's upbringing, he always gives the wrong impression. Gus, his uncle, takes an instant dislike to him, gibing at his assumptions of superiority, making sure Peter knows he has been nick-named Little Lord Fauntleroy, sneering at Peter's attempts to please him. These undeserved humiliations both swing the reader onto Peter's side, and open his own eyes to the image of himself he is presenting. Drawing on depths of courage and determination, which should have been apparent in his successful plan for running away, he sets himself to change his image; so that the boy who once primly refused to sit on a doorstep, ends by coping magnificently with a stable fire. Noel makes his progress absolutely convincing, demonstrating, as she did with Nicky, that heroes and heroines can be carved from the most unpromising materials.

Santa is more readily likeable, but there are setbacks and lessons for her as well. She too has tried to improve her image by boasting that she can play the violin, and the revelation of her ineptitude is as wounding as any of Peter's humiliations. The circus world is fiercely honest. No one makes false claims about themselves, and gay little Santa has to learn about seriousness of purpose and genuine achievement.

Some of the first reactions to *The Circus is Coming* missed the point Noel was making – that Peter and Santa have to be fitted, not just for ordinary life, but for the supremely demanding life of the circus. 'Peter and Santa – what horribly incredible children!' exclaimed one review. 'If only Noel Streatfeild had . . . killed them off, instead of trailing them through the book and nearly spoiling her excellent material.'[6] Regretting the lack of a new Arthur Ransome story in 1938, another comment was – 'It will appeal to adult purchasers, especially those looking for something new, but I back the more heroic atmosphere of cleats and halyards for the majority.'[7] But as a serious and successful writer, Noel felt justified in her unorthodox approach. She did not believe in easy heroism for her characters, or easy options for herself. Children's books were already full of readymade characters, tailored to fit run-of-the-mill day-dreams. She wanted to put forward something more challenging to the reader's intelligence. Nothing shows this more clearly than her treatment of Gus. It was one of the traditions of children's fiction that, while fathers were a liability and best excluded, uncles could be picturesque, warm-hearted if occasionally hot-tempered, but basically full of good will. Like their counterparts, the scatty artistic aunts, they are ideal children's book guardians, providing the security of an adult presence without demanding any deep emotional commitment from their charges. Above all uncles, from the Bastables' 'poor Indian' to the Amazons' 'Captain Flint', are fun to have around.

Gus is very different, a complex character, unpredictable and hard to like. He is no well-disposed, fun-loving figure, but a touchy, self-sufficient man, with no wish to assume responsibility for two children who will only get in his way. He blames them for things which are admittedly irritating, but not really their fault – their expectations of special privileges, or their ignorance about their family. Even at the end of the book he does not understand them; it is they who have been obliged to make most of the adjustments. The relationship is dissected in an uncompromisingly adult way, untouched by easy sentiment, or any wish to make the reader comfortable. Those who wanted to believe that circus life was all tinsel and cosiness could read Enid Blyton's *Mr Galliano's Circus*, which was also published in 1938, and provides a startling contrast.

The Circus is Coming is highly original, the most penetrating, if not the most accessible, of Noel's children's books. Most reviews praised it warmly. By the time it was published, Noel was immersed in other things. She had moved out of Shepherd's Market, and taken a charming maisonette at 11 Bolton Street, near Piccadilly. Fanny Burney had lived there when she was a lady-in-waiting to Queen Charlotte, and 'she must have been a delightful person, for the house radiated happiness,' Noel wrote.[8] Everything inside was as perfect as Noel could make it, and she spent her mounting royalties on the beautiful furniture and exotic carpets she could never afford before.

With a bedroom to spare, she could employ a maid to live in, and she engaged her first secretary, Susan Montagu. But life was still hectic, for besides her writing and all her engagements, she had enrolled for a short Civil Defence course; and, when that was over, and *The Circus is Coming* was safely launched for Christmas 1938, she longed to escape again. So she and Susan set off for St Juan-les-Pins in the south of France, to work on Noel's next adult novel, *Luke*, a psychological thriller about a boy murderer; and here, at the beginning of February 1939, she received an exciting cable. 'You have won the Carnegie gold medal. Many congratulations. Carey.'

The Carnegie gold medal, awarded by the Library Association for 'a distinguished contribution to children's literature', had been instituted two years earlier, one of the random signs that critical interest was at last being taken in children's books. Arthur Ransome, with *Pigeon Post*, had predictably won the first medal in 1936, and Eve Garnett the second with *The Family from One End Street*. Noel had been a runner-up in both years with *Ballet Shoes* and *Tennis Shoes*; and despite strong competition in 1938 from Kitty Barne's *She shall have Music*, Patricia Lynch's *The King of the Tinkers*, T. H. White's *The Sword in the Stone*, and Eleanor Graham's *The Children who lived in a Barn*, it was Noel's turn to win outright. The gold predicted by the Mexican fortune teller was hers.

An article in *The Library Association Record* of March 1939 to mark the award, enthused about the way Noel had written *The Circus is Coming*. 'She sees; she makes us see; but she does more. It is not just a panorama that she spreads before us; it is a life she shows us. We begin to breathe circus air, we catch a glimpse of circus ideals; and before long we feel that we too would like to shed our London habits with our London gloves, and, like Peter and Santa, learn to play our parts in this strange but worthwhile world.'

'It is impossible to predict,' the article ended, 'where Miss Streatfeild's talent will lead her next.' This certainly warranted speculation. With a mere eight years as a writer behind her, and a tally of six novels, three children's books, a full-length play, a set of children's plays, and a number of short stories, she seemed poised to soar upwards in any direction she pleased. But what she might have achieved, given absolute freedom, must remain hypothetical; for within six months of her receiving the Carnegie gold medal, war had broken out, and disrupted her writing career.

12

Wartime Worker

Before the outbreak of war, Noel had never been much interested in news or politics. She was to say of her friends in the
1920s – 'had they ventured to discuss a serious subject they would
have been accused of bad manners. Blasphemy could be fun . . .
but who wanted to know about the Means Test?'[1] When she
began her work at Deptford, she saw the problems as personal,
not political. None of her lectures advocated state welfare. In the
tradition of her father, she believed that help should be given
voluntarily, from one human being to another, and not as part of
an impersonal system.

The early signs of trouble from Nazi Germany passed her by as
well. She was in California for the first half of 1938, and because
she never mastered American radio dials, or found a newspaper
which covered European affairs adequately, she missed the rising
tension with which people in England watched Hitler march into
Austria, and threaten Czechoslovakia. But when, in July, she
decided to return home, she knew enough to decline a passage
on a German boat. 'It was roomy, empty, apparently comfortable. I could get a good single cabin and a bathroom. I turned
the offer down without a breath of hesitation. I would not, I
told myself, pay money to Nazis. I would not travel under a
German flag. Driving home from the dock I suddenly knew
something else, which made my heart miss a beat. I would
not risk travelling on a German ship because war might break
out. I believe that was the first moment that I had honestly faced
the fact that we might be in for another war. Like the majority
of English people I wanted to believe in a miracle, to snatch
at straws of hope – I could have known what was coming,
but I did not want to part with my hard-earned income

in taxes to pay for guns. I did not want to make sacrifices.'[2]

She travelled home on a Norwegian boat, and at first forgot her worries in the excitement of Richenda's wedding, which took place soon after her return. The Munich crisis of September 1938 revived her fears, and she doubted Chamberlain's message of 'peace for our time'. Instead she prepared for the worst by enrolling in the Westminster City Council's Civil Defence course, to train as an air raid Warden.

Wardens were local volunteers who, in the event of war, would take responsibility for a particular area. They were people to whom others could turn for help and advice, and who must set an example in times of danger. They learned fire drill, first aid, and how to cope with bombs and gas. All these points were covered in a series of lectures which Noel attended. 'We had a good, clear and amusing lecturer. He tried, especially when dealing with the more devastating forms of bombing, to strike the note, "of course we hope there never will be a war, but – " though as a rule he talked as if the horrors he was describing were certain to happen to us. It was no end of good for me, though my hair stood on end, and my eyes were popping out. In the end I was expecting a war of such horror that no matter what the enemy has inflicted on us, or may inflict, it will always fall below what I was taught to expect.'[3]

When the course was over she retreated to France to work on *Luke*, the story of a child pianist who poisons his unsympathetic stepfather. It is another example of the immense technical skill Noel so much enjoyed exercising, for it is written almost entirely in dialogue, and Luke himself remains offstage, a sinister, lurking presence. Detached from the international problems of 1939 as *Luke* seems, perhaps something of the tension Noel felt is reflected in the tense drama of the murder hunt, with its unresolved ending. It demonstrates too, from an unusual angle, Noel's preoccupation with the gifted child. If genius is thwarted, she asks, will it turn to violence?

Unluckily for Noel, the publication of *Luke* coincided with the beginning of the war; and although the reviews were excellent, sales were badly affected, as they were of *Dennis the Dragon*, an amusing short fantasy, illustrated by Ruth, which Noel also published in the autumn of 1939. Dennis, a lonely dragon, longs for a more sophisticated life, but a dip into high society convinces him, in the best traditions of the moral fable, that there is no place like home.

The early months of the war were strangely frustrating. Full of energy and patriotism, Noel was eager to get into action, but there was nothing for her to do. She took a refresher course in her Warden's training, and waited for the air raids which did not happen, as Hitler's air force was engaged against Poland. London stood prepared but idle, with windows blacked out, buildings sand-bagged, barrage balloons in the sky, and rumours rife. 'They're ready for thirty thousand casualties a night . . . They say they have bombs to kill everyone within twenty miles.'[4] But the 'phoney war' stretched on past Christmas 1939.

At the beginning of 1940 Noel started to keep a diary. Prompted by the feeling that she was living in historic times, she decided that the daily events of the war should be recorded, for her own interest and posterity's. The diary continued sporadically until August 1942, after which it was partly replaced by the WVS newsletters that Noel wrote during the later stages of the war. The contents of the diary vary considerably. At first it is a very brief, factual document, recording public events – a calling-up decree on January 1st, the pooling of butter on January 2nd, a speech by President Roosevelt and the fixing of the bacon ration on January 3rd. For several months this kind of entry predominates, sometimes reduced to a mere 'no news', but gradually personal details creep in. The bitter cold of the 1940 winter comes somewhere between the personal and the impersonal, Noel describing 'frost like snow on the roofs and a thick fog' (12 January), and observing 'apparently all the pipes in London are frozen up' (18 January).

With the ending of the 'phoney war' in the spring, the diary begins to expand. Noel recounts not only the news but reactions to it, as with the fall of Holland and Belgium on 10 May. 'In the evening directions broadcast as to what steps the public should take in the event of a parachute landing by the Germans. This provided comic relief on a taut day, no British citizen being able to consider a German trying to land from the skies as anything but funny. Much talk about – "I'll be waiting with a kitchen knife", or "My husband says he'll get a pitchfork, that'll give them something to land on." . . . The news that Hitler is in command on the western front taken as good, as he is no general. Widespread hopes expressed that he might get killed.'

At the beginning of September 1940 the diary slips into top gear, with daily accounts of Noel's war work, and of life in London during the Blitz. In February 1941 she put these entries together as a book, *London under Fire, a Woman's Diary*, which she showed to her new publishers, Collins. William Collins, the director, liked it, but felt that it should be kept until after the war; by which time Noel had moved on to other things, and *London under Fire* was forgotten.

The entries for 1941 and 1942 lack the freshness and vivid detail of *London under Fire*, for the strains of daily life sapped even Noel's vitality, but they contain much interesting material, and give a fascinating picture of her character and her activities at this important time. And it was an important time, for although her writing career inevitably lost some of its momentum, the war brought Noel personally to the summit of her powers. 'I don't think I exaggerate, or am mistaken,' wrote Storm Jameson, 'when I say that the Second War brought to life in her a spirit she may not have known was hidden in her.' It was a spirit of tremendous courage, and imaginative leadership.

During the freezing calm of the 'phoney war', Noel remained in Bolton Street, writing. She had recently, after trying two disastrous refugees, acquired a splendid maid, Nellie Thompson, who took complete charge of the flat. She cleaned, washed and cooked, with slow thoroughness, to the rhythm of the hymns she perpetually sang; inspiring Noel, who was always economical with her material, to introduce hymn-singing domestics into several of her books, like Hannah in *Curtain Up*, and Mrs Gage in *The Bell Family*. Nellie's predecessor, a self-pitying Austrian Jewess, reappears too as the dismal Gerda in *I Ordered a Table for Six*.

The invasion of Holland and Belgium, suddenly bringing the war much closer, stirred Noel, as well as her diary, to new vigour. Storm Jameson was staying with her at the time, and breakfasting in the sitting room, when Noel came in 'smiling, and said – "Well, we're on. Germany invaded Holland and Belgium this morning. I've just been told." She had her breakfast tray brought in from her bedroom, and we talked. How gay she was, how alive and self-possessed, with the self-possession both of an actress and of the well-bred daughter of a suffragan bishop. Her voice had not changed from that of the reckless young girl – it was strong, very clear, with light traces of a tart accent, learned in the nursery, I'd think. I listened to it with pleasure when she was ringing up a friend. "Yes, yes, my sweet, but what *sort* of help are we giving them? The sort we gave the Poles? – This is where I get into the war. It's true the only weapon I could handle is a pitchfork – Yes, yes, anything is better than going on waiting." No stranger listening to this nonsense would have supposed that she was an extremely efficient ARP Warden.'

'This is where I get into the war'; the words were prophetic. Still the expected air raids did not come, but fears of invasion were real and widespread, and, using her Child Care contacts, Noel began going daily to South London, to help with organizing Civil Defence, and with evacuation plans for mothers and children. The courage of the Londoners, as they faced up to the horrors which seemed to lie ahead, filled Noel with admiration. A visit to Bermondsey was 'an absolute tonic. (The people are) so tough, so certain that one Briton is a match for ten foreigners' (28 May). Noel thought so too. She thrilled with patriotic pride over Churchill's speeches, and considered the RAF pilots as 'more like Gods than men' (25 May).

It was a hard summer, with the evacuation of Dunkirk, the Battle of Britain, and the first, long-awaited air raids on London to keep nerves at full stretch. Somehow Noel combined her writing with visits to Deptford, and nightly patrols when enemy aircraft flew over. In the stress she found her figure reverting to its old modelling statistics. 'Delighted with my own lost stone, but sorry to see extra thinness on the already thin,' she wrote (5 July). The inside of a week on Roland Pertwee's Devon estate was all the holiday she managed, apart from occasional free Sundays of piercing enjoyment. 'Went to Sussex, the road bristled with guns but the downlands lay in their age-old beauty with the corn ripening on their sides, and cloud shadows scudding across them, and small blue harebells and scabious to give them colour . . . Coming home the moon was like a golden balloon, and even the road barricades had a dark charm. London felt more stuffy and oppressed than usual, and because the day had been so beautiful, the war fell on one like a blanket, and one's morale slipped to zero' (21 July). As the Blitz increased in fury, bringing an endless sequence of interrupted nights, Noel wrote – 'I spend more and more time thinking about sleep, which one never gets, and barges drawn very very slowly by aged white horses' (31 August).

By September 1940 Noel's life had settled into the extraordinary pattern it was to maintain for months. The air raids gave a background of continual fear, danger and exhaustion; noise, smoke and destruction. 'There was a raid yesterday about tea-time,' she wrote on 8 September. 'Even from my flat could smell burning. Nellie said, "Looks as if he's hit something." Went up on my roof, the smell was stronger, but I could see nothing, but I could hear the ringing bells of fire engines tearing through the streets. Came down feeling anxious, there was too strong a smell of burning, and too endless a clanging of fire engines. The siren went again, and (I) hurried to the (Warden's) post. The sky was flaming with the reflection of fires. Fire engines could be heard clanging along from north, south, east and west, felt that was encouraging, it seemed all England was rushing to help the capital.'

To go immediately to their post when the warning sirens blared was a Warden's first duty. Grabbing her gas mask and tin hat, Noel would set off, perhaps through darkness shot with flames, not knowing what appalling tasks lay ahead. The sequel to the sirens of 8 September was fairly harmless. Noel and another Warden were trying to calm and shelter a lorry-load of frightened people from the Docks, when a young prostitute appeared off the street, and gave invaluable help, with utter casualness. 'She had on a little inadequate green coat, a brown skirt, and high-heeled shoes, and no hat. We offered her tea, she seemed embarrassed as if it was undue kindness that we should ask her to have tea with us. I went up to the door with her, to see her on her way. The sky was still a pitiless crimson. It was a particularly noisy moment. I said, "wouldn't you like to wait until it quietens down a bit, you've no tin hat?" She tripped off on her silly heels, merely remarking, "I never wear a hat!" '

Comforting the desolate was one of the easier tasks; surveying flattened buildings one of the worst. 'Saw something very nasty,' Noel recorded on 14 September. 'Suppose one must get used to seeing things, but would have been glad to have missed that.' The blasted houses, their furnishings glimpsed through gaping holes, depressed her terribly; and she had a lucky escape herself when the house of some friends she was visiting was nearly blown up by a landmine, leaving Noel and her friends trapped inside amidst broken glass and debris. They waited in darkness until the morning, and then climbed with difficulty out of the wreckage. But at least they were alive and unhurt. They might have been in hospital, 'if not harping on a cloud' (19 September).

Day after day, and night after night, the checking of bombed houses, summoning of ambulances, and tiresome but necessary paperwork had to go on. Only a day after her ordeal in the collapsing house, Noel had to cope with a Warden in a state of severe shock after he had helped in some gruesome incident. 'He repeated, with dreadful graphic details, his story over and over again, until we felt like screaming. The deputy post warden drew me into a corner, and said with truth that the poor man ought not to be allowed to go on like that . . . I agreed with him, and as we were not at that moment busy, he and I held the floor for what felt like hours with the dreariest travel talk I have ever heard. Through the guns and the rain we went solemnly round the world remembering fatuous things about the loveliest spots. I know I was guilty of – "Coming into Java in the morning the light was so lovely it was like gliding into an opal." We succeeded in our purpose, our poor invalid couldn't get a word in edgeways' (20 September).

London seemed to be crashing in ruins. Rubble blocked the streets; mains sources were cut off. With no gas for her fire, and no hot water, Noel wrote at home with an eiderdown pinned round her shoulders. To add to her misery, all the windows in the flat were blown out on 11 October. But air raids strengthened the bond between her and the South Londoners she still diligently visited, united in suffering as they all were. 'The streets have always been grey and shabby,' Noel wrote of Deptford, 'but the devastation, the pitious (sic) remains of household Gods, the heaps of rubble with tiny Union Jacks waving on top of them, brought me disgracefully near tears . . . It was worth keeping one's mind on the number of bed bugs killed nightly' (9 October).

Late every afternoon people left their homes to spend the night in cavernous underground shelters, and this caused a problem which they confided to Noel. It was impossible to have a meal, or a cup of hot tea. Noel discussed the matter with another helper. 'I suggested mobile canteens, or a travelling kitchen, would meet the case, and it was agreed that I should write to the only powers I know, and see if something could be done. Came back and wrote as fervently as I could' (9 October). Nothing happened until, a week later, she was invited out to lunch. 'What is a miracle? I saw one at lunch yesterday,' the diary entry for 16 October begins; for, in a noble attempt to make herself amusing, she was chatting to a fellow guest, 'about my letter to the powers that I know, and the futility of such efforts, when, quite suddenly, he stopped me by putting a hand on my arm, and he said, "I will buy you a canteen. How much money do you want?" '

That was the beginning of what was to be Noel's most important war work. From then on, as well as keeping up her Warden's duties in Mayfair, she ran a regular canteen service for the people in the Deptford shelters. She linked up with the Women's Voluntary Service (the WVS), who were just starting to organize their first mobile canteens; but the large van with its sink and burners, and its rota of helpers, remained under Noel's personal control; and she arranged her own round through the blasted streets of Deptford. As darkness fell, the canteen would set off with its supply of tea, cocoa, Bovril, buns and rolls, stopping at every shelter, where the helpers would plunge into the subterranean depths with loaded trays, pushing through curtains of sacking which covered the doorways. Noel gave a vivid picture of the work in her novel *I Ordered a Table for Six*, in which one of the characters, Claire, runs a mobile canteen.

'She much preferred to be wearing a tin hat to a beret when she had to push aside the sacking over the entrance. "I'll get," she thought, "something awful in my hair one day." At the bottom of the greasy wooden stairs was another piece of sacking. As she moved it she met the smell of too many bodies in too confined a space, carbolic, and the indefinable odour found in hurriedly-dug and not well-finished shelters, of wet earth, roots and worms. Claire braced her shoulders and smiled. "Canteen," she called. She was rewarded by the pleased smiles which passed along the people. "Here's the mobile." '

All through the war, from the early raids to the flying bombs and doodlebugs, Noel's mobile canteen distributed food and hot drinks. The work grew, for besides visiting the shelters, the canteen served rescue parties, fire brigades, and demolition squads at many terrible incidents, as well as shocked relatives, called to identify mangled bodies. She fell on her knees, or was blown off her feet, as bombs crashed around her. She passed round sweets with such shaking hands that the sweets rattled in the tin like castanets. She endured the grumbles when some bush telegraph seemed to send messages to the shelters ahead of her – 'Tea's horrible tonight.' Unconquerable, she kept on.

The connection with the WVS increased her work load, for its leaders soon realized that she was an experienced speaker, and asked her to lecture for them about a new project, the House-wives' Service. That housewives should help in a war was a revolutionary idea; but the WVS believed that women could be organized, not just to help injured or distressed neighbours, but to offer the myriads of tiny services which could smooth the disruptions of war. The idea appealed to Noel, and busy though she was, she undertook a huge programme of speaking engage-ments, often involving very awkward journeys, to recruit women for the Housewives' Service. Once again she drew strength from the courage and selflessness of others. 'Let us praise the housewife,' she headed an article she wrote for the *Evening News*, for the housewife, besides looking after her family through the difficulties and shortages of the war, often housing bombed-out relations as well, also 'serves on mobile canteens, garnishes camouflage nets, lends a hand in wartime nurseries, twists and turns secondhand clothing into something wearable for the emergency clothing stores, helps on the land, makes jam, collects salvage . . . '[5] Noel concludes her article with the throat-catching anecdote of a housewife, already half dropping under her burden of work, who somehow makes time to alter a coat, so that a child shall have something respectable to wear at the funeral of his brother killed in a raid.

Noel suffered her own personal disaster on 10 May 1941, exactly a year after her cheerful efficiency had so impressed Storm Jameson. The Blitz had continued relentlessly through the winter and spring, with all its accompanying fatigue and sapping of morale. 'Pitifully conscious of my own moments of abject terror, can only hope they were unnoticeable,' she wrote on 19 March after a gruelling night fighting fires and helping casualties. One of her terrors was of being alone at night. Nellie always slept in a shelter, and Noel hated coming off duty in the small hours, and returning to an empty flat. She rationalized this as her 'burglar complex', but fear of more than burglars lay at its root; and quite soon she stopped trying to force herself to be brave, and arranged sleeping quarters in the coal cellar of a Mayfair mansion, Bath House.

Noel's handwriting was never very good, but the script in which she recorded the events of 10 May is shakier and more illegible than usual. That evening she had done her usual round in Deptford, though 'feeling wretched with a cold. Siren about eleven, and soon it was clear we were having a London raid. Drove home about midnight, missing a bomb by inches. Went straight to Bath House as raid very fierce. Bomb dropped very near, and later another which brought down part of the house. Smoke and sparks drifted through. Warden arrived to know how many had been in . . . (illegible) . . . Could not help, but could hear the screams of somebody trapped. The place well on fire, so chance of saving anybody remote. No hope of fire engine. Later several bombs near us, last of which struck us on the side of the house. Beecham (the butler) hurt. Through a strange major and a drunk I got a stretcher car, and took him to Adelphi dressing station. Took stretcher bearers home to my flat to have drinks, and found place practically demolished. Went back at day-break and looked round. A sad scene, my flat is no more.'

The shock was appalling, intensified, no doubt, by the events of the whole terrible night. Noel's first reaction was to rush to Daphne, who wrapped her in rugs, and drove her to another friend, who lived in the comparative peace of East Grinstead. For a few days Noel felt ghastly, cold and shaking, and oppressed by nightmares, but there was little time to rest with legal and insurance complications to clear up; and by 19 May she was back on her round in Deptford. But she had lost nearly everything – all her beautiful furnishings, including a white, handmade carpet, all her clothes. Like other bomb victims she turned for help to an emergency clothing store at the English-Speaking Union, and nothing could have been better for her morale.

'Got a coat and frock. Feel much better. Coat enchanting. Took it and frock to dressmaker to be altered. Dressmaker said, "Worth £35 if a penny, Madam." Must say when she had cut out the lining in the sleeves so that it fitted I felt a new person. So delighted to have something to tide me over as have, apart from finance, no inclination nor time to struggle with shops . . . To bed in Bath House deffinately (sic) accepting my fate. My coal cellar looked almost human' (22 May).

From then until the end of the war she had no satisfactory home. Sometimes she stayed with friends, sometimes she slept in Bath House, and eventually she rented a tiny flatlet in Pont Street; but all her work was henceforth done against this background of temporary or transient accommodation. She accepted her lot with cheerful and courageous resignation, thinking how lucky she was compared to Rose Macaulay, who had lost her flat the same night, together with a manuscript she had been working on for six years. 'If I had lost a six years M.S. I should feel like an elephant must feel when it has a mis-carriage . . . I don't know Rose Macaulay except to admire her work, but now she's never out of my mind' (26 May).

Naturally strain and exhaustion took their toll of Noel. The diary is peppered with mentions of colds, flu and liver trouble. But it also shows the extraordinary resilience of her spirit. She was in her late forties, writing all day and working in the blitzed streets most nights, but usually she was too busy thinking about other people to waste time pitying herself. The plight of her brother Bill, with his wife and daughter, now interned by the Japanese in Siam, preyed on her mind during 1941 and 1942. News of Japanese atrocities trickled through, and Noel seriously wondered if the family should try to commit suicide. With no contact apparently possible, she pestered all the relevant authorities unceasingly, and hers was eventually the first cable to reach the internment camp from the outside world in over a year. 'All well, including parents' was all that it said, but the relief to Bill and his wife was never forgotten. When, later in 1942, they were released, Noel was the person who met them at Liverpool docks, having commandeered an ambulance for them, which was luckily not necessary. When they were installed in the attic flat of a relative's house, she insisted on relinquishing Nellie, so that they could be looked after.

Tired though she often was physically, her mind was always alert, grappling with the many problems she saw around her. She worried about evacuation, and whether families should be separated; and about the children who stayed in London with no schools to attend. Could there be hostels for children on the outskirts of London, she wondered; and hostels too for the elderly who could not hurry to the shelters when the siren wailed? Could bands be organized to cheer people with light music in the badly blitzed streets? She involved herself in raising money for naval war libraries. She organized a scheme of salvage collecting by the children of Honor Oak, and she ran children's parties in Deptford. Never did she show herself more to be the daughter of her selflessly dedicated father.

And inevitably a good deal of social life was fitted in too. This was impossible at the height of the Blitz, but during lulls hardly a day passed without Noel's having a lunch or dinner engagement, or entertaining friends to tea or drinks. Daphne remained her most constant companion, though a little of her elegance was submerged beneath a new enthusiasm for the WVS. 'Daphne, for all her niceness, getting tinged with that frightful "women in uniform playing at soldiers" business,' Noel wrote regretfully (30 January 1941). Roland Pertwee remained close as well, and chose Noel as his confidante when his marriage failed. 'Talk about bombs, divorce seems more disrupting,' Noel observed after dining with him (22 May 1941).

A new friend was Theodora Newbold, who gave Noel hospitality in her Pavilion Road house after Noel's flat was bombed. Generous and kindly though she was, she provoked Noel to occasional tart comments. 'She is uncontrolled emotionally, which is fatal in war, and leads to confused thinking' (30 April 1941). Noel's Vicarage upbringing ensured that she was never 'uncontrolled emotionally'; indeed exhortations to herself to keep up morale recur frequently in the diary.

The entry for 6 Mary 1942 – 'Dined luxuriously with Elsa on lobster and chicken soup, and planned her magazine' – marks both a new venture and a new friendship. Noel had visited Lady Reading, the Chairman of the WVS, to ask if PEN Club members could be of use to her, and the question was passed on to Elsa Dunbar, 'a very efficient young woman', as Noel described her (7 January 1942), whose job was to keep in touch with all overseas organizations sending help to Britain through the WVS. She wanted to launch a monthly magazine, which would give WVS supporters at home and abroad some picture of what was being done, and PEN Club assistance sounded ideal. 'Noel coerced every kind of woman writer to help in this way, from the highbrow to those who catered for the most romantic kitchen maid', but 'they took a great deal of cossetting and encouragement to get their efforts available on time,'[6] and in the end Noel wrote most of the newsletters herself.

Elsa had a weekend cottage in Bicester, to which Noel occasionally retired for what was meant as a rest, but seldom proved to be one, for with her usual vitality she threw herself into whatever was going on. 'Noel tells a story,' Elsa Dunbar wrote, 'that when she arrived there to spend Christmas with us, the first thing I said to her was – "please will you make me a robin for the Christmas tree." She did, but the idea seems to have tickled her over the years. She loved dogs and was great friends with ours, and in fact trained a new arrival of three months to walk properly on the lead. She loved gardening, and we worked hard in the garden, and one memorable, gloriously hot August weekend even built a haystack which I was left marooned on top of while it swayed about, and Noel instead of getting help collapsed into fits of laughter.'

Hard pressed though she might be, Noel only needed small things to raise her spirits. Any plant or flower was a source of almost disproportionate joy. 'Put catkins in a blue vase. They look exquisate (sic). Hyacinths too lovely to be true' (23 February 1941), is a typical diary entry. When Nellie spoke disparagingly of some snowdrops Noel had bought, the diary comments wryly – 'How odd is the wish of people to kill happiness in others. I've so often seen women do it to each other about clothes. "It's a lovely hat, darling, but not your colour." Why say such things? It's always puzzled me. Anyway no one can kill my pleasure in my snowdrops' (2 March 1942).

While flowers were a perennial delight, clothes were a source of regret and nostalgic longing. In October 1940 she describes going out to lunch, and how 'I felt that I've let appearances slip a bit lately. I wore my best (which is not saying much) and I had my hair done yesterday morning, but I don't think my face is up to much, though carefully made up. There was too much of, "I'm sure you're overdoing it, darling". Wish I felt justified in buying a really doggy winter outfit. Walked home chewing over this point. But my old fur coat will do, I have enough frocks, there's no excuse . . . But I can't help feeling that something like a mink coat would be a great help to my morale' (6 October). Having always aimed at smartness and sophistication, her increasing shabbiness caused her many genuine pangs. An article she wrote for *The Evening News* in January 1944 about the difficulty of getting shoes mended, illustrates her despair – and brought a sheaf of letters from indignant cobblers.

Still the war work went on. She began to lecture all over the country for the WVS, she worked on the newsletter, and she ran her canteen, travelling precariously through the bomb-cratered streets on a newly acquired motor bike. One of the worst experiences of the war was at the end of 1944 when a rocket bomb hit the Deptford branch of Woolworth's when it was packed with children, who had heard that ice cream was on sale. No one in the building was left alive; and Noel was quickly on hand to provide hot tea, and any comfort possible, to the grief-stricken parents, the Wardens and the rescue workers. 'I can't to this day pass the place where that incident took place without a shudder,' she wrote nearly ten years later. 'I can still see the immensely long queues waiting for news of relatives, I can still hear the cranes working . . . But when the war was over, and VE Day was celebrated, what did the people do? They built an enormous bonfire on the Woolworth site, and round it they danced "Knees up, Mother Brown" most of the night'[7]. Such a strange gesture of defiance was something Noel never understood.

Towards the end of the war, scarred, dilapidated London was roused to new life by the arrival of the American troops. They brought gaiety, energy, and gleaming white tin hats, for which they were nick-named 'Snowdrops'. Their appearance inspired both hope and thankfulness in Noel. How much they were the natural heroes of 1945 is clear from Noel's book about the end of the war, *Party Frock*, when the arrival of American soldiers in jeeps brings a historical pageant to its climax, and the audience rises to wave and cheer; cheers which Noel echoed from the heart.

The ending of hostilities did not quite mean the ending of her war work. In December 1945 she went with a WVS party to the Channel Island of Alderney, to organize Christmas celebrations for the returning or liberated islanders. Noel was asked to produce some Nativity tableaux for Christmas Eve, and found herself faced with an absolute dearth of materials. The island's clothing store could only offer a hat with red roses and a morning suit. Even pins were unobtainable, but, determinedly undeterred, Noel improvised with paper and sheets, and the tableaux were ready on time.

Last of all her commitments was the Victory Parade, in June 1946, at which the King took the salute. Representatives of every organization that had helped to win the war took part, and Noel was invited to march with the WVS contingent. She was drilled beforehand by a sergeant-major, and given her instructions. 'I don't want sweets sucked nor apples eaten on the march. I don't want you ladies to carry handbags, and if you must have your umbrellas, you'll carry them at the slope.'

Next morning the parade assembled in pouring rain. Noel, with the WVS, lined up behind the Red Cross and St John's Ambulance members, under the eye of a senior Guards officer. 'He was quite unmoved by what must have been the rather dismaying appearance of us green sheep. After all, lines had been held by cooks and cleaners before now.' Then at last they were off, into the packed London streets.

'It was hard to say what we expected. Certainly not what we got. We were not ourselves, of course. We stood for over a million women. Even then the thanks of the crowd were surely more than our due. They started to clap before we were even out of Hyde Park. They shouted to us from the kerb and from windows. "Thank you, dears, for everything. Thank you for your canteens." And over and over again: "Give the WVS a cheer. Thank you for the tea." '[8]

13

Historian of the Age

Noel's diary entry for 11 September 1940 begins – 'Tried abortively to write throughout the day. Blitz or no blitz, must earn my bread and butter.' All through the war this was to be her predicament. Her Warden's duties, her canteen round, her writing and lecturing for the WVS, were all voluntary and unpaid. She still had to support herself, a maid and a secretary, and this meant a gruelling schedule of work.

A writer in wartime faced extra difficulties. In February 1940 paper was rationed, with a limited allocation going to each publisher; and in April 1940 it was further limited. 'Paper to be cut by 30% of what we had,' Noel wrote on 14 April. 'I suppose courage by writers needs no greater effort than courage of millions of others, but one cannot prevent an inward faltering.' The paper ration precipitated Noel's move to a new publisher. Already annoyed by what she considered Dent's failure to promote *The Circus is Coming* properly, after it had won the Carnegie medal, she was still more dismayed to hear how little paper they were prepared to allow her for a new children's book. She knew, as Dent's did, that the demand for her books would far outstrip the numbers that could be printed; but, trying to be fair, Dent's would not increase Noel's paper allowance at another writer's expense. Usually Noel would have been equally concerned about fairness, but now she felt only desperation at the prospect of reduced sales and reduced royalties.

The ration was based on pre-war paper consumption; and because the publishing firm of Collins had always printed diaries as well as books, their allocation was much larger than Dent's. When Noel heard from her agent that Collins could offer a more generous paper allowance, she decided to move. She was helped to sever her links with Dent's by the knowledge that Mabel Carey was doing the same. Already she was a part-time ambulance driver. Soon she was to become a full-time Red Cross worker, and would ultimately be one of the first people to enter Belsen concentration camp after it was liberated from the Nazis. At this point Noel broke her links with Heinemann's too. From 1940 onwards, Collins were her main publishers.

Another cause for depression was the purchase tax imposed on books in July 1940, which also, inevitably, damaged sales. 'The budget,' Noel wrote on 23 July. 'Most people think it doesn't go far enough. To me, with a 12% tax on books, and a shilling on ordinary income tax, it went paralysingly far. There are moments when I think the struggle is too great, and relapse into dreams of the beauty of sudden death by bombs.'

She was hampered too by difficult physical conditions for writing. When bed was a mattress in a coal cellar, there was no lying scribbling comfortably in the mornings. She had to get up, and write in cold, uncongenial surroundings, battling against the fears and anxieties of wartime, and the weariness induced by her voluntary work. 'Felt ill all day . . . wrote deplorably,' is a characteristic diary entry, made on 6 March 1942, the day following an exhausting canteen round through the icy, blacked-out streets of Deptford. Somehow she found the courage and determination to go on, even through the daylight raids towards the end of the war. Her secretary remembered – 'When we heard a doodlebug coming we would crawl under the desk, and then come out with Noel saying, "Where was I?" '[1]

The one factor which worked to her advantage was that she had established her reputation so firmly before the war. Unlike new writers, she got a reasonable share of the rationed paper, and people were prepared to buy her books, in spite of the purchase tax. Indeed, far from the void she had anticipated, her problem soon was being asked to do too much. Newspapers, magazines, and the BBC, all asked her to write for them; and small unexpected commissions came her way, like the 'telephone call asking me to write a fairy story for children in connection with a war weapons week' (3 January 1941). She managed to fit everything in, but it was wearing. 'I have so much to write,' she recorded plaintively on 6 February 1941, 'and only one me, and not always boundless energy, and now and again no application. Shall now do diary slowly, and get on with novel and children's book, and synopses for Johnson's serial, and another short story. I'll put in for some quiet work in Heaven.'

This entry follows William Collins' decision to postpone the publication of *London under Fire*, the book Noel compiled from her diary. Noel's readers were thus robbed of one of her sharpest, liveliest pieces of writing. The chief value of *London under Fire* is its vivid picture of beleaguered London, but almost as interesting is the self-portrait of the harassed writer, trying to goad herself on through an unending succession of hindrances.

Noel admired a contemporary woman novelist, E. M. Delafield, whose *Diary of a Provincial Lady* (1931) had achieved considerable popularity. The tone of *London under Fire* echoes that of E. M. Delafield's diarist – the maladroit, undomesticated 'provincial lady', floundering through the quicksands of everyday family life. Noel too casts herself as a comedy heroine, recounting her setbacks and misadventures with ruefully honest humour.

A perpetual source of comedy is her relationship with her two most constant companions – Nellie, the maid, whom she calls 'Millie', and 'Joan', a new, hard-working, but austerely highbrow secretary, who disapproves of Noel's magazine fiction. The interplay between these three brings light relief into the account of London at war, while shedding a revealing incidental glow on Noel herself.

'Not being on call did a good day's writing. Discouraged by Joan. Secretaries should take a course in tact, it can't be pleasant for the author who for once thinks she's done well, to hear, "I wonder who on earth reads serials?" Snapped at her. Millie evidently heard the snap, for I then heard Joan being given a cup of tea and a bun. No words seemed to pass between her and Millie, but I know what volumes of pity Millie's face expressed. Bit down my rage with difficulty' (3 September).

'Made an immense stride with the serial yesterday,' Noel wrote on 24 September. 'Can see the end of it. Thought a page was missing, and blamed Millie or Joan or both. Millie said, "I never touch a paper, even to dust," and shut the kitchen door. Joan searched noisily, slamming drawer after drawer. Presently I heard the chink of teacups, and knew Millie was being a ministering angel, and they were both sympathizing with each other by looks and sighs at my door for having to work for me. Found the page wasn't missing at all. Told Joan, who said nothing, but put back the drawer she was searching in a very meaning way. Told Millie, who said, "I wouldn't be your secretary Madam for a lot." Went back to the serial in a very bad temper, wishing I'd never found the sheet. Hope I shall frequently re-read this entry, as obviously good for my soul.'

But next day the shared discomforts of life drew them together again. After sleeping on a mattress in a friend's kitchen, Noel started writing early as she had arranged to go to Deptford. 'It's chilly so Millie has lit my (paraffin) stove. It looks a bit like a ship, perhaps that's because it's painted grey. It's obviously never supposed charm to be any part of its mission in life. I suppose I must be wrong, but I can't feel any heat coming from it, in fact it seems to me to dispense cold like black magic. Millie says, "I never held with them Madam. It'll be better with a kettle on top." She's put a kettle, but it isn't. Joan surprisingly sympathetic, and said she did hope the gas would be back before winter. In fact she looked so sympathetic, that I took my glass out when she had gone, and saw my nose red and my face yellow. Feel very low.'

The serial Noel was writing was *Under the Rainbow*, one of twelve full-length stories she published under the pen-name Susan Scarlett. Noel seldom spoke about these stories, and did not include them in authorized bibliographies of her work, for she rightly considered them to be very much inferior to her serious novels. They were romantic pot-boilers, of a type which Noel had deplored before financial necessity drove her into writing them. 'I don't myself care for books which come under the heading of "a strong romance". I don't believe in idylls of that ilk,'[2] she declared in 1937. By 1939 she had written her first, *Clothes-Pegs*.

The publishers for Susan Scarlett were Hodder and Stoughton. They were perfectly aware of their author's true identity, and arranged serial rights for her with Amalgamated Press, who owned a number of women's magazines. Worried as she was about sales and paper shortages, Noel was thankful to have this extra source of income; and as she completed her dozen stories without a great deal of effort, she modified her earlier strictures. The novels might be 'sweetly pretty', as she herself disparagingly labelled them;[3] Joan might sneer at them as ideal reading for air raid shelters, where 'you can't concentrate enough to read a good book';[4] but Noel gradually came to distrust literary snobbery, and to believe that 'the great thing is that people should read',[5] although, even then, she never quite brought herself to speak openly about these secret progeny.

Noel wrote nine Susan Scarlett novels during the war, and three shortly afterwards. All have hackneyed, sentimental plots, usually built around the rivalry of two sharply contrasted girls for one desirable man, and ending in a stilted proposal for the heroine, and disappointment for her thwarted competitor. The characters are manoeuvred briskly through the story without ever taking on a real life of their own. Noel was never good at evoking romantic love, and even under the disguise of Susan Scarlett she could not conquer her inhibitions. Instead the books convey the same breezy, spinsterish conviction that love is 'sloppy', which can be found in *Tops and Bottoms* and *Shepherdess of Sheep*, and which effectively destroys the credibility of her lovers.

The only interest of the stories lies in their backgrounds, for, as in her serious novels, Noel used settings which she knew well – the world of modelling in *Clothes-Pegs*, a munitions factory in *Murder while you Work*, a third-rate theatre company in *Poppies for England*, a Vicarage in *Under the Rainbow*. *London under Fire* is laced with humorous references to this country Vicarage, where the governess and the local Lady Bountiful battle for possession of the delicate, unworldly Vicar. 'Finished the serial after lunch,' Noel wrote on 19 October. 'Bathed the Vicarage in the rays of the setting sun. Toyed with letting a bird sing, but decided that would over-do things. Didn't like the parson to kiss the girl although he had asked her to marry him. Feel that in the world of escapist Cinderella fiction parsons have no bed life. Kisses even following an engagement would probably read in bad taste.' No doubt she was right, for magazine fiction of the 1940s was scrupulously chaste.

Susan Scarlett was a useful money-spinner, but Noel's real interest lay in more serious writing. During the war she began the practice, which continued for over ten years, of publishing alternately children's and adult novels. She approached the two categories differently. Her adult novels were based on genuine war experiences, so that they were both immediately relevant, and ultimately valuable social documents. Surprisingly, considering the realism of *Tennis Shoes* and *The Circus is Coming*, her children's books tend to shy away from actuality; and it was thirty years before she used her memories of air raids and evacuees in *When the Siren Wailed*.

Of *The House in Cornwall* (1940) and *The Children of Primrose Lane* (1941), Noel was to say – 'I have only written two thrillers for children and they were both wartime books, because it was impossible at that time to travel around to get information for my usual type of book for children.'[6] Tied by her war work, Noel had lost the freedom she had needed in her research for *Tennis Shoes* and *The Circus is Coming*, but instead of looking round for interesting new material, she fell back on the clichés of the commonplace adventure story. Only a mixture of anxiety, utter fatigue, and the driving need to earn money quickly can explain why, after her penetrating analysis of the relations between children and grown-ups in *The Circus is Coming*, she succumbed, in *The House in Cornwall,* to the myth that a family of children could outwit a gang of criminals. Nor are they ordinary criminals. Including among them the children's Uncle Murdock, they are the conspirators who have been ruling the imaginary country of Livia, and who, after a revolution, have kidnapped the boy king, and fled to Uncle Murdock's Cornish estate, where they improbably hide behind spiked walls, and iron gates patrolled by uniformed guards. Everything Noel usually stood for in children's books – well-observed characters, a basis of solid fact combined with realistic detail, sheer good sense – are lost in this morass of unlikely inventions. The book which it uncannily resembles is Enid Blyton's *The Secret of Spiggy Holes,* also published in 1940. Both use a stereotyped Cornish setting, both revolve round the rescue of a child monarch from cardboard desperadoes, and both concentrate on unremitting action at the expense of character and atmosphere.

Noel never liked creating villains, and on the whole her books are remarkably free of them. Flossie Elk and Nicky Heath cause trouble, but through egotism rather than deliberate wickedness. Luke, the boy murderer, never appears. When Noel decided, in *The House in Cornwall*, to present two monsters of evil, Uncle Murdock and the dictator Manoff, the result was ludicrous. The war, by reinforcing feelings of patriotism, meant that children's book villains were generally foreign; and Manoff, with his enormous bullet head, slobbering mouth and gorilla arms, is the archetype of the whole absurd species, and quite unworthy of Noel.

As the grip of war tightened, affecting every area of life, children's writers began to draw on many aspects of it for their stories. The best books arise from naturally dramatic situations. The German invasion of the Channel Islands is the background for Mary Treadgold's *We Couldn't Leave Dinah*, the exciting Carnegie medal winner of 1941; while in 1942 Kitty Barne published *We'll meet in England*, a brilliant account of how two children escape from occupied Norway, evading a chillingly sinister Nazi snooper. But other writers, like Malcolm Saville, and M. Pardoe of the *Bunkle* books, imposed imaginary heroics on wartime life, often concerning the unmasking of spies or traitors; and Noel's next children's book, *The Children of Primrose Lane*, must be included with these.

The Children of Primrose Lane, while an improvement on *The House in Cornwall*, falls far short of Noel's pre-war trio of children's books. Writing through the Blitz was a wearisome task. 'The spirit is willing to finish the children's book, the flesh is very laggard,' Noel wrote on 11 March 1941. The final result was a competent book which never quite catches fire. It tells the story of a group of children who find a German spy hiding in an empty house, accidentally betray to him the date on which a troopship carrying one of their fathers is to sail from Southampton, and then shadow him for several days to prevent his passing on the information. The spy, with his fat, bristling neck and broken English, is the usual stereotype, and the mechanics of the plot are clumsy, showing again that Noel had no particular flair for a straight adventure story. Where the book succeeds is in the characterization of the children, especially Millie Evans, a pretty, quick-witted, bumptious child, a mixture of Flossie Elk and Nicky Heath, who, without any particular gifts, shares something of their star quality. Confidently, maddeningly, she is always one step ahead of the other children, and it is entirely characteristic of her talent for exploiting her own charm that, while all the children help to trap the spy, it is Millie's photograph alone which adorns the front pages of the newspapers.

The paper shortage meant that fewer books were reviewed, but because Noel was well-known *The Children of Primrose Lane* attracted quite a lot of attention. Some critics pointed to a feature unfamiliar in children's books – that the characters came from the working class. Apart from Eve Garnett's *The Family from One End Street,* where the parents are a dustman and a washerwoman, working class characters very seldom took a prominent place in children's fiction. They were, in their own way, as much aliens as the bulging-necked Nazis, and far less common. Eve Garnett used her observations of London slum life as the basis for her portrait of the Ruggles family, who, in 1937, were hailed as strikingly original; but Noel, with equal opportunities for observation, failed to follow her example in her children's books. She was inhibited by knowing that her books were bought by middle class parents, who would not be happy to see their offspring reading about bed bugs, meals eaten on doorsteps, and babies with dummies in their mouths – features of slum life with which Noel was well acquainted. So the Primrose Lane children are given a kind of negative, bloodless, working class status, which could offend nobody, boiling down to not much more than an absence of maids and nannies, and a taste for tinned lobster and cream buns.

Noel found it much easier to present life as it really was in her adult fiction. She still frequently referrred to her children's books as a 'sideline', and concentrated her main energies on the novels which she hoped would eventually place her in the top rank of

English authors. *The Winter is Past* (1940), *I Ordered a Table for Six* (1942) *Myra Carroll* (1944), and *Saplings* (1945), represent the substantial achievement of a highly professional writer, who handles large casts adroitly, and moves convincingly through many settings.

The diary entry for 28 March 1941 records an 'interesting argument' between Noel and an archaeologist friend of Daphne's, about 'the place of the novelist in the world. I stood up for their value as historians of their age. She distrusted anything which uses imagination, feeling facts and yet more facts are all that can be trusted.' Noel's wartime novels are a good illustration of her case. Through her imaginative recreation of her own time, she can swiftly transport a reader back into the world of raids, and commandeered houses, and roped-off streets. Her wartime books are, in fact, excellent history.

The Winter is Past is set in a country house, where a wealthy family with middle class standards of etiquette and self-control receive, as evacuees from Deptford, a Cockney family, portrayed with all the realism lacking in *The Children of Primrose Lane*. Noel demonstrates the attitudes of both sides with absolute honesty, balancing good and bad. Domineering Mrs Laurence may try to interfere with Deptford ways of child-rearing, but she is a tower of strength when little Tommy contracts pneumonia. Cockney Mrs Vidler certainly has her vulgar side, but her warmly natural relationships contrast favourably with the stiff reticences of middle class society. Noel treated the problems of evacuation with much greater sympathy than many contemporary writers, who openly despised evacuees. Even Kitty Barne spoils *Visitors from London* (1940) by her condescension to the aggressive, sniffing, chattering Cockneys who invade the home of her 'nice' middle class characters. This was probably the outcome of Kitty Barne's own experiences as the unwilling hostess to some families of evacuees, who, she considered, had vandalized her beautiful home; but *Visitors from London*, and many similar stories, serve to highlight the breadth of Noel's sympathies.

Noel's diary gives the origin of her next war novel, *I Ordered a Table for Six*. On 8 March 1941 a bomb fell on a popular London restaurant, the Café de Paris, killing a number of people. Two days later the diary records briefly – 'The idea of my novel came'; and the next day – 'Shall call that book *I Ordered a Table for Six*. Very enthusiastic about it, and look forward to writing it.' For no apparent reason Noel was afterwards, in *Beyond the Vicarage* and elsewhere, at pains to deny any connection between her novel and the Café de Paris, but the diary provides its own clear evidence, as does Noel's careful saving of a newspaper account of the tragedy.

In the book a party of six well-assorted characters assemble at a restaurant called La Porte Verte. During a raid which destroys the restaurant, three of the six who would be glad to die survive, and three who have everything to live for are killed. 'The book was suggested to me,' Noel wrote in the blurb, 'by the fact that over and over again I have noticed in this war that it never seems to be the people who would be thankful to go who are killed by bombs;' and the novel illustrates this poignant irony. The narrative is gripping, and Noel brings blitzed London alive with abundant details of shelters, searchlights, barricades and guns, all forming a dark background to the edgy pleasures of a night out.

Noel wrote *I Ordered a Table for Six* at top speed, for by 9 May, in spite of constant interruptions, she was able to read it aloud to Daphne. 'She cried, and said the whole book was wretchedly sad. This surprised me, as I thought tone slightly amusing. I suppose nothing much is amusing today, however hard you try.' When the book appeared in January 1942, the reviews were ecstatic. 'It is strikingly original, and deserves a place of its own in the literature of war,' declared the *Times Literary Supplement*.[7]

Her next novel, *Myra Carroll*, the life story of a beautiful, unhappy woman is disappointing; but its successor, *Saplings*, is a powerful denunciation of some of the evil and tragic consequences of war. While *The Winter is Past* dealt with the disorientation of moving to new places, and *I Ordered a Table for Six* with the disorientation of losing people and possessions, *Saplings* presents the paralysing disorientation of broken relationships. Separated or divided families had always aroused Noel's anger; that was why divorce seemed to her so particularly harmful. *Saplings*, in a long sequence of brief scenes, charts the effect on a family of sensitive children of all the disruptions of war, as they shuttle between preoccupied relations and overcrowded schools, neglected by their mother, and denied a proper chance to mourn their dead father. Brought up in the stiff upper lip traditions of their class, the children are never encouraged to express all the hurt and bewilderment they are feeling, and can only find release in anti-social behaviour which leads to further disgrace. Noel's crisp characterization and witty style make her sombre narrative compulsive reading; and, among many glowing reviews, *Saplings* was pronounced by Pamela Hansford-Johnson to be Noel's 'best book to date.'[8]

To complete four long novels amongst all the fatigues and vexations of war was an astonishing achievement, especially as each has a complex structure and a large cast. Noel described in an interview how she squeezed the planning into any spare moments, 'fitting together her ideas as she went about on trams and buses and even a motorcycle'.[9] And besides the four novels, there were her children's books – *Harlequinade* (1943), a short, unsatisfactory fantasy, and the much more ambitious *Curtain Up* (1944).

Noel received many letters from her readers asking for sequels to their favourite books. Even reviewers of *I Ordered a Table for Six* begged to know what happened next. Noel did not care for sequels, but somehow the Fossils had stayed stubbornly alive, and *Curtain Up* re-introduced them, if rather grudgingly and at second hand, as the donors of scholarships to Madame Fidolia's Academy. Noel was more interested in reviving the Academy itself, with its familiar staff. *Curtain Up* shows it in wartime, surviving precariously in a half ruined Bloomsbury square, its pupils reduced to a makeshift uniform of shorts and bathing costumes, instead of the old white tarlatan dresses and black satin tunics, its shows performed to wounded servicemen.

But *Curtain Up* is also Noel's most detailed look at the serious theatre. The story centres on the theatrical clan of Warrens, from Grandmother, a once famous actress now struggling to keep up a pretence of stardom, through children and children-in-law in various branches of the profession, down to her five talented grandchildren. As the story begins, three of these, Sorrel, Mark and Holly, are sent to live with their grandmother, and are plunged into the exciting, disturbing world of the stage. It is a bran-tub of a book, crowded with characters, and including, amongst the Warrens, an amusing gallery of theatrical types, with their speech and mannerisms acutely pinpointed. For a stagestruck child the kaleidoscopic scenes of auditions, rehearsals, first nights, performances and broadcasts make fascinating reading. The weakness of the book, which puts it well below Noel's highest level, is its central character, Sorrel.

Sorrel is a close copy of Susan Heath, the nice elder sister in *Tennis Shoes*. The choice of D. L. Mays to do the illustrations again accentuates the likeness, for he gives both girls the same neat plaits and slim build. Susan failed through her lack of star quality, and the same lack is clearly apparent in Sorrel. Noel tries to present her as a great actress of the future, the natural heir of the Warrens, and the account of her gradual discovery of what acting is all about, is convincingly done. But to the end, her personality remains colourless. The boldness of Noel's character drawing seems somehow to have evaporated.

Sorrel is continually compared with her unpleasant cousin Miranda, to Miranda's disadvantage. But the reader, who is expected to dislike Miranda, cannot fail to see that her determined egotism will get her a good deal further in the theatre than Sorrel's gentleness. This confusion over the exact roles of the characters throws the whole book slightly out of gear. Noel does not seem quite in control. *Curtain Up* lacks shape too. Outline and movement are clouded; some characters remain undeveloped. Despite vivid moments it seems – not surprisingly – a tired book. Indeed *Harlequinade*, *Myra Carroll*, and *Curtain Up*, three books following each other, represent something of a trough in Noel's work, suggesting a time when writing was a wearisome chore, and not the joy it had once been; when the energy to think of fresh characters and events had drained away; when Noel, more shaken than she would care to admit, would emerge from under her desk saying – 'Where was I?'

Together *Saplings*, and the next children's book, *Party Frock*, mark a revival in Noel's powers. *Party Frock*, actually published after the war, in 1946, is the best of Noel's children's books of this period, and as fine a piece of craftsmanship as she ever achieved. The story arises naturally from wartime conditions, specifically from the impossibility of finding a suitable occasion to wear a new dress.

This tragedy – and to clothes-loving Noel it was a tragedy – had befallen Ruth's daughter, thirteen-year-old Nicolette Gervis. Her godmother in America had sent her an organdie party dress with a matching pair of shoes. 'It was Nicolette's first long frock, and she could hardly wait for the right occasion to put it on. But no occasion turned up. There was at that time almost no transport. So little heating that if it was a winter party something warmer than organdie would have to be worn. Food was difficult, and every grown-up person too busy to arrange a party of the making-do sort it would have to have been. The frock hung in the cupboard and hung in the cupboard. A most depressing place for a first long party frock.'[10]

Noel was very fond of her nieces and nephews. Earlier in the war, when Nicolette had flu, Noel sent her from London a staggeringly opulent basket of fruit, accompanied by a charming letter about 'the influenza germ . . . a long, pale grey beast', who can only be exorcized by the sight of his victim eating heartily. Later in the war she wrote a Nativity play which the Gervis children put on for charity; and remembering how, in Eastbourne days, she had rewarded her young performers with bags of sweets, Noel arranged for several of her friends to go to Harrods, and buy the special little cakes which were rationed to one for each customer, so that she could send a box full of them to the cast in Dorset. So now, with Nicolette's plight in mind, she wrote *Party Frock*.

A close scrutiny of *Party Frock* reveals Noel's tremendous technical expertise. She manages a large cast and a complicated story with such ease that the very real difficulties are never apparent. A family of children decides to write a historical pageant, to give their cousin Selina an opportunity to wear her new party frock. Initially the children write brief scenes which illumine their own characters. One of them, bumptious Phoebe, chooses to be the child Anne Boleyn. Another, ballet-loving Sally, devises a masque to be danced in front of Queen Elizabeth I.

The story then shows how each scene develops from its embryonic beginnings to its culmination in the hands of an experienced director, who transforms the original simplicity into a much more ambitious production which involves the whole village. From the lively opening chapter to the surprise ending, the story never flags. Characters are neatly pinned down; the vastness of the final structure is encapsulated in quick snatches of dialogue and cleverly selected details; and a whole colourful panorama is unfurled with masterly control.

Always in the background is the war, an English battlefield, full of everyday difficulties which have to be overcome. There is the problem of supplying all the costumes without clothing coupons, of keeping children clean when soap is rationed, of getting people together when buses are sporadic and often full. *Party Frock* aligns itself with the best wartime children's books, for the struggles it records are as compelling, and far more realistic, than any struggles with spies and secret agents. And, reflecting Noel's own attitude, everything American is spangled with glory, from the original parcel with its scarlet and green ribbons, to the beneficent Colonel who buys the Abbey where the pageant is staged, as a hostel for young American visitors, 'to keep alive for ever the bonds of friendship forged in these last years.'

How, amongst her numerous voluntary undertakings, did Noel achieve in six years the phenomenal output of four adult novels, five children's books, nine Susan Scarlett stories, a diary, a series of WVS newsletters, a handful of short stories and newspaper articles, occasional radio scripts, plays, and even some book reviews? Looking back on this time, Elsa Dunbar, the wartime friend who saw Noel more often in WVS uniform than at her desk, summed her up. 'She was a dedicated writer. Nothing else really mattered.' Writing was necessity and a joy, the stimulant by which Noel survived her many horrifying ordeals. Wearying though it might sometimes be, the escape it offered enabled her to endure the war.

14

Post-war Adjustments

The first thing Noel needed after the war was a new home, and it was not long before she found one. 51 Elizabeth Street was a tall old house in the heart of London, near Chester Square and Buckingham Palace Road. Above a car showroom the floors were let off in flats, and Noel first rented one, and then added a second, making herself a lofty maisonette which faced another Georgian terrace across a narrow, bustling road. On summer mornings the music of the Guards' band drifted in from Chelsea Barracks, and on State occasions the ceremonial guns could be heard firing in Hyde Park. Next door was an excellent restaurant where Noel entertained; and she was handy for her publisher, her club, and the theatres and cinemas of London's West End. The worst feature of the maisonette was the dark, narrow, twisting staircase by which it was approached – 'lethal', some of her friends stigmatized it – but Noel did not mind. She installed a speaking tube so that callers could announce themselves from below; and, energetic as she was, flights of stairs did not worry her. 'I can still hear Noel shutting the distant door and climbing the stairs rapidly, humming as she approached,' her post-war secretary, June Allen, recalled.

The luxurious furnishings of the Bolton Street flat were never replaced, though the sitting room was pleasant enough, with three elegant built-in bookcases, and flowers and plants everywhere. After the bombing Noel had rather lost interest in possessions. 'They are roots, and tie you down,' she had reflected in her diary.[1] Her most eccentric object was the stuffed cat which lay on the hearthrug. Noel longed for a pet, but the stairs and lack of garden seemed to present insuperable obstacles, so she compromised on the cat, which caused shivers down the spines of some of her guests, but, for her, completed the homeliness of the room.

For the next thirty years 51A Elizabeth Street was the hub of Noel's life, and here she settled down to endure the rigours of the new peace, and write her next novel. *Grass in Piccadilly* brings post-war London vividly before the reader. In a once stately mansion, now divided into flats, a motley collection of people is gathered, whose stories intertwine; and if the plot is at times too melodramatic, it is underpinned by some extremely perceptive characterization. The range of characters drawn by Noel in her novels of the 1940s is wide and effective. Amongst the inhabitants of this Piccadilly mansion she includes a German Jewess, humbly self-effacing, racked with guilt over her husband's greed and selfishness, but so kind that she involuntarily becomes the person to whom everyone else turns; an upper class stepmother and stepdaughter, locked in their own secrets, but groping towards friendship with each other; a struggling writer; a promiscuous actress; and, on the fringe of the book, raffish 'Mumsie' with her homosexual boy-friends. Most brilliantly drawn of all are the two maids – Hannah, a starchy, respectable prude, and Mabel, a cynical, inquisitive woman of easy virtue – who, through the long, enforced intimacy of their service, have become totally dependant on each other. The lives of servants had fascinated Noel since she had watched them long ago during family prayers at Chart's Edge. The kitchen scenes in *Luke* and *The Winter is Past* are compelling, but the subtle dissection of the relationship between Hannah and Mabel in *Grass in Piccadilly* shows a remarkable understanding of the by-ways of human nature.

In the background of the book are all the difficulties and privations of life in 1946 – the shortage of everything, from food to bathroom fittings, and the scrounging and black-marketeering which were the inevitable consequence. And Sir John Nettel, the owner of the mansion, reflects Noel's own despondency as he gazes sadly at the battered streets. ' "I suppose London will stop looking shabby and drab when we all do something about it," ' remarks his wife . . . ' "We ought to have window boxes." ' And she finds some, and fills them with geraniums, as Noel had done in Elizabeth Street.

Many aspects of post-war life troubled Noel besides the shabbiness – the problems of evacuated children, often returning to broken homes; the crisis in housing. A little story that she sent out as a Christmas card in 1947 makes the telling point that 'There's millions would think it smashing if they could have their kid in a nice dry cattle shed.' Food was still rationed; clothes almost impossible to obtain. To boost her morale Noel exchanged the waterproof jacket and trousers she had worn on her shelter rounds for an evening dress Elsa Dunbar had made herself out of a pair of gold damask curtains. As she wrote in 1947, in the last of the WVS newsletters, the accumulation of frustrations sapped the spirit. 'The laundry that tears, uses bad soap, and loses things . . . The sheets that wear out, top and tail them as you will . . . The shabbiness of the house, the desperate need for paint and repairs, and the impossibility of getting a permit to have these things done . . . The carpets that wear out and are frayed, and can never be replaced. The dreary monotonous utility china which is all that is on sale in the shops . . . Standing in queues . . . ' The doleful list goes on and on.

Noel was tired out, suffering a reaction from seven years of hardship and intense struggle. Suddenly even writing seemed impossible. 'It was as if something had dried up in (my) brain,'[2] she said of herself. She longed to get away from pinched, dilapidated England, and refresh herself with beauty and luxury. There was nowhere to go in Europe. She had seen something of conditions there when, in February 1946, she undertook a month's lecture tour in Holland for the WVS, describing what British housewives had accomplished during the war. The tour was a nightmare. The weather was so bitter that, on one occasion, Noel recorded in her diary – 'I had to hold my chin so that the audience wouldn't see my teeth chattering.'[3] But the cold was nothing compared with the devastation of the country, and the effects of the Nazi occupation on the Dutch people. At times, crossing 'mile after mile of dead grey land,' with 'dead trees, fallen down telegraph poles, ruined villages, not even a bird,'[4] she felt as if she were travelling through Dante's Inferno. And when she reached each destination, there were stories of torture and execution to appal her.

Undomesticated Noel found herself harried by all the practical difficulties of life in Holland. She had to set her own hair, and wash her own clothes – monumental tasks for someone who always depended on hairdressers and laundries. It sharpened her sympathies towards the Dutch people as they laboured under crippling handicaps. 'Sat and talked to my hostess,' she wrote towards the end of the tour, while she was staying in an apparently wealthy house. 'Discovered that she wanted night cream, brown sewing silk and white cotton. Asked if there was anything else I could send, she said she would pay. Thinking she wanted a motor car, I asked what for. She then told me that they had no hairbrush. I hurriedly unpacked mine. She took it with tears of gratitude in her eyes. The amount of need of little things in all Dutch houses, even a very rich one such as I was in, is heartbreaking.'[5]

The country for which Noel, like many other exhausted Europeans, yearned, was America; and when, in the summer of 1947, her agent suggested that she might visit her American publishers, and research for a book with a film background, Noel seized the chance with alacrity.

America, and especially California, both restored her, and reinforced her enthusiasm for everything American. She revelled in the beauty of the cloudless skies and sapphire sea, and the white houses garlanded with flowers. 'The sun here isn't like any other sun. It's a golden haze which covers everything,'[6] she wrote, and she soaked herself in it. She marvelled at the smart clothes and exotic foods – the waffles with maple syrup, the banana splits, the hamburgers, all unbelievably lavish when contrasted with British rations. She loved the welcoming friendliness of the people, and the easy sophistication of their parties. On later visits she was occasionally more critical, but in 1947 she accepted everything with rapture. America, she declared proudly, was her second home.

Her chief purpose was to visit the film studios of Hollywood, and watch the child stars at work. A film of *The Secret Garden* was being made, with Margaret O'Brien in the leading role, and Noel spent several weeks in close observation. The film children fascinated her, as the pantomime children of Newcastle had once done. 'Star children, particularly film stars, have a sense of responsibility even at a very early age, that is startling. Not to remember a line, or not being on the spot the instant their director calls them, is a deadly sin. I remember . . . Margaret O'Brien filming when she was about ten years old. Between shots she played some thrilling game with her stand-in, but no matter how absorbing the game, a quiet "Margaret" from the set, and she was gone, her whole attention immediately focused on the scene she was about to play. There was no need to call her twice, or to remind her to be quiet on the set, in fact except that she was obviously a small girl, she was treated and expected to be treated as a responsible person.'[7]

As ever, such professional dedication gripped Noel, interesting her far more than anything else in the studio. She watched the film children doing lessons, having costume-fittings, giving press interviews, rehearsing, and, of course, filming. 'It is very hard for them to have a normal home life,' she reflected. 'They have to be taken care of rather more than ordinary children, for a scratched nose or a broken front tooth may hold the picture up for days, and cost the film company a fortune.'[8] Yet they responded readily to all the demands made upon them.

She filled her notebook with jottings about every aspect of studio life. The technique of filming, with its concentration on short scenes, was very different from stage acting, and seemed to her less satisfactory; but the same total identification of the actor with the part was needed. The first threads of a new story were beginning to weave themselves together as she booked her passage back to England.

She came home early in 1948 with her energies recharged. Some restrictions in Britain were at last being lifted. There was more freedom to plan ahead. During the war Noel had spoken poignantly about leisure. She had it now, to use as she liked, and unexpectedly she found herself at a loss. The war had accustomed her to having some purpose larger than herself. Without one, life seemed empty. The Welfare State had taken over her voluntary committees. As Noel returned to her old routine of writing, she was aware of the need for a cause.

An immediately obvious one was London itself, which

appeared even drabber after California. Noel loved London, and its dereliction really hurt her. 'Flapping canvases still covered roofs,' she was to recall of this time. 'Half rooms could be seen where buildings were split in two. The city so many had fought to save was looking an old hag.'[9]

On a corner between Elizabeth Street and Chester Square was a particularly noisome bombsite, a ruined pub choked with unspeakable litter. Noel loathed it, but what could be done about it she could not imagine. The solution came to her after a chance conversation with an Irish maid who worked in the flat above hers, and who passed on to Noel a tip for the Grand National. It was for a horse called Sheila's Cottage, an outsider whose odds were 66-1. Noel risked a pound, and won sixty-six more when Sheila's Cottage came first in the race. Such money, Noel decided, was too special to fritter away on ordinary expenses. She would use it to transform the bombsite.

Few of her achievements ever gave Noel more satisfaction. First she cleared away all the rubbish, and then she filled the concrete foundations of the pub with sixty-six pounds' worth of rich country earth. The plants she put in were, to begin with, devoured by the woodlice which infested a crumbling wall nearby, but Noel battled against them with DDT, counting woodlice corpses in their thousands. Gradually she brought order out of chaos; and her laburnum and lilac, her rose bushes, daffodils, chrysanthemums and michaelmas daisies filled the sordid corner with beauty.

As a cause, however, it was not enough. She needed something bigger. The encounter which transformed her from a simple writer into a crusader, happened when she boarded a train, and sat down opposite an unknown man. 'He was in that mood when he had to talk to somebody,' Noel recalled, 'and since I was the only person there, he talked to me. We talked about Australia. The birds, the flowers, people, the colour and the smell. And it would be truer to say he talked, and I put in a word now and again. When I was getting out of the train, I said to him: "When are you going back to Australia?" He said: "Back? I've never been there." I was amazed, for after all I had been there, and he knew far more than I had ever dreamt of. Then he told me his story; he had been a prisoner of war in Germany for four and a half years. He said: "I never read much as a kid," but while he was a prisoner a box from the Red Cross brought him a book about Australia. He said: "Then they sent me more and more books on Australia, and I read so much about it sometimes it seemed there was no barbed wire, and I was on my way there. So when the war was over, and I was liberated, I went to Australia House and told them what I'd read, and asked them to get me a job. And now they've got me one, and I'm going next week. And when I've got there, thanks to what I've read, I shan't be a stranger." '[10]

Noel found his story deeply moving, and quoted it often. More importantly, it strengthened her consciousness of the power of books. All writers would like to believe that books influence people, and here was some telling, independent evidence that they did. Without even knowing she was a writer, the man had told her about the effect she might have. He set her thinking seriously about reading and writing. Could books be a way of helping to build happier, more meaningful lives for other people as well?

Natural inclination turned her mind towards the children's book world, and with the thoroughness she always brought to research, she began to investigate every possible aspect. She studied the contents and appearance of books, magazines and comics, and she became convinced that standards needed to be raised. On children the future rested – and, living in the immediate shadow of the atomic bombs dropped on Japan, the future looked as alarming to Noel as it did to almost everyone else. Surely it would be good, she thought, if children could be taught to identify and value the best things in life.

The post-war children's book world was in the doldrums. Publishers were still bedevilled by paper shortages. Being unwilling to risk their precious paper on books that might not sell, they played safe with sequels and repetitive annuals, while Enid Blyton, with her insistence on huge print runs, grabbed an unfair share of the market. Noel never cared for Enid Blyton. 'I think one of Miss Blyton's great qualities is that she doesn't strain any child's brain,'[11] she once remarked acidly.

But there were no satisfactory means, she discovered, of sorting out the good books from the commonplace, the indifferent and the bad. No newspaper or magazine gave regular attention to children's books. Reviewing was left to the editor's whim. Consequently, through publishers' caution and the lack of informed discussion, writers had little incentive to improve. The state of children's books in 1949 was summed up by *Punch*. 'Most of them are "Bloods" without much blood, and novelettes purged of love interest. The young heroes and heroines scamper after spies, yatter in old-fashioned slang, find hidden treasure, get stuck on ledges or cut off by tides, and are much more clever than grown-up people, and drearily like each other.'[12]

Noel was excellently placed to take a lead in this situation. Her status as one of the best-known children's writers was undisputed. In 1948, for instance, *Ballet Shoes* and *The Circus is Coming* were listed by the Library Association as 'books which should always be in print.' Previously, in 1947, the broadcasting of *Ballet Shoes* on the radio programme Children's Hour, in a version scripted by Felicity Douglas, brought Noel wide publicity; and so did her involvement with *Collins Magazine for Boys and Girls*, a lively monthly which was started in 1948. 'In this magazine she does not need any bush. She is different from everybody else,'[13] the magazine's literary editor, Viola Garvin, wrote of Noel.

In the late 1940s Noel did not yet speak or write much about children's books – that was still to come; but she was busy gathering material. She toured bookshops, noting with disfavour those which indiscriminately labelled all children's books 'juveniles', and pushed them into corners. She was alert for piles of cheap, gaudy annuals; trashy picture books with vulgar illustrations that could corrupt a child's taste; and unalluring, badly-printed school books. All her impressions were stored in her retentive memory, to be brought out and used at the right moment. Books, she believed, were like doors, opening onto different worlds. It was vital for children that the worlds should be beautiful, truthful, and, in the best sense, magical. In 1937 she had had to resort to the London Library for help when asked to speak about children's books. In 1949 she delivered her first post-war lecture on the same subject to a writers' summer school, and it was knowledgeable and trenchant, advocating a boycott of tawdry books and ignorant booksellers.

Meanwhile she was working hard on her own books. For the first issues of the new *Collins Magazine* she contributed a four-part serial, *The Sadler's Wells Ballet School*, about imaginary children in a real institution. The school had opened just a year earlier, under the direction of Noel's old friend, Arnold Haskell; and it offered what seemed to Noel an ideal combination of classical ballet training and general education. Her enthusiasm glows through the simple narrative which, beginning with auditions, traces the progress of two children, Rose and Edward, through their first year at the school.

Even in the blackest months of the war, Noel had watched ballet whenever she could. 'When the war came I was on night work, and seldom had an evening off,' she recalled, 'but when I did, I was at the New Theatre. This was the wartime home of the Vic-Wells Ballet. The Company danced there accompanied by two pianos, and though the wardrobe grew shabbier and shabbier, and almost all the men were called up, for me and for many it was the ballet which kept our souls alive in our darkest hours.'[14] Years of ballet-going had made Noel far better informed about ballet training than when she casually created Posy Fossil. She now knew the realities of hard work and discipline, the dangers of growing too tall or too heavy, and these were the ingredients of the story, with a sharp warning to aspiring dancers not utterly dedicated to reaching the supreme peaks of classical ballet. 'Nobody at Sadler's Wells wants to train children to appear at matinees while their admiring relatives say: "Oo, isn't she wonderful!" ' Such frivolity is rightly despised when the goal is Covent Garden.

Up to a point *The Sadler's Wells Ballet School* is lively and instructive, with an interesting emphasis on the importance of boy dancers. Whether Arnold Haskell could have been entirely satisfied with it as a picture of his school is debatable. Rose and Edward seem to dance in a vacuum, for any account of the school's everyday routine or atmosphere is buried under the combined weight of too much information, and too much enthusiam. This is in no sense an 'inside story' of a school; it is a gush of uncritical ardour. And the same fault mars Noel's next book, *The Painted Garden*, also serialized in *Collins Magazine* in 1948, and published in 1949.

This is the Hollywood book, the story about film-making which Noel had researched in California, an ambitious enterprise which, in the end, disappoints through being overloaded with excessive adulation for everything American. Gone is the controlled narrative of *The Circus is Coming* and *Party Frock*. Instead, *The Painted Garden* sinks at times to a mere colourful travelogue with its lengthy descriptions of the Atlantic crossing and the trans-continental train journey, and its rhapsodizing over California. Well over a hundred pages must be read before the real theme of the book is reached – the story of how plain, contrary Jane Winter is spotted by a Hollywood director, and chosen by him for a part of Mary in a film of *The Secret Garden*; and how, through her difficulties with the part, and her contacts with the other film children, her prickly character is softened.

The aura of Hollywood glamour – still very potent in 1949, when film stars were universal pin-ups, and movie magazines the favourite reading of millions – perhaps helped to disguise the flaws in *The Painted Garden*. The reviews were mostly good, though there was little competition from other books. 'Noel Streatfeild stands out as clearly as a rose among weeds,'[15] one reviewer remarked. But when the Hollywood romance and fervid travel writing are stripped away, the disquieting truth that Noel was merely repeating old themes and old stories is laid bare.

The Painted Garden is a kind of transmuted version of *Tennis Shoes*. There is the same ineffectual mother – rather more ineffectual, indeed, than Mrs Heath – supported by the same genteel dogsbody, though the Winters' Peaseblossom is considerably nastier than the Heaths' Pinny. After *Tennis Shoes* and *Curtain Up* the musical small brother is coming dangerously near to cliché, as is the resolutely nice elder sister, trembling modestly on the brink of successes which fate may snatch away. Jane is the Nicky Heath character, but a Nicky Heath with no genuine star quality, without even the charm which had made Millie Evans the focus of unwilling attention. It is a weakness of the book that Jane is introduced as difficult on the first page, unlike Nicky whose difficult nature is only slowly revealed.

A writer's imagination tends to run in grooves, but character drawing had been one of the great strengths of Noel's adult novels and early children's books. *The Painted Garden* was a respectable achievement by the standards of its day, but not by Noel's own standards. It is disappointing to find her shying away from the bold imaginative leaps she had once taken so confidently, and settling – perhaps through pressure of work and other commitments – for the well-known and well-tried. Just as she discovered children's books as a cause, her own seemed, paradoxically, to be declining.

As usual her life was crammed with activities. She wrote articles and short stories, there were three Susan Scarletts between 1947 and 1951, she took up work for charities like the Invalid Children's Aid Association, and in 1949 she was chairman of the Society of Authors. Perhaps the most important personal event of the late 1940s was making a new friend.

When Noel met her, Margot Grey was running the Clifton Hotel behind Selfridges. The two women liked each other immediately, but at first a strange constraint lay over the acquaintance, for Margot was reluctant to talk about her past. So reserved was she, that Noel began to suspect that her father must have been a murderer; but trust was slowly built up, and one day Margot confessed the truth. She did not know the identity of her parents. Her mother, she believed, had been a wealthy society girl, who had fallen in love with a groom on her father's estate. When she was found to be pregnant, she was banished to France; and as soon as the baby, Margot, was born, she was taken away from her mother, who never saw her again. All this Margot partly deduced from hints, partly guessed. She was brought up in an isolated country house by two godmothers, who stifled her questions by pretending that her parents were dead, but the mystery hung over her childhood, a perpetual shadow. Although she was beautifully dressed, and much petted, 'there was an undercurrent of "poor little thing" which she resented bitterly.'[16] At school there were whispers, nudges, and cruel gossip. She was so frequently treated as inferior to the other children that one day she walked out, and refused to return. Other schools were tried unsuccessfully, and at last it was discovered that the godmothers had so mismanaged the trust fund left for her education that no more school fees could be paid, whereupon teenage Margot thankfully seized the opportunity to break her links with the people whose secrecy and pretence, however well-meaning, had blighted her life. She went off alone to France, and trained as a hotel manager.

As a novelist, Noel was fascinated by this story; as a person, she responded warmly to Margot's strength of spirit. The friendship grew. Margot had a house on the coast at Hythe, which Noel liked; and presently they arranged that Margot should live at 51A Elizabeth Street during the winter, and Noel would be free to stay in Hythe as much as she wished during the summer.

Margot filled a gap in Noel's life, for, by the end of the war, her old friendship with Daphne had sadly crumbled. Theodora Newbold, who had once been so kind to Noel, had been captivated, in her turn, by Daphne; and the two had embarked on a strongly possessive friendship from which Noel was excluded.

In many ways Margot was the exact opposite to Daphne, homely and unsophisticated where Daphne had been cosmopolitan and smart. Probably because she was an excellent cook, she was too fat; and she had what some of Noel's friends considered disreputable tastes. Noel did not mind Margot's appearance, or that she was a compulsive gambler, addicted to horse-racing and greyhound-racing. Under her influence Noel, always ready for a new experience, bought herself two greyhounds, Primrose and Periwinkle, and watched them run whenever she could. An evening's racing at Harringay or the White City became a familiar pleasure. She and Margot would dine at leisure in the glass-fronted restaurant overlooking the track. The trainer would join them for a chat, and girl runners would place their bets, and collect their winnings. To Noel it was all tremendous fun. Even the shadier dealings of the racing world amused her, and she described them with gusto in her novel *Aunt Clara*, published in 1952.

Possibly it was through the greyhounds that Noel's buried longing for a pet dog began to surface. Though she had never risked buying one, her books are full of dog lovers, from the children in *Parson's Nine* to Jane in *The Painted Garden*. Margot kept a dog in Hythe, and when it died Noel suggested that they should buy another one jointly, keeping it mainly in London, but taking it to the seaside whenever they could.

Together they chose a black miniature poodle, Pierre, who was for many years the recipient of Noel's extreme devotion. Her passion for him, expressed in fancy coats, diamanté collars, piles of Christmas presents, even the services of a 'dogsitter' when she went out in the evenings, seemed absurd to some of her friends, another of the excesses inspired by Margot. Their opinions did not trouble Noel. She loved Pierre as if he were the child she had never had.

Her real family were immensely important to her, more so as time went on. The war had reinforced her belief in the need for stable family life. She loved to spend Christmas with Bill and his wife, or gather a party of relations at Elizabeth Street. When Ruth's teenage son had a day off from Winchester, she would invite him to visit her, and offer him meals, drinks and cigarettes, in an agreeably sophisticated way. She even took him to the Windmill Theatre to see the famous showgirls – an unprecedented treat from a spinster aunt. She was the only woman in the theatre, her nephew remembered, but she enjoyed herself. For a new nephew, Richenda's son, she brought home from America a collection of stylish baby clothes, which were the envy of other mothers. To her nieces she gave the same kind of practical advice about fashion she had once given Richenda. She liked people to make the most of themselves, and look their best – it was shortly to be the theme of her anthology, *The Years of Grace*.

So, with family and friends, a home and a solid reputation, she was comfortably set to begin what she later remembered as the happiest part of her life.

15

Halcyon Days

'Without doubt the fifties and early sixties were halcyon days,'
Noel wrote in *Beyond the Vicarage*. At last everything she had
wanted seemed to have come to her. She had all the assurance of
being known as one of the stars in the literary firmament. Her
sales were so great that Susan Scarlett, the extra money-spinner,
could be quietly dropped. Her books were enjoyed throughout
the English-speaking world. It was to Noel that the National
Book League turned when they needed a well-known writer to
launch their new 'book tallys' – sixpenny vouchers to be used like
book tokens. It was Noel who was invited to open an important
London exhibition of book illustrations, *The Child and the Artist*,
as well as a new branch of W. H. Smith's, and countless charity
bazaars. She was one of the 'sixteen principal literary figures in
Britain today', who, with Bernard Shaw, Compton Mackenzie,
J. B. Priestley and others, autographed a teacloth which was sold
to raise funds for the PEN Club. She spoke at Book Weeks and
on Brains' Trust panels. She gave away prizes at school speech
days.

With her actress's training she played the part of a celebrity to
perfection. Tall and stately, and carrying considerably more
weight, she would sail onto platforms, and hold audiences
spellbound with her wit, her vocal range, and her theatrical
gestures. Now that she could afford to spend lavishly on clothes,
she chose for her public appearances striking outfits which
caught the eye of every newspaper reporter. 'Miss Streatfeild
wore a sage green dress and a tiny hat of blue and pink feathers'
. . . 'Noel Streatfeild wore a décolleté dress of kingfisher blue,
long black gloves, and large drop ear-rings' . . . 'She was smartly
dressed in black with a gay little pink hat' . . . 'Miss Streatfeild

wore an intriguing hat made entirely of flowers.' She used a special cigarette holder fitted with a loop which ringed the little finger of her left hand, a decorative property which enhanced her gestures. Even the spectacles she used for reading and writing had coloured, zig-zag frames. But behind the dazzling hats, the glasses and the cigarette holder, was a kindly, humorous, determined face, illumined by the blue eyes which everyone remembered.

In 1950 she was fifty-four, still full of vigour and energy, and keeping to a strict routine of writing. Every morning her housekeeper brought in her breakfast tray, with *The Times* and her letters. A leisurely bath followed; the bath, Noel said, was a good place for thinking. Then she put on a stylish négligé, added ear-rings, make-up and a touch of scent, and returned to bed to write. Her best working time was between half past nine and one o'clock. She wrote by hand with a fountain pen, covering sheets of unlined paper in a huge, dashing scrawl. Her aim was to complete a thousand words a day. Sometimes a whole day's output had to be scrapped, but on the whole she worked as a disciplined professional, knowing exactly what she wanted to do, and pacing herself to achieve it. Any interruptions maddened her, but her housekeeper and secretary guarded her devotedly, answering the telephone and warding off visitors. The only distraction she allowed herself was background music on the radio.

Unless she had visitors she lunched in bed, and often worked into the afternoon, dictating and signing letters, and going through the previous day's writing which had been typed out by her secretary. Presently she would get up, and perhaps take Pierre for a walk, keep an appointment at the hairdresser's, or at Elizabeth Arden's beauty salon where she would have a facial and a manicure, or go shopping. The evening was the time for speaking engagements, for entertaining, and for going out to parties, or – best of all – to new plays, films and ballets. If she was tired she stayed at home to have supper on a tray, read and watch television, then in its early, pioneering stage.

The physical writing was only part of the job. Into her tight routine she fitted a good deal of reading, borrowing extensively from Harrod's Library and the London Library. She was a perfectionist over research, checking the smallest details. She liked, as well, to keep abreast of current novels and biographies, and they filled her shelves, together with her many reference volumes, and her collection of books about ballet. Still more books flooded in to be reviewed. 'This year, as every year at this time,' she wrote in November 1957, 'each room of my small flat is full of children's books waiting for review . . . I am a scrupulous reviewer, and read each book in its entirety.'[1] Afterwards she sent her review copies to children's hospitals and deprived parishes.

As important in the creation of a book as reading and writing was thinking time. Since the days when Noel played Circe in the Amberley nursery, ideas and characters had thronged her fertile mind, but they had to be worked out carefully before they were committed to paper. Sometimes it seemed that the hardest part of a writer's life was 'the struggle towards tomorrow's output when the pen is laid down,'[2] but it was the most essential. In the bath, in the park with Pierre, in the manicurist's chair, she brooded on her books. 'If you don't know a character,' she told an interviewer, 'how can anyone else? You've got to live with them in your head. Very often the characters are closer to me than the people I'm meeting,'[3] a familiar experience for a creative writer.

The flash of inspiration which produced *I Ordered a Table for Six* was rare. Long incubation was much more usual for her. She enlarged on the theme in a letter of 1957 to two teenage girls who had sent a story they had written to her for her comments. 'Before you write anything, find out about your characters. Make charts. Who are their grandfathers and grandmothers? What are *they* like? How many traits of theirs have the children inherited? What are their parents like? What have the children inherited from them? What, when they are alone, do your characters think about? Everybody has hopes and fears, what are your characters secretly afraid of? What are their ambitions? What are their faiths? There is no end to this business of knowing the people you write about. I find it takes me nearly a year of thinking about my people before I know them well enough to write about them.'[4]

Noel's popularity as a children's writer reached its peak in the 1950s. Her sales might not equal Enid Blyton's, but there was hardly a newspaper reference or library poll which did not place her in the first flight. Her success was helped by the wide age span of her readers. A decade later this had contracted to the seven to twelve age group, but teenagers in the early 1950s were fairly unsophisticated, and girls of fourteen and fifteen still read Noel's books.

Children's fiction of the time was tediously monochrome, with innumerable pony books and outdoor adventure stories, constant additions to the interminable sequences of writers like W. E. Johns and Elinor Brent-Dyer, and a scattering of worthy but pedestrian career stories. The emphasis on enjoying physical activities and keeping a stiff upper lip, encouraged in the 1930s, still lingered on; and there was much outdated snobbery, with pony and ballet books in particular subjecting their unlucky *parvenu* characters to merciless attack. Naturally there were no stories of working class children. New gleams of light were just beginning to shine on the distant horizon in 1950. C. S. Lewis's *The Lion, the Witch and the Wardrobe* piled new imaginative riches before its readers, and Noel's old friend, Roland Pertwee, gave interesting depth and complexity to the outdoor adventure story with *The Islanders*; but such books were rare.

Against this background Noel's books glowed. Other writers might imitate her stories of child professionals, but, lacking Noel's tough reality of characterization and genuine understanding of what working out a vocation meant, their actresses and ballerinas are merely pretty paper dolls, who demonstrate their genius by pirouetting compulsively in moonlit glades. Adventure stories Noel had wisely avoided since *The Children of Primrose Lane*. Instead, with *Party Frock* and the immensely popular new radio serial *The Bell Family*, she showed that ordinary life could be colourful and absorbing, its small incidents as much packed with drama and suspense as the most hectic inventions of the Blyton school. Unlike most of her contemporaries she wrote books without villains, yet she offered a firm scale of values, with a secure, loving family life as the highest of all. 'What I always want in a book is a family,' she told a fellow writer, Rumer Godden – and a proper family, she might have added, not one from which parents were compulsorily excluded. A complete family interested her far more than the conventional story book children on the loose; and she was equally good at conveying the rubs of family life – shared bedrooms and handed-down clothes – and its simple pleasure of pets, holidays and Christmas.

Nothing increased Noel's fame more than the Bell family stories. They were broadcast in six-part serials on Children's Hour every year from 1949 to 1953, appeared in book form in 1954, were revived in a new setting for Children's Hour in 1955, and finally wound up in another book, *New Town*, in 1960. Television was still uncommon, and radio immensely influential. It was estimated that two million adults and four million children listened daily to Children's Hour in 1950 – a vast audience for the Bells.

Noel's first impulse for the series came after *Ballet Shoes* was broadcast in 1947. She had not believed that the book could be adapted, but Felicity Douglas's script worked so well that Noel listened entranced, and was fired with the ambition to try a radio script herself. She approached May Jenkin, the Head of Children's Hour, and told her 'that I would like to write something specially for that medium, about an absolutely ordinary family of children, who don't catch burglars, find jewels down wells, or have any of those extraordinary adventures peculiar to children in books and plays. About six months later May Jenkin telephoned me and said, "Have you thought any more about that ordinary family, because . . . we'd like to have a play like that next year".'[5]

The Bell Family was one of the most popular of all children's radio programmes, frequently voted top play of the year in Children's Hour Request Weeks. In weaving her stories about a poor clergyman's family in South London, Noel mixed several strands from her own past. The setting is clearly Deptford, grimy and overcrowded, but full of sterling characters. The poverty is that of Noel's childhood, where traumas over clothes can coincide with the employment of full-time domestic help. The morality is staunchly Victorian. High standards of manners, loyalty and unselfishness are displayed by everyone, giving the serials, even in the early 1950s, an old world charm which appealed as much to adults as to children. They are unashamedly stories about people who try to do the right things.

The father of the family, the Reverend Alex Bell, is a softened version of William Streatfeild; as devoted a priest as his prototype – 'he thought the place where he was most needed the loveliest place to be' – but much more relaxed. Contentment and tranquility radiate from him, making him the nicest clergyman Noel ever drew, just as his wife Cathy, loving, brave, and touchingly dependent on her domestic help, Mrs Gage, is Noel's most attractive mother. Of the four children, the most memorable was the younger daughter Ginnie – 'Miss Virginia Bell' as she liked to call herself. The Nicky Heath outline was remodelled in her into something gentler and more engaging. Ginnie is plain and plump, with a tendency to point out embarrassing truths, and a genius for running into trouble; but since all her difficulties arise from well-meaning attempts to help the family she adores, listeners were always on her side. 'Ginnie was very very popular all over the country,' Noel remembered, 'particularly, I noticed, with Women's Institutes. When I went to speak to them, their first question always was – "What's the news of Miss Virginia Bell?" '[6]

The Bell Family was successful because it presented a family who were idealized and yet credible – the sort of family every listener would like to belong to. It followed a simple formula of loosely connected stories, stemming from the temperaments and interests of the children, and their relationships with each other. Concurrently Noel was writing one of her most tightly constructed and exciting stories, *White Boots*, published in 1951.

Having covered theatre, ballet, films, tennis and the circus, Noel had been looking around for a new background. Children who sent her fan mail sometimes mentioned that they were taking part in ballets on ice, and, in an unguarded moment, Noel floated the idea of a skating book with her American editor, Bennet Cerf. To her consternation he seized it enthusiastically; and she found herself committed to a subject about which she knew nothing, and which demanded an enormous amount of research. The preparation of *White Boots* demonstrates both Noel's thoroughness, and her close relations with her staff. People who worked for her always became linked by strong bonds of loyalty, caught up in her interests and pleasures. On this occasion, having decided that she was too old to learn to skate herself, she persuaded her secretary, June, to undertake a course of lessons, and report both on skating technique, and on all the happenings at an ice rink. Meanwhile Noel studied books on skating, and contacted an expert about the figures required for each graded test. With a background of knowledge, she began observing skaters in training; and when figures had been traced, 'I knelt on wet, cold ice, studying the tracings, trying to find out what made them faulty or otherwise. Then I began to fly high. I attended every stage of first the European and finally the World Championships. People were very kind. They sat by me for hours on end, explaining why one skater would get more marks for a figure than another. Finally I reached the grand state of being able to guess reasonably accurately exactly what marks a skater would get.'[7] When the book was finished, Noel sent it for approval to a famous skating judge, before submitting it to the publishers.

Such exhaustive study gave Noel confidence, and confident *White Boots* certainly is, one of Noel's best books. After a rather shaky start, introducing the Johnson family who make an improbable living by selling unwanted vegetables from a rich relation's estate, it develops into an enthralling account of the progress of two child skaters – Lalla Moore, orphan daughter of a famous ice champion, destined by her ambitious aunt to follow in her father's footsteps; and Harriet Johnson, who takes up skating first for her health, and then to be a companion and spur to Lalla. There is an almost Victorian contrast between rich, admired Lalla, who has everything except a happy family life, and delicate Harriet, 'all eyes, hair and legs', poor and shabby, but cradled in love.

The greatest triumph of *White Boots* is the character of Lalla. Charm is a difficult quality for a writer to convey, easy to assert, but hard to evoke, but Lalla has charm in abundance. At times cocky, at times self-pitying, she is always loveable and real. Her dashing style of skating conceals for a long time the horrible truth that she will never be good enough to reach the top. Gradually, while Harriet's skating improves, Lalla begins to fail her tests, and falls ill with nervous strain. As in *The Circus is Coming*, the climax of the book is not some breath-taking triumph, but the moment when Lalla has the courage to admit of those bogey skating figures – 'I just couldn't do them. They were too difficult.'

White Boots contains many of Noel's favourite themes – the importance of family life; the lesson that hard work and determination are quite as essential to success as flair and personality; the varied opportunities within every field, so that Lalla can look forward to a thrilling future starring in ice shows while Harriet pursues her dedicated path towards the Olympic Games. Its richness of character and plot captivated readers and reviewers alike. 'Miss Noel Streatfeild has the joy of being a classic in her own lifetime,'[8] wrote one critic after *White Boots* followed *The Bell Family* as a radio serial in 1954.

Such adulation was perhaps a little too intoxicating. A shade of pomposity now tinged Noel's stateliness. Friends noticed her tendency at parties to begin every remark, 'Of course, speaking as a writer – ', and to strangers her strong, even flamboyant personality could be intimidating.

But her self-assurance was never more than a veneer, the outward sign of how far the plain Vicarage child with her crippling inferiority complex had come. Underneath she remained generous and warm-hearted. It was characteristic of her that once she had a reasonable income she charged no more than expenses for her speaking engagements; characteristic too that she answered every letter of her enormous fan mail. She read and commented on all the manuscripts hopefully sent her by aspiring writers; she signed autographs; she supplied personal details to endless children doing English projects about her; she provided an explanation to the American child who wrote plaintively – 'What are trifles and what are drawing pins?' She dealt kindly with the anguished letters of would-be actresses and dancers – 'Please can you help me to act! I must act, I know I must!' 'I want to be a dancer. I have not told anybody my feelings, just you' – advising them to contact drama schools and reputable ballet teachers, whose names she would even supply. More difficult were the agony column letters – 'From your books I realize how understanding you are. My problem is that my mother does not realize that I need a bra' – but she tackled them with patient good sense.

She became a popular advice-giver, the sort of person to whom editors turned for an instant, readable opinion. She gave her views in print on television for teenagers, careers for girls, clothes for fishing, children's pocket money, and other such topical matters. But her chief subject was always children's books, every aspect of them, from their contents to the way they were sold.

Remembering herself as a small child, poring over the exquisite water colours of *The Tailor of Gloucester*, she stressed repeatedly the value of good illustrations. Pictures were the first way into a book, and far too many seemed to her crude and flat, offering no stimulus to the imagination. 'I like a lion to look as if he could eat people,'[9] she commented. Badly illustrated books led to a corrupted taste which would see no harm in comics, and comics were anathema to her.

In the early 1950s a flood of American 'horror comics', pouring into Britain, galvanized Noel to action. She foresaw just how they would spread, for she had no illusions about children automatically enjoying books. Long ago, at a Christmas party in Deptford, almost all the books she had chosen as prizes had been handed back with the words – 'Could I have a toy, miss? I don't read books.'[10] In the pre-television, pre-video age, such children were the natural market for thrill-provoking horror comics.

Noel determined on a crusade. She would organize a band of like-minded people, to be called 'The Company of New Elizabethans', who would campaign against the comics. 'Their subject matter is violence, crime, plus a little sex on the side,' she declared. 'They are atrociously illustrated, their morals are nil, their trend is to build up in the minds of children and young people the idea that violence is the best way out of any situation.'[11] Noel's aim was not simply to have such comics banned. She wanted to see formulated a set of critical standards, which would encourage discrimination by parents and news-agents; and she wrote to the press, and to church and social organizations, propounding her ideas. In a bold bid for support she challenged *The Daily Express* to print a selection of pictures from some of the worst comics, but *The Daily Express* prudently declined.

Plenty of people were sympathetic to her cause. Enid Blyton, for example, opposed the comics in paradoxically violent language. 'I want to whip out those who pollute the innocence and goodness in the hearts of children.'[12] The problem of the horror comics was canvassed in the media, and debated in Parliament. But somehow the Company of New Elizabethans never got off the ground. Noel had too many other interests to give it the exclusive attention needed for a nationwide movement, and few pages of the cuttings book she prepared for the cause were filled. She was not, in any case, a natural member of organized movements; she was an individualist who worked best on her own. She did, however, have the satisfaction of knowing that she must have provided some of the ammunition for the Children's and Young Person's Harmful Publications Act, passed in 1955, which banned the most objectionable comics.

At first the contents of books worried her less than the illustrations. Brought up herself on the classics, she had innocently believed that once children had acquired the habit of reading, they would naturally choose good books. Her eyes were opened when, in 1952, she was asked to judge a children's book-writing competition, run by *Collins Magazine*. The two hundred entrants were presumably the novelists of the future, the cream of teenage narrative talent, yet the low level of their productions appalled Noel. Their literary taste seemed totally uneducated, as if they had never read anything but the most conventional rubbish. She waded despairingly through piles of hackneyed adventure stories, school stories, pony books and Ruritanian romances. 'Only a very small percentage showed a spark of originality, and the majority wrote poor imitations of someone else's work . . . Do both schools and homes prefer rows of jellies from the same mould?'[13] she wondered.

The competition gave impetus to her work as a reviewer and writer about children's books, for she saw how vital was the need to widen children's horizons. Fortunately she had a special platform in *Collins Magazine*. Through its attractive and comprehensive book pages the editor, Pamela Whitlock, had already done more for children's literature than anyone else; and in 1952 she invited Noel to select a regular 'book of the month' from the entire range of newly-published books, fiction and non-fiction, for children or adults. Noel took up the idea with enthusiasm, and in contrast to the more orthodox recommendations of the magazine's main literary pages, her choices were unusual and idiosyncratic. Working on her favourite principle that books should be doors, leading children into unfamiliar worlds, she turned most frequently to adult non-fiction, picking for her first six, books about early sailing ships, inventors, fifteenth century Scotland, Canadian whaling, ghosts and grizzly bears.

Her 'book of the month' selections show Noel at her best as a critic, perceptive and original as she explains her choices. But because there were few recognized experts on children's books, and Noel's was a well-known name, she was consistently asked to do far too much reviewing, so that she was sometimes almost lost beneath the weight of books she was expected to evaluate for newspapers, magazines, and Children's Hour. Good though it was that children's literature was beginning to command more attention, the result for overworked Noel was an inevitable lack of discrimination. Often she liked the books she read, sometimes she detested them, but within the categories of good and bad she seldom attempted to define shades, showing equal enthusiasm for Winnie the Pooh and Andy-Pandy. Her taste was catholic, with a slight preference for books based on solid fact, and an understandable bias against the candy-floss confections which passed for serious ballet stories. But in spite of the amount she read, and the range of books she recommended, she was never able to stand back and make a detailed analysis of trends, or to spot a rising talent before it was generally recognized. Indeed the immense volume of her reviews adds up to disappointingly little, except to show her addiction to books, and her belief that they should reinforce traditional moral values.

Yet for her, reviewing was important, part of her crusade to encourage children in their reading; and if she did not apply strict critical standards, that was because she was ready to like almost anything. Her enthusiasm for books was infectious. It was to her that Independent Television producers turned for help with the very first series of children's book programmes, launched in 1956. *Book Choice* featured Noel discussing newly-published books with a group of children. She prepared conscientiously, ploughing through still more piles of books, but the programmes were not a great success. Faced with Noel's theatrical, larger than life personality, the children were overawed. Inevitably they let Noel dominate the discussions, and dismiss briskly opinions that differed from her own. There was such an aura of certainty about her, that the discouraged children were left struggling in her wake.

Believing as she did in wide horizons, she began to extend the scope of her own children's books. She edited two compendiums of advice for teenagers, *The Years of Grace* (1950) and *Growing up Gracefully* (1955); an anthology of short stories, *By Special Request* (1953); and a fascinating collection of brief memoirs of life at the beginning of the century, *The Day before Yesterday* (1956). Noel loved editing. She chose her contributors carefully, briefed them on exactly what she wanted, and then bound the contents together in a personalized running commentary, in which she addresses the reader directly. Chatty introductions precede stories and articles. 'Catherine (Gaskin) is a very interesting person. When she was fifteen she had to sit for a school examination. You know what that means, the last minute cramming, the way it hangs over you and haunts your days, at least that is most people's feeling, but Catherine evidently despised examinations. What do you think she did at the same time as sit for hers? She wrote a first novel.'[14] Sometimes familiarity topples into sentimentality. 'I have written so much to you in this book, I am beginning to know and see you, so it is hard to write the word "goodbye" '[15]

This personal style made the books immensely popular. They were glowingly reviewed, and *The Years of Grace* particularly, with its fifty chapters of advice on appearance, social skills, hobbies and careers, sold in enormous numbers, and influenced a whole generation of teenagers, filling the gap which teenage magazines – as yet hardly in existence – were later to plug. Another of Noel's books to receive tremendous acclaim was *The Fearless Treasure* (1953), a social history of England. When the suggestion for it came from the publishers, Michael Joseph, she was temporarily nonplussed. History had never appealed to her greatly. 'Odd to live outside your own period',[16] she had observed when her friend, Theodora Newbold, was immersed in a course on the Victorian novelists; and, for a person of imagination, she was oddly indifferent to the romance of her ancestors – Elizabeth Fry, the Stuart regicide and royalist, the de Morville who had murdered Thomas à Becket. The present and future mattered to her, not the past. Unwilling though she was to refuse, Michael Joseph's idea seemed outside her sphere.

Then, by chance, she remembered how, on the Sussex Downs, her father had once found a flint arrowhead, and described to her the civilization of the man who had made it. 'As he talked . . . I saw the man's hut, I smelt his food cooking. Almost I saw him.'[17] The memory gave her a shape for her book. Six children would journey back in time, and experience the daily lives of their ancestors in different generations. The plot mechanics are, in fact, clumsy; the conclusions about the greatness of England, though no doubt chiming with the mood of Coronation year, now seem sententious; but the feel of the past, which Noel conveys with apt details of sights, sounds and smells, is immediately convincing. Research and imagination dovetail into a whole.

'She was a devil for work,' one of her secretaries remembered, trying to explain the staggering quantity and range of Noel's output. Somehow in the 1950s she found time for three more adult novels – *Mothering Sunday* (1950), *Aunt Clara* (1952), and *Judith* (1956); a play, *Many Happy Returns*, which she wrote in collaboration with Roland Pertwee in 1950, but which, to Noel's disappointment, never received more than occasional single performances; a television serial, *The Thompson Family* (1957); a biographical study of E. Nesbit, *Magic and the Magician* (1958); *The Royal Ballet School* (1959), an ambitious successor to *The*

Sadler's Wells Ballet School, which includes several chapters on the history of ballet; at least twenty short stories for children and adults; several minor plays, and a serial, *The Emerald Island* (1954), for the *Nottingham Evening News*. She edited a *Ballet Annual* for Collins in 1960, and contributed introductions to a number of books.

Such a list was only possible for a writer very much cushioned against the frets and inconveniences of everyday life. Noel never made a meal, or washed an item of clothing for herself. Library books were ordered by telephone; taxis were summoned when she had to go out. Her entertaining was done either at her club, the Hanstown, or at a restaurant, frequently the one next door to her. She had a wide circle of acquaintances from the worlds of books, ballet and the theatre, and she liked to repay the hospitality that she received.

Not that she accepted indiscriminately every invitation. 'I do hope we can meet again sometime,' Noel Coward wrote to her. 'I hope to be in London for Christmas, and shall be at the Dorchester. If you are about, do let me know.' Noel replied a little coolly. 'It would be delightful if we could meet, but no doubt you will be buried under your friends who have heard the good news that you are back.'

She had been exchanging letters with Noel Coward over his reminiscences of E. Nesbit, which she had used in the biography *Magic and the Magician*. The letters had been warm and friendly, and she had much appreciated his contribution, but she did not want to pretend that there were any close bonds between them. A certain restraint lay beneath the surface gaiety of many of her relationships. She had 'writing friendships' with a number of other authors. She would send them pleasant, chatty letters, often hung on the peg of a request for help with some project like an anthology. There would follow occasional meetings for drinks or dinner, and a veneer of easy intimacy would be established. After she had given a lecture, or presented prizes, her hosts would be left with an agreeable impression of friendliness, of shared jokes and cigarettes.

But apart from Margot, her relations and her devoted secretaries, really close friends were rare. One of the few was Kitty

Barne, who was still writing children's books, and who always visited Elizabeth Street when she came up from Eastbourne. She was now distressingly deaf, and conversation with her was difficult, but Noel made time to see her, and somehow, over lunch, they would manage a conversation about their books.

And all the time, critics and reviewers vied with their eulogies. 'Noel Streatfeild, best beloved of children's writers.'[18] 'No one else has controlled as persuasive and skilled a pen.'[19] 'Hosts of young readers everywhere bless Noel Streatfeild.'[20] For anyone less mentally tough the volume of work, the chorus of praise, the heaps of fan mail, the eager commissions, might have got completely out of control; and even Noel, after a run of excellent books, stumbled over *Wintle's Wonders* in 1957.

She had not written about professional theatre children since *Curtain Up*. The children who put on the pageant in *Party Frock* are amateurs in the hands of an experienced director. Jane, in *The Painted Garden*, steps into her film part by the mere accident of looking 'black doggish' at a lucky moment. But *Wintle's Wonders* is set again in a stage school, to which come orphaned cousins – pale, serious Rachel, and lively extrovert Hilary, for whom a splendid dancing future is prophesied. There was to be no repetition, however, of the ethos of *Curtain Up*; Mrs Wintle's Academy is very unlike Madame Fidolia's. Noel returned to the world of *The Whicharts* and *It Pays to be Good*, to a cheap, secondrate establishment, where children in cutely infantile outfits cartwheel and kick their way into pantomime troupes.

Noel imagines an interesting situation. Rachel has promised her dying mother that Hilary will prepare for an audition at the Royal Ballet School; but, to her dismay, Hilary is captivated by the Little Wonders' style of dancing, and only wants to tour seaside resorts with them. Unfortunately, instead of finding a proper solution, Noel muddles herself and her readers. Because Hilary has been labelled 'nice', she cannot be condemned outright for her choice of cartwheels and high kicks, yet Noel clearly despises them, surrounding them with all the attributes of conscious vulgarity. The result is a chaotically shifting viewpoint, left unresolved when attention switches to Rachel's discovery of her talents as an actress.

For the first time Noel's technical ability seems in decline. Climaxes are prepared, and then feebly slithered over. The once subtle dissection of character is lost, while incidents rattle past at breakneck speed. Noel almost seems afraid that she will lose the reader's attention if she does not keep up a rapid pace. There are too many echoes of *White Boots*. Rachel and Hilary are paler versions of Harriet and Lalla, surrounded by a similar cast of domineering aunt, well-meaning uncle, cosy nannie, and intellectual governess.

Mesmerized, apparently, by the name Noel Streatfeild, most reviewers were ready to praise. Only the critic of *The Times Literary Supplement* searched beneath the frothy surface of the book, and found no real core. 'Having set an excellent pattern with *Ballet Shoes*, Noel Streatfeild now seems content to join the ranks of her own imitators, using stock characters, stock scenes, stock coincidences . . . (She) is too good a literary craftsman for her skill to be wasted on turning out replicas of her own early efforts.'[21]

One of the most attractive aspects of Noel's character was that she never made exalted claims for herself. 'Let's face it,' she wrote in *Beyond the Vicarage*, '(I) never had more than what Noel Coward's song called "a talent to amuse". (I) never belonged to the great.' Considering all that was said about her, this is amazingly modest; and it seems possible that she took to heart an occasional bad review far more than all the good ones. Evidence for this can be derived from the aftermath of those cutting remarks in *The Times Literary Supplement*. Stage schools, dancing troupes, aspiring child actresses ceased for a long time to feature in her books, and only reappeared in the undistinguished *Gemma* stories, and *Ballet Shoes for Anna*, written after she was seventy.

Noel may well have realized that her theatrical seam was now worked out. Nearly thirty years had elapsed since she had been on the stage. Attempts to return as an author had failed. She was still an ardent theatre-goer, but her knowledge of the magical world of pass doors, call boys, and dressing rooms was lamentably out of date. Unquenchable as ever, she widened her search for new fields.

16

The Autobiographies

Throughout the 1950s Noel made frequent visits to the United States, her 'second home'. Her children's books were published there in what Random House called her 'Shoe series', with *Curtain Up* renamed as *Theater Shoes*, *Party Frock* as *Party Shoes*, even *White Boots* as *Skating Shoes*. They were favourably reviewed and sold well, and Noel was invited to make several lecture tours, which included Brains' Trusts, book-signing sessions, and television appearances. She enjoyed them, though she remarked ruefully that she wished half the questions after her lectures were not invariably about the British royal family. But she made audiences laugh with jokes about her accent, and she pleased them by praising America.

Not caring for flying, she preferred to cross the Atlantic in the comfort of a liner. A glimpse of her on board the *Queen Mary* came from another writer of ballet stories, Mabel Esther Allan, who happened to see Noel's name on the passenger list, and sent her a note suggesting they should meet for drinks.

'It was extraordinary how deserted those great ships could be. There wasn't a soul in the lounge when suddenly the doors swung open, and a figure swirled in – a largish figure wearing a hat with a brim and a billowing cloak. She swooped down on me, and I rather began to wish I hadn't written that note. A very formidable woman, but a friendly one, and we had a lot to talk about. After that first drink we ended up in her state room, making inroads on a magnum of champagne. For the rest of the voyage I saw a good deal of her, and visited her several times in Elizabeth Street. The first time I seemed to climb for ever, but a voice encouraged me from above. She seems to me to have had a rather loud voice, very commanding. I have another memory of her in a hat and cloak, whirling away through a swing door. She really always did seem to bring drama into arrivals and departures.'[1]

Closest among Noel's American friends was Helen Hoke Watts, a partner in the New York firm of Franklin Watts which had commissioned three books from Noel – *The Picture Story of Britain* (1951), *The First Book of the Ballet* (1953), and *The First Book of England* (1958). The two were not unalike, both vigorous women with strong personalities, who felt naturally akin to each other. Helen Watts sponsored some of Noel's American tours, and Noel enjoyed returning her hospitality when Helen was in London.

On one such occasion, in 1961, the two decided to visit Brighton. '(Helen) said we would go by car, having had sad experiences with our country trains,' Noel recalled; 'but I said, oh no, we'd go by train, because the Brighton Belle was magnificent and always punctual. The day I took her to Brighton was the day the Brighton Belle went wrong. It huffed and puffed, and stopped and stopped. What she said was nobody's business. To keep her quiet I told her about my childhood and upbringing in an English Vicarage – a world of which she knew nothing. Hours later, coming off Brighton Pier, she, sucking candy-floss, said – "Will you write a book about it for me?" '[2] And with those casual words, the idea of the autobiography was born.

For most of her life Noel had despised nostalgia, and prided herself on keeping up to date. Eagerly, thankfully, she had shrugged off her childhood with its spartan living and religious observances. Determinedly modern, she had been among the first women to have her hair bobbed, use make-up and wear trousers. From *The Whicharts* onwards her books had startled readers with their daring subjects and outspoken language. Even as late as 1947, a review in *The Spectator* said of *Grass in Piccadilly* – 'strait-laced persons are warned not to attempt more than the first few pages';[3] presumably because they would be distressed by a promiscuous heroine, and passing references to homosexuality and prostitution.

But in the post-war years, the rejected past began slowly to re-assert itself. Her own enormous popularity, and her widening knowledge of children's books, increased Noel's awareness of herself as a specifically children's writer, whose books were intimately connected with her childhood.

The question why someone, whose memories of youthful miseries and humiliations were so bitter, went on to write books commending family life, was one that Noel never answered explicitly. In view of her childhood, it would have seemed natural for her characters to find happiness by escaping from the iron clutch of home; but nearly always the opposite is true, and the fledglings outside the nest are wretched. For somehow, though she had been in perpetual rebellion as a teenager, Janet's training had had its insidious effect on Noel's personality; and when her revolts were over, and her wild oats sown, she began to reflect very much the same values that her parents had held dear.

Noel seems never to have been quite aware of this irony, though she knew there were many links between her stories and her childhood. *Ballet Shoes* provided the information she had longed for when she watched Lila Field's Little Wonders. *Tennis Shoes* arose from her teenage ambition to be a tennis star, and contained the first character based on her childish self. In *The Years of Grace* she drew an acknowledged self-portrait in the autobiographical connecting passages – a characteristically dramatic self-portrait of a plain, badly-dressed, temperamental misfit. 'I was hideous,' she tells the reader; '. . . I was horrible to have about the house . . . I argued and argued.' Piled-up details of spots, lank hair, and habitual defiance are made the justification for the book. Noel would not have been so unattractive, she suggests, if *The Years of Grace* had been available for her guidance.

Once the first lines had been sketched in, Noel grew fascinated by self-portraiture. All through the 1950s *A Writer's Life* was one of her favourite lecture titles, and audiences were enthralled by colourful accounts of her upbringing. She did not dwell on the horrors of a Vicarage Sunday, or the mortification of wearing the wrong clothes, merely to amuse. She wanted to point out how her writing was the outcome of her early experiences. Unhappiness, she claimed, had made her unusually objective. She had watched other children keenly, trying to discover why she was different from them, and that observation was the basis of her character drawing. A sense of inferiority had sharpened her memory, as she vowed never to forget the injustices she had suffered. In retrospect a happy childhood blurred into a golden haze, she believed. An unhappy one was remembered with stinging clarity.

From her pinnacle of success, Noel could afford to be tolerant. She looked down with a mixture of humour and sympathy on the child she had once been – a rebel certainly, but everybody's butt as well. It was all there at her fingertips – the descriptions, the anecdotes, the wry comments – when she needed to distract her American guest from the shortcomings of British trains.

The suggestion of a new subject for a book pleased Noel. Recently she had come to the sad conclusion that she would have to give up adult novels. They were more trouble than they were worth, harder to write than children's books, and much harder to sell. Her last, *The Silent Speaker* (1961), a not very convincing exploration of the reasons why an apparently contented woman committed suicide, had received disappointing reviews; and Noel recognized that her style of well-constructed, middle class novel was going out of fashion. She was being left behind, too, by a strong new tide of permissive morality. Certainly she had written about adultery, divorce and drugs herself – but not to assert that they did not matter, which seemed to her to be the attitude of young, liberalized novelists. Then she was conscious of how much her range of experience had narrowed. In the 1930s she could choose her subjects from many spheres – the theatre, modelling, Deptford, the munitions factory, the homes of the country gentry, Vicarages. Now she was out of touch with them all. Suddenly it seemed safer to retreat into the past, where – almost unaccountably – she now felt more at home.

Partly concealed by the originality of her material, there had often been an old-fashioned strand in Noel's children's books. Nannies and governesses were perhaps appropriate for child dancers and skaters, but they were hardly commonplace among the readers of the 1950s. Clergymen were not as poor as Alex Bell, or, if they were, they did not employ full-time domestic help.

Apple Bough (1962), the children's book which precedes the first of the autobiographies, has a strongly old world flavour, despite its accounts of global travel, its scenes in Moscow and California. The story revolves round Sebastian, a child violinist, not working his way to the top, but recognized as a genius from the age of eight. Noel concentrates mainly on the plight of his sisters and brother, as they cope with the strains and disruption of Sebastian's endless concert tours; but when Sebastian does appear he seems like a character from Juliana Ewing or Frances Hodgson Burnett, painted in the darker shades of Victorian romanticism, and trembling on the brink of an early grave. As she wrote *Apple Bough* Noel was already digging back into the past, perhaps recalling her father weeping as he read aloud *The Story of a Short Life.*

With *Apple Bough* out of the way, Noel turned to her auto-biography. It had been easy to tell stories of her childhood to Helen Watts or to audiences around the country; but, as she thought of writing it all down, she was overcome by a strange self-consciousness. The exposure involved alarmed her. She might pretend to disregard the traditions of restraint in which she had been brought up, but they were ingrained and inhibiting. Then there was her family. Could she portray them as they really were? Would they want to be put in a book? Streatfeilds instinctively shrank from publicity. 'Isn't it very unpleasant seeing your name in print?' an uncle had inquired when *The Whicharts* was published.[4]

One of her favourite books provided Noel with the solution to her difficulties. Though she was bored by horses, and hunting was a mystery, she loved *The Memoirs of a Fox-Hunting Man* by Siegfried Sassoon, with its evocation of Edwardian country life. Now she saw that Sassoon's technique of writing autobiographically behind an assumed name would exactly suit her. She could guard herself and her family with pseudonyms.

In a brief introduction to the account of her childhood, *A Vicarage Family* (1963), Noel wrote – 'It is because of my awareness that the portraits of my family are probably faulty, that I have used no real names. The thin shield of anonymity helped me to feel unselfconscious in drawing them, and in approaching the facts of my own life.' The Streatfeilds become the Strangeway family. Noel called herself Victoria, or Vicky; Ruth and Barbara were Isabel and Louise; Bill was Dick, and their parents were Jim and Sylvia.

'The thin shield of anonymity' liberated Noel in other ways. Dates need be no more accurate than names; events could be subtly altered or re-arranged. Janet, after all, had been adept at embroidering small incidents, an inherited talent most service-able for a writer. Consequently, *A Vicarage Family* is more a novel based on Noel's childhood than the unvarnished truth of conventional autobiographies.

Noel decided to focus on the traumas and misunderstandings of her teens, and the theme dictated the shape of the book. All the happy earlier years are discarded. Amberley is only briefly referred to as the village where her father had his first living. There is no mention of Noel's childhood delight in books and games of pretence, no hint that she ever encountered a ghost, or enjoyed snowdrop gardens and walnut plantations. Such details would have thrown the book out of key, by lightening the sombre impression she wished to create. So she opens her story at the moment when her expulsion from the Hastings and St Leonard's Ladies' College is only averted by the move to East-bourne. It is to be clear from the first page that Vicky is a problem child.

A Vicarage Family traces the Strangeways from their new beginning in Eastbourne to the First World War which ended so much. Within this framework, the portrait of Vicky fills most of the canvas. A variety of highly dramatized misadventures show her as a victim, sometimes of her own difficult nature, but more often of the injustices of other people. Imagination plays as large a part as memory, for airy structures of fantasy tower up from slender foundations of fact. Certainly Noel wore Ruth's out-grown dresses, and they seemed shabby and ill-fitting, but the appalling green velvet with its unmatching sleeves, which Vicky is compelled to wear in *A Vicarage Family*, is quite fictitious. Certainly too Noel was naughty, but Vicky's ferocious punish-ments – the darning of old church hassocks, the early rising to saw logs – were never inflicted on her. Such examples can be mutiplied throughout the book, where grains of truth are puffed into lurid horror stories.

Nevertheless, there is a sense in which it is all true. It is an authentic picture of how life might appear to an unhappy teenager with a strong disposition to over-react. 'I'll always see myself on this day, and remember how it felt when people were cruel and I was thirteen,' she vows dramatically, when an aunt takes her sisters out for tea and cream cakes, and she is left behind.

But while she projects herself easily back into old miseries, she judges her situation more by the standards of 1963 than 1911. She expects her readers to recoil, aghast, from aspects of life which were not really uncommon in those days, whether they were unheated bedrooms or restricted Sundays. Plenty of other children lived very much as the Streatfeilds did, but the emphasis of *A Vicarage Family* is to present their austerities as unique. Similarly she condemns the strictness of her parents, without allowing for the Victorian attitudes in which they were inevitably encased. Noel's inadequate sense of history failed her completely here.

The portrait of Sylvia (Janet) is another distortion of the truth. Clearly to the adolescent Noel she was an unsympathetic mother – that was fact; but the pattern of consistent unkindness attributed to Sylvia was an unfair exaggeration. The ineffectual mothers of *Tennis Shoes* and *The Painted Garden* resemble Noel's memories of Janet more than Vicky's spiteful, snubbing mother. Of course it heightens the drama of Vicky's plight to paint her mother as black as possible, but it runs counter to reality.

The portrait is the more surprising because, once she had grown up, Noel and her mother had become quite close, and not only through a shared love of flowers. After her widowhood Janet had depended very much on her unmarried daughter to solve her problems with companions and accommodation. References to her in the war diaries show Noel's admiration for Janet's self-control. 'Mother would be loathe (sic) to admit she is anxious, so we have a nice conversation on bulb-planting or some such.'[5] But Janet had died before *A Vicarage Family* was written; and, peering into the murky past, Noel only saw her as she had once seemed, unloving and uncomprehending; and the extenuating circumstances of her mother's poor health and time-consuming duties are hardly mentioned.

Jim Strangeway is much closer to William Streatfeild. He is truthfully presented as a dedicated clergyman, a priest first and a husband and father a long way second. Life with a saint is not easy, but the ironic picture of *Parson's Nine* has been softened. In the 1950s Noel, the wanderer, had returned to the Christian fold. It had always been her practice rather than her faith which had lapsed. 'A lapsed Christian need not be an agnostic,' she wrote. 'He can probably still remember how much richer life seemed when he was still part of the church.'[6] Settled in Elizabeth Street, she was drawn back to the nearby church of St Michael's; and, following her father's pattern of regular worship, she felt very close to him again. A tremendous warmth of affection glows through *A Vicarage Family*. 'Victoria loved her father so much that sometimes it almost hurt.' Nevertheless, since her theme is her misunderstood adolescence, she ruthlessly exposes William's basic weakness – that he idealized the family without managing to see its members as individuals. She does not pretend that he was a perfect father for difficult Vicky. If he had prayed about her less, and thought about her more, she might have been happier.

A Vicarage Family is above all a book of strong feelings. Those who are nice are very very nice; those who are not are hateful. Louise shares the latter category with Sylvia; Isabel and Dick the former, with their father. And nicest of all, unfailingly kind and understanding, is Vicky's cousin John, in creating whom Noel departed furthest from the truth.

Most unhappy teenagers long for a close, trusted friend, and this is John's role in the book. He was, of course, loosely based on Noel's cousin, Derek Baumer, but in most ways he is quite fictitious. Since, for the purposes of the book, John has to spend his holidays with his Strangeway relations, he is given, not an artist father, but one who works in India. There were Streatfeild relatives with Indian links; there was also a girl cousin, younger than Noel, who lived for some time at Eastbourne Vicarage; and Noel used these two facts when she drew John. But Derek's home was actually in London, and he never stayed at the Vicarage for longer than a week. Nor, when they looked back, could the family remember his showing any special preference for Noel. Yet *A Vicarage Family* suggests that some tiny, perhaps half forgotten incident, had endowed him, in Noel's eyes, with romance. It might have needed no more than an enchanted evening at a dance, in that emancipated winter of 1914, for Noel to turn him into a fantasy figure, as much dearest friend as lover, adoring but chaste; and then, working backwards in time, to create a whole series of imaginary events, in which he alone sympathized with her troubles, and shared confidences with her.

John is a type of boy familiar in Noel's novels, from Baruch in *Parson's Nine*, through Tony in *Saplings*, to Peter in *Mothering Sunday*. They are sensitive, imaginative, often delicate boys, unfitted for the demands to be tough and extrovert which life, or their relations, make upon them. Faced with anything physically unpleasant, they may be sick, or faint. Noel treats them with loving tenderness, for the frail heroes of several Susan Scarlett stories also suggest that she was robust enough herself to find delicacy attractive. John, and the other boys, are allowed one great strength – a potent inner life, never exposed to adult scorn. Baruch has a fantasy world originally derived from *The Pilgrim's Progress*, Peter has an imaginary farm, and John has a secret longing, only shared with Vicky, to be an actor.

Besides being Vicky's only friend, John's crucial part in the structure of *A Vicarage Family* justifies his presence. The book is cleverly planned, with a sense of movement, for its story is Vicky's growing up. At the beginning she is just a naughty child, alert to spot and resent injustices. As time passes her wayward-ness and bitterness increase, culminating in her furious reaction to the Confirmation which her father forces upon her. After that, things improve. Helped by John she acquires an interest in books; she has successes in parish entertainments; she grows prettier; and a promise is held out that she may make something of her writing. During a blissful summer holiday her relationship with John deepens. Then, tragically, war is declared, and John, as a territorial officer, is despatched to France. His one leave is enough for him to confide in Vicky all his revulsion at trench warfare. Five weeks later a telegram announces that he has been killed; and his death brings with it the end of Vicky's childhood.

The choice of the war to bring Vicky's early life to its conclusion was dramatically apt. 1914 was so much the closing of an era. The difficulty, from Noel's point of view, was that her childhood had finished well before Derek was actually killed. She had left school, taken her domestic economy course, fluttered her wings in Eastbourne's social circles, and started working in the hospital kitchen. To make John's death synchronize tidily with the end of her childhood, Noel was obliged to push her dates backwards, and make herself three years younger – twelve rather than fifteen when she arrives in Eastbourne. The earlier age also puts a more favourable gloss on her explulsion from the Ladies' College. Miss Bishop's behaviour seems more harsh to a mere twelve-year-old.

A Vicarage Family is a powerful book, pulsing with vitality and immensely readable. By her light touch, Noel holds the reader's sympathy for misunderstood Vicky, without lapsing too much into bitterness and self-pity. As a novel, it ranks high. Unfortunately Noel did not call it a novel. The cover proclaims it as a 'biography of myself', while her introductory remarks about the 'thin shield of anonymity' reinforce the impression that this is the true story of her early life.

Reaction amongst Noel's family was adverse. In particular the portraits of Janet and Barbara were disliked and resented. There was indignation that they should have been pilloried for posterity as if they had no redeeming features. As for John, they could not understand how he could have got into a book that was supposed to be autobiographical. No one in the family was happy to have such a mixture of exaggeration and blatant romance passed off as fact. Nothing much was said, restraint triumphed, but close relations showed their feelings by staying away from the party given to launch the book.

Old Eastbourne parishioners were upset as well. William's memory was still too precious to be impugned by hints that he had been an inadequate father. They consoled themselves by remembering how troublesome his actress daughter had been, and discounted what, in this case, was the truth.

Undeterred, for once a book was finished she put it behind her, Noel began to plan a sequel. As usual many other things were competing for her attention. She judged the 1963 E. Nesbit award for a children's book, and joined in agitation about the public lending right for authors. She published two rather undistinguished children's novels, *Lisa goes to Russia* (1963) and *The Children on the Top Floor* (1964); edited *Confirmation and After* (1963), a collection of articles for young Christians by various theologians; and kept up her torrent of reviews and articles.

Heaps of toys now jostled the review copies in her sitting room. She had visited a Care and Protection Home in East London, and discovered that although, while they stayed there, the children could take the Home's toys to cuddle in bed, they had to leave them behind when they were moved to foster homes. The image of insecure children, bereft of the toys that had comforted them, horrified Noel. 'She immediately went into action,' her secretary remembered, 'and wrote a letter to the press, appealing for toys that the children could keep for ever. I cannot tell you the shoals we received – beautiful ones from Women's Institutes, and equally precious ones from the humblest homes. Each one was personally acknowledged.'[7]

But most of Noel's thought was devoted to the second part of her autobiography, *Away from the Vicarage*, which was published in 1965. This time there was no need to impose a structure on her experiences, with altered dates, for her ten years as an actress, which the book covered, made a natural framework. Again she chose an interesting theme. It was of herself, torn between two worlds, trying to shake off the influence of the Vicarage, but unable to do so, and realizing, against her will, that her family matter quite as much to her as the theatre.

The book moves in a circle. Ignoring her work at Woolwich Arsenal, Noel introduces herself again as Vicky Strangeway, the girl who longs to act, and who leaves home in order to study at the Academy of Dramatic Art. The story of her acting career is punctuated by her visits home, and the feelings these evoke. At first she records disappointment. 'The family is going on just the same without me. I doubt if I am even missed.' As she tastes the glamour of London, 'what Vicky felt about her home was pity. The pity, she believed, of an experienced, orientated adult looking at the undeveloped.' She drifts further away, 'conscious, as never before, of how detached she had become from her family.' But after the appalling African tour, the magnetism of home begins to reassert itself. The Vicarage and its family now represent love and security in a world that seems to be rejecting her. A sensation of panic sweeps over her as she leaves for Australia. 'It's ridiculous, at my age, to care,' she tells herself, but she cannot shake off her homesickness. Regrets coalesce with a growing urge to write a book, in safe family surroundings. 'So odd that I, who always wanted to be free, should now want to go home . . . but I do, I've never wanted anything more.'[8] Her dream of returning to write is shattered, on the last page, by her father's death.

The outline of the book is factually correct; the emotions, on the whole, genuine, though a comparison with Noel's Australian diary shows some divergences. There is no doubt that in 1919 Noel was eager to leave home, and, by 1929, equally eager to abandon the theatre and start a new career. Once again members of her family occupy central positions, but this time the portraits are kinder. She has warmed towards her mother. 'Almost I think she's beginning to like me,' Vicky reflects with some bewilderment. Observing her father from an adult viewpoint, Vicky now feels quite protective towards him, trying to shield him from the excesses of his own asceticism, and becoming, to some extent, his confidante. Experience teaches Vicky to appreciate her family. The wholeness of her father's life contrasts with the messiness of her own; the security her sisters and brother know counterpoints her restless insecurity.

Indeed while *A Vicarage Family* was a case for the prosecution against the family, *Away from the Vicarage* is very much a case for the defence. It demonstrates the change of mood which led to her putting so much emphasis on the value of family life in her books. But her concentration on the family means that the theatrical sections of the book seem, by comparison, shallow and perfunctory. Comment on the state of the theatre in the 1920s, on other actors and plays, even on her own performances and parts, is disappointingly scanty. No productions are described, no notices quoted, and there is no assessment of Noel's skill as an actress. Livening with every visit to the Vicarage, the narrative flattens again, becomes hurried and thin, when Vicky returns to work.

The fictitious interpolations are mainly about love affairs. Although there is no one like John, two men have particular significance in her life. Robert is presented as a fellow actor on the South African tour. The close relationship which develops between him and Vicky, derived from their shared homesickness, arouses the jealousy of Arthur Bourchier. He picks a furious argument with Robert in a Johannesburg hotel, and Robert suffers a heart attack and dies. A little less dramatic is Vicky's love affair with Claude, a sybaritic young man with a mania for white things, who periodically visits London while on leave from abroad. He seems to be promising marriage, but finally reveals that he is a homosexual, and can never marry.

In *Away from the Vicarage*, Robert and Claude are as much Vicky's inventions as John had been; indeed more so, for Noel's friends were unable to guess at a basis of real identity for either. Although, during her years on the stage, many men had flitted through her life, and perhaps some had loved her, for she treasured an anonymous love sonnet which had been written to her, she had never truly fallen in love with any of them. They were often pleasant as companions, and useful as escorts, but she had shrunk from closer contact with them. Somehow she had concealed her sexual coldness; she was the charming young actress, Noelle Sonning, to be seen dining in fashionable restaurants and dancing in night clubs, the centre of a throng of admirers. And just as she had covered up the truth when she was living through those days, so now, writing about them, she did the same.

Robert and Claude provided her with a useful way out of a dilemma. There is no doubt that by far the strongest feeling she had for anyone during this period was for Daphne. 'I like her more than anyone I have met for years,' she had confided in her diary. But Daphne is never mentioned in *Away from the Vicarage*. The unorthodox passion which she inspired did not fit into the picture of Vicky as a girl who is only, conventionally, attracted by men. Private person that she was, unwilling – as Storm Jameson recalled – to talk about the dark spaces in her life where love and marriage might have been, Noel felt it safer to credit Vicky with imaginary loves, and to close down the hatches on the real one. Robert's death, and Claude's homosexuality, provide reasons that are valid, if somewhat far fetched, for Vicky's marrying neither of them.

She may not have realized that Claude in particular strikes a false note in the book. She had never been good at drawing lovers, and Claude, with his endless talk of white farms and white animals, is credible neither in himself nor as an object of devotion for Vicky. But then Vicky, apart from her love for her family, is not a girl of deep emotions. She skims over the surface of life, leaving its depths unplumbed.

Judging, as in *A Vicarage Family*, by the standards of the 1960s, Noel is harsh on her youthful self for her thoughtless frivolity. Looking back, she saw the fun she had shared with Moxie and Sunday as deplorable in an era of hardship, and blamed herself for being caught up in what was, after all, the prevailing mood of the time. 'Victoria plunged head over heels into the mad, wild night life of that date. It was a hectic world; she seldom went to bed quite sober. Anybody would do anything for kicks . . . That a large part of the country was living at starvation level escaped her . . . If in the quiet of the night she felt shame, in the morning she dismissed it with a shrug or a laugh. "I must have had alcoholic remorse." '

Everything in the end turns to dust and ashes – the acting career, the gaiety, the dream of a real family reunion. *Away from the Vicarage* is, in the final analysis, a sadder book than *A Vicarage Family*, lacking the indignation, the vitality and the romance which blaze through the earlier volume. The central portrait of Vicky is still clearly and convincingly drawn, but for all the crowded details of her doings, the reader is left with the impression of her standing alone in a wilderness, her talents for love, for acting, for family life, all somehow wasted.

The last part of the autobiography, *Beyond the Vicarage*, was published in 1971. The old Vicarage family life had, of course, been conclusively left behind, but the word in the title linked the volume to its predecessors. With the task of covering forty years, Noel could not prevent the book becoming something of a shapeless scramble. Once she is a writer, Vicky seems too close to Noel to be observed with the clarity of the earlier books; and the nearer the narrative approaches its actual time, the scrappier it grows. There is a straightforward account of Noel's start as a novelist, fascinating vignettes of her experiences in Deptford, and during the war; but then *Beyond the Vicarage* degenerates into the random chit-chat of a letter home, with disjointed thoughts and events pulled loosely together. Fiction is avoided, but its absence demonstrates how much the other two volumes gained in shape and content when Noel's imagination took control.

The death of William, who was so important in the previous books, leaves a gap which nothing can fill. Janet, in her widowhood, is both pathetic and a nuisance. Noel's sisters have virtually dropped out of the story, while the two most substantial presences in Noel's life, Daphne and Margot, remain in the shadows. A bustle of activity hides an emotional emptiness at the heart of the book. There are no loves, and not much indignation either. Noel's writing career is no more seen in context than her acting career was in *Away from the Vicarage*. There is no attempt to assess her own works, or trace the development of her thoughts about children's books.

Put together, the general effect of the autobiographies is puzzling. Purporting, behind the 'thin shield of anonymity', to record the facts of her own life, and 'to draw myself – as I hope I have done – with truth',[9] Noel produced a selective, fictionalized work, which sends the reader down false trails, and hides as much as it reveals.

Yet Noel enjoyed writing and speaking about herself. Her lectures and articles, the linking commentaries in the books she edited, the many interviews she gave, all form a continuous autobiography, and disclose, in a casual manner, much fascinating information. Measured against these, there is a contrived air about the autobiographies. They are not about the real Noel, the tireless writer, the perfectionist over research, the clothes-loving ex-model, the lineal descendant of crusading ancestors, the patient signer of autographs, the receiver of confidences. They are about a woman called Vicky, a diminution of Noel herself, a watered-down, weaker, more limited version of the real person, devoid of wide-ranging enthusiasms, and eager responses to new challenges.

17

A National Monument

Since the tour of South Africa with Arthur Bourchier's company, travel had been one of Noel's greatest pleasures. She was not especially interested in history or architecture, but she loved to see new places and meet new people. She travelled by boat, any sort of boat, from enormous liners to squat cargo ships; and she had a store of amusing anecdotes, about the Jamaican banana boat where the care and attention lavished on the bananas far exceeded anything offered to the passengers, or the Polish cargo boat on which nobody but herself spoke English. She visited every continent, and most European countries; and in 1960 she even went to Russia, an unusual adventure in those days.

Her aim was to gather information about Russian ballet schools, but the Russian tourist officials misled her – accidentally or deliberately – and she arrived in June when the schools had closed for the summer. The trip was not a success. She tried to be tolerant as, day after day, arrangements she thought she had made were changed or muddled by the authorities, when food was inedible, and the thin trickle of bath water icy, but the constant frustrations were exhausting. It was characteristic of Noel's intensely economical methods that, drawing on the diary she kept during those three unsatisfactory weeks, she was able to write six articles for *The Elizabethan* (the old *Collins Magazine*) on Russian schools and young people, two for *The Nursery World* about Russian baby care, and a book, *Lisa goes to Russia*.

Though she travelled so extensively, and particularly loved America, her favourite place of all was Ireland. With a strain of Irish ancestry from Janet's mother's family, the de Butts, she thrilled to the country's wild beauty, and to the Irish traditions of fantasy and story-telling. 'They have a most unfair advantage over the rest of the world,' she wrote; 'that glorious brogue which, together with the Irishman's gift for piling word on word in a golden heap, makes the simplest story sound entrancing.'[1]

During the war Noel had met Rachel Leigh-White, an Irish-woman working for the WVS, who occasionally delivered china or urns to the mobile canteen. She remembered with admiration how Noel had been unfailingly cheerful and courageous in times of danger; and when, soon after the war, Noel crossed to Ireland, to attend a PEN Club conference in Dublin, Rachel invited her to stay in her pretty white house on the west coast in County Cork. Soon Noel was making regular, annual visits, revelling in the spectacular landscape, and enjoying the country pursuits of shrimping and lobster fishing and hunting for wild flowers. To her unending satisfaction she and Rachel together hauled in the biggest lobster ever caught in the local bay; and equally satisfying were her discoveries of many rare plants, which she painted into her grandmother's wild flower book.

Ireland meant freedom from the routine of work and the pressures of fame. 'She never really forgot (in the nicest possible way) that she had made a name for herself,' Rachel Leigh-White recalled; 'but I do remember her roaring with laughter when our postmistress, on being told that she was a well-known authoress, said to Noel, "Really! I've never heard of your books."

'Noel was extraordinarily unpractical,' Rachel Leigh-White continued, 'even in the most ordinary things of life. I wouldn't have left her in the kitchen to boil an egg! Not only was she unpractical, but she was physically the most clumsy person I have ever met. Everything got knocked off tables, got lost or broken, and when she walked about the room if there was anything – including the dog or the cat – that she could stumble over, she invariably did – but all this with immense good humour and much laughter. She did care about her looks, clothes, etc., just as much in Ireland, but being without her maid, the results were sometimes funny.

'She was an exceptional personality – at times a bit vain and self-satisfied, and socially aware of herself as important; but all the traits were somehow very endearing and childlike. I think that is why she wrote such marvellous children's books. In some ways she never quite grew up.'[2]

Back in London with all her comforts attended to – her housekeeper to hook her into her corsets as her bulk increased, a manicurist visiting weekly to do her nails, a woman coming in specially to wash her expensive underwear – Noel saw Ireland as symbolizing magic and freedom. It was, she wrote in an unpublished play which she and Rachel drafted together, 'a sort of prehistoric fairyland.'

The contrast between the scattered white cottages of Bantry Bay, and the crowded homes of London and its suburbs, struck her forcibly as she listened to a popular song of the mid-1960s. Pete Seegar's *Little Boxes* was a protest against urban life, where everyone lived identical lives in identical, boxlike houses, reduced to 'rows of jellies from the same mould', as Noel had said of the writers in the *Collins Magazine* competition. Suppose, she thought, some children were taken away from their monochrome suburban existence, and exposed to the glorious anarchy of Ireland. What would happen to them?

This idea was the germ for *The Growing Summer* (1966), the last of Noel's really outstanding children's books. It is a celebration of the enchantment of Ireland. The four Gareths, ordinary children with not a youthful ballerina or budding actress among them, are sent to County Cork, to spend an entire summer with their eccentric Great-aunt Dymphna. They find themselves in a ramshackle country house, festooned with cobwebs which Great-aunt Dymphna calls 'fairy lace', with an open garbage heap outside the back door, and a barn full of mildewed junk. Great-aunt Dymphna expects them – unskilled though they are – to cook for themselves, wash their own clothes and spread them on the fuchsia bushes to dry, and entertain themselves in the strange, planless, un-timetabled days which stretch dauntingly ahead. How the children grow and develop in response to the challenges of absolute liberty, and how Great-aunt Dymphna changes imperceptibly from something like a witch to a kind fairy godmother, is the theme of this entrancing, unusual book. Its charm is cumulative. At first the reader, like the children, is alarmed by a lifestyle that seems so odd, but no one can resist for long the persuasive delights of Irish pastimes and people, or the superstitions which Noel gleefully embroidered into still richer fantasies. And, as clearly as in *The Circus is Coming* and *White Boots*, Noel points her characteristic moral: children must not expect things to fall into their laps, but difficulties can be overcome, and the harder the effort, the greater the reward.

Noel too shows that she has learned something – how to cope successfully with a book of shifting viewpoints. Where *Curtain Up* and *Wintle's Wonders* were muddled, the changes of angle in *The Growing Summer* are brilliantly handled, giving the book a unique, prismatic quality. Are the children surviving well under ghastly conditions, or are they – as someone devastatingly puts it – 'a hopelessly incompetent lot'? Is Great-aunt Dymphna right to scorn their suburban preoccupation with domesticity, or are they right to be alarmed by her chaotic ways? The Gareths expect to hear news of their parents by telegraph; Great-aunt Dymphna expects to hear it from the seagulls. Both methods of trans-mission seem equally effective. The children appear at first to be making all the concessions, but, in reality, Great-aunt Dymphna too is having to adjust to them. All the angles and attitudes are valid, all only partial. Life in a 'prehistoric fairyland' is a puzzling, stretching, growth-provoking experience.

Apart from an unnecessary sub-plot, *The Growing Summer* is a wonderfully rich and lively book, crammed with poetry, folk-lore and fun. It topped the children's bestseller lists, and the reviews were as enthusiastic as any Noel had had. 'Miss Streat-feild is in excellent form',[3] 'Noel Streatfeild is as skilful as ever'[4] 'Noel Streatfeild is a master of her craft, and has surely written a children's classic.'[5] Two years later it was filmed for television, with Rachel Leigh-White's house as the setting.

By then Noel was recovering from a serious illness, to which the pressures of work must have contributed. In 1966, the year after her seventieth birthday, when she might justifiably have slackened her pace, she published, besides *The Growing Summer*, a shorter children's book *Old Chairs to Mend*, and two books needing research, *Enjoying Opera* and *The Thames*. Two more books were published in 1967, and four in 1968. The 1960s were, in fact, her most prolific decade. It seemed that she could not stop working. Of course she liked luxury. She shopped at Harrods, and took taxis everywhere, and she had to pay the salaries of her staff, but her income should have been sufficient. The writing had become obsessional.

Early in 1968 she awoke one morning, and found she was paralysed down the left side. She had suffered a massive stroke in her sleep. The virtually complete recovery which she made was due partly to the care of nurses who took up residence in Elizabeth Street, and partly to Noel's formidable willpower. Almost as soon as she knew what had happened she was working with physiotherapists and speech therapists to recover the use of her left arm and leg, and to restore her speech. All her life she had admired courage. Now she showed it herself – incredible courage, her friends remembered. A few months after the stroke, apart from a slight limp, and a blurring of speech when she was tired, she was herself again.

Or almost. With that lethal staircase it was much more difficult to go out, and the minor speech impediment put an end to her lecturing. She stayed indoors a good deal, but she found plenty to occupy her. Besides *The Times* every day, she read three Sunday newspapers, scattering their pages all over her sitting room; and books still poured into the house. She enjoyed television, and had a curious ability to watch a programme and talk on the telephone at the same time. Flowers and plants remained a joy. There was a miniature garden inside a glasshouse on her windowsill, which she tended with tiny, improvized tools.

But other shocks followed her recovery. Her aged poodle, Pierre, had to be put down, and her friend Margot died suddenly. Barbara and Bill were already dead; and, of her closest literary friends, Kitty Barne had died in 1961 and Roland Pertwee in 1963. The world, at the beginning of 1970, looked sad and depleted.

A little earlier Noel had made herself a list of rules, which she quoted in *Beyond the Vicarage*.

1 Never willingly mention your health. People may ask how you are, but they don't want to know.

2 When your health and strength fail to such an extent that

you can't pull your weight at parties, don't go. NB People like to laugh.

3 Never, never, never criticize those younger than yourself. If tempted, remember yourself at their age, and blush.

4 Go to church regularly, even if you don't feel like it. God understands it's tough growing old, and will help you to be pleasant about it.

5 Make your motto, 'Keep right on to the end of the road.'

The most difficult rule was the third. There was much in the modern world which Noel disliked. She was out of sympathy with fashionable trends in the theatre, and with much that was being done in literature. 'The novel has become a close-up camera searching around for every bit of grime that can be scratched up anywhere,'[6] she protested, forgetting that this was very much what she had done in *Tops and Bottoms*. Then, keen Christian though she was, she found it hard to adapt to the new services and new ways of thought in the church. She hated to be considered a back number, yet more and more it seemed easiest to retreat into the past.

All her best writing in the 1970s was linked to, or evolved from, recollections retained in her blotting paper memory. *Thursday's Child* (1970), the first children's novel completed after her stroke, seems on the surface all breathless melodrama, with its story of Margaret Thursday, a late Victorian foundling baby, left in a church porch. When lack of money compels the elderly ladies who have adopted her to send her to a repressive orphanage, Margaret runs away, takes refuge on a canal boat, and ends in a travelling fairground theatre, captivating the audiences with her performances as Little Lord Fauntleroy. But between the crowding horrors and excitements are strewn numerous small memories from Noel's childhood. She relives ancient agonies in Margaret's trials with her boots and orphanage clothes. The village where Margaret goes to school is very like Amberley, even to the old custom when the cruel orphanage matron is 'rough-music-ed'. The country house scenes, with their details of family prayers and servants' routines, are a recreation of Edwardian life at Chart's Edge. In the last chapters Noel seems to be drawing on memories of the Victorian nursery classic of fairground life, *A Peep behind the Scenes*; while the story which runs parallel to Margaret's adventures, about an orphan scullery maid who proves to be a Marquis's grand-daughter, is the very essence of late Victorian children's fiction, echoing Frances Hodgson Burnett's *A Little Princess*, and Mrs Molesworth's wilder flights of fancy. Above all, *Thursday's Child* brims with recollections of Margot Grey. The little girl of mysterious origins, full of courage and determination, is Noel's last tribute to a beloved friend.

Compared with Noel's best books, *Thursday's Child* is not so much a work of imagination as of fertile invention; indeed its very fertility gets in the way of a proper imaginative realization of events. The writing is hurried, the climaxes muffled. The leisurely control of the earlier books has given way to an anxious sense that on no account must the action be allowed to slow down. A loss of confidence seems to lurk behind the hectic pace.

These faults were not new. Glimpsed first in *Wintle's Wonders*, they are even more glaring in the four *Gemma* books published in the late 1960s, and recur in Noel's next story, the disappointing *Ballet Shoes for Anna* (1972). They arose partly from Noel's awareness of the changing state of children's fiction, and her understandable fears that her own pre-eminence was under threat. After *The Growing Summer* reviews of her books became shorter and cooler. 'Nowadays,' said *The Times Literary Supplement* of *Thursday's Child*, 'we prefer fiction for children to be stronger and less predictable.'[7] *The Observer's* review of *Ballet Shoes for Anna* condemned its 'easy snobberies' and 'facile assumptions about virtue and talent.'[8]

Now nearly eighty, Noel saw herself beginning to be patronized as a writer stuck in a groove, outstripped by younger writers with soaring reputations, and blamed for being out of touch with a new generation of readers. She was regarded, she complained, as 'a national monument',[9] of great age and prestige, but little relevance to modern life – she, who had been considered a daring trend-setter. It was the price she had to pay for living and writing so long.

Children's books had changed vastly in her lifetime, while the number of experts on them had proliferated. To such critics, accustomed to the searching historical stories, fine-spun fantasies, and psychological dramas of the 1960s, Noel's recent books looked very ordinary. Her part in extending the frontiers of children's literature was often forgotten; her middle class outlook was noticed and condemned.

Stung by criticism, Noel fought back with one unassailable weapon – her continuing enormous sales. 'Naturally I write about the world and people I know best,' she explained in 1972. 'But I don't think children categorize, erect barriers in the way adults do. What could be more foreign to children today – even middle class children – than the world of *Ballet Shoes*? . . . (But) no child has ever written complaining about this. No, what they *all* want to know is what happens next.'[10] Firmly she turned down suggestions that she might seek contemporary backgrounds for her stories. 'I can't write about industrial or working class families because I don't know them intimately, and unless you know how people will react in certain circumstances, you can't write about them.'[11] Rounding on her critics, she frequently asserted that she did not believe children wanted to read about housing estates and downtown schools. She was sure they would far prefer the inside story of the Buckingham Palace nurseries.

Her actual popularity was immensely reassuring. Despite some unfavourable reviews, *Thursday's Child* was a bestseller for Christmas 1970, was shown on television in 1973, and repeated its success in paperback in 1974. Library polls of favourite authors throughout the 1970s show Noel continuing to score highly with the seven to eleven-year-olds; below Enid Blyton, but on a level with C. S. Lewis. Her long association with the Puffin Club kept her in touch with book-loving children, while, year after year, *Ballet Shoes* maintained its prime position among Puffin books. Noel was a regular attender at Puffin Club parties, talking to children, and patiently signing often very tattered copies of her own books. Asked for their opinion of her in 1981, Puffin Club members answered with a resounding burst of praise. 'She is my favourite author'. . . 'I am a devoted fan'. . . 'I enjoy *all* Noel Streatfeild's books.' As Noel said in 1976 – 'The letters I received when *Ballet Shoes* was first published in the

1930s are almost replicas of the letters I am getting today.'[12] Time could not destroy the credibility of the Fossils, or tarnish the romance of their lives.

In 1972 Noel stunned her critics with a brilliant new book, *The Boy Pharaoh, Tutankhamen*. Timed to coincide with a British Museum exhibition of Tutankhamen's treasures, this was a book for both children and adults to enjoy. Noel, who had never cared much for history, suddenly, in her late seventies, produced a historical masterpiece. She had slaved over the research, building up a formidably convincing picture of everyday life in ancient Egypt; but it had been really hard. 'I think this was the toughest work we ever did,' she wrote on the title page of the copy she gave her secretary, still wincing at the memory of how the fourth chapter, on Tutankhamen's childhood, had had to be revised and rewritten eleven times. Yet, in the end, the impressive scholarship is carried lightly, the different angles of history and archaeology are perfectly integrated, and, by a justifiable use of imagination, the boy pharaoh and his cousin-wife, become totally believable people. Magnificently produced and illustrated, the book was another bestseller.

Still Noel did not rest; sheer professionalism carried her on. She edited five anthologies for Dent's in her old style, with linking commentaries; and she turned back to her memories of the war for another story, *When the Siren Wailed* (1974). Unlike the Primrose Lane children, the central characters here were authentic Cockney children of the 1940s. There was no need now for pussy-footing hints about cream buns and tinned lobster to convey working class culture; the reader is introduced directly to a world of slums and searing poverty. The young Clarks are the sort of children Noel remembered from her Care Committee days, and she shows exactly how their home régime of treats, threats, and casual hours, hinders their adjustment when, evacuated to the country, they are billeted on a retired Colonel. Noel is scrupulously fair to both sides – to the Colonel who believes hot baths and regular letters home are essential to civilized living, and to the chidren who honestly cannot see the point of his evident peculiarities. Flawed in parts, *When the Siren Wailed* nevertheless gives an interesting picture of wartime ways and attitudes.

Cushioned and protected by her staff, Noel wrote on and on. To have a pen in her hand, to compose, kept her going. As she grew feebler and less co-ordinated, the awkward stairs trapped her still more, and she welcomed her occasional outings with enthusiasm. One of the last was to Rye, to speak at a dinner. 'The talk was at the Mermaid Hotel,' a friend and fellow-writer, Rumer Godden, recalled, 'and Noel presided, no other word, sitting in a great carved chair. My home, where she stayed, was just opposite, and we had a difficult time getting her down my narrow steps and across the cobbles of the street. She was always large, but had become really unwieldy, and she must have suffered a good deal of pain, as she was so ill, she was almost immobile – but she only chuckled and egged us on. The spirit was marvellous.'

Her eightieth birthday was marked by one of the accolades of English life, an appearance on the radio programme *Desert Island Discs*. In the accepted way she looked backwards, choosing, among her records, music from Wolf-Ferrari's *Jewels of the Madonna*, which had introduced the Children's Hour broadcasts of *Ballet Shoes*; Saint-Saens' *The Dying Swan* as a reminder of Ninette de Valois, that unforgettable Little Wonder; and Tschaikovsky's fifth symphony, to which her other favourite, Irina Baronova, had danced *Présages*. The book she chose was John Galsworthy's *The Forsyte Saga*, and her luxury was a set of gardening tools.

In 1976 she published her last two books of any value. *Gran-Nannie* is a memoir of the old nurse who had been loved by three generations of Streatfeilds. Noel could see her still, upstairs in the Chart's Edge nursery, the prototype of the cosy nannies of so many books – *The Whicharts, Parson's Nine, Ballet Shoes, White Boots*, and *Wintle's Wonders*. For the last time Noel told the story of 'brotherly love' and the French boots, and still she sympathized passionately with Grand-Nannie's belief in the right clothes for the right occasions.

Far to Go, also published in 1976, is a sequel to *Thursday's Child*, a slighter story, but remarkably well-plotted and coherent for a writer of eighty. And now it almost seemed as if writing were keeping her alive. *Meet the Maitlands* (1978) was planned as the first of a series of stories about the Maitland family, and even if it was only published on the strength of Noel Streatfeild's name, it still contains a few strong flashes of invention.

Between July and Christmas 1979, a series of small strokes induced her finally and regretfully to give up her home in Elizabeth Street. Established in a nursing home, she still tried at times to write, but the shadows of old age were creeping over her.

One last triumph remained. For many years her friends had wished that she might receive some public recognition for her work for children's books, and finally it came. In the New Year's Honours List of 1983 she was awarded the Order of the British Empire. Letters of congratulations poured in, and, disabled though she was, she managed to go to the Palace to receive the decoration.

And now her extraordinarily full life seemed to be drawing towards its close. She had packed in enough for several lifetimes. She had had ten years as an actress and nearly fifty as a writer, with over eighty books to her credit. She had adored clothes, dogs, gardens and the ballet. She had loved reading, travelling and fishing. She had revelled in her status as a celebrity, not least because it had fulfilled her deep childhood need to be valued and important.

Although she had never been a wife or mother, she had found compensation in many friendships. Marriage, she could see, might have cramped her exceedingly satisfying career. There were nieces and nephews, and more than fifty godchildren, to care for and pray for; and perhaps childlessness too had been an advantage. 'It's much easier to get a clear picture of children if you are not nursing them through measles, or putting on their nappies,'[13] she once observed. She had overthrown many of the Vicarage standards – lived above her income, wallowed in luxury, cultivated her appearance – but the most valuable things had stuck, belief in God and in family life.

Not many people can have lived to her great age, with such a record of successes, and incurred so little resentment and hostility. The memories of her friends were warm and affectionate. That she was occasionally pompous, and sometimes a little vain, were the worst things anyone could find to say about her. She sailed through her adult life, confident that people would like her – and they did.

For Christmas 1981 the members of the Puffin Club made her a special present. It was a 'loving tree', a ball of holly to which were tied many small, beautiful things which children had made and sent – miniature ballet shoes, violins, skates, apple boughs. She had given so much happiness to children, and this was their way of saying thank you. There was one advantage in being a national monument. She could be certain she would not be forgotten.

Notes

CHAPTER 1
1   *Evening Standard*, 18 May 1955.
2   'Raising the standard of children's reading', *Young Wives* (Mothers' Union magazine for St Alban's diocese), August 1954.
3   Introduction to *Tanglewood Tales*, Collins New Classics, 1957.

CHAPTER 2
1   'Books as friends', Talk given by N. S. at Women's Institute Book Day, Preston, 1957.
2   Unpublished notes on the Streatfeild family, compiled by Ruth Gervis.
3   *The Day before Yesterday*, Collins, 1956.
4   Unpublished notes on the Streatfeild family, compiled by Ruth Gervis.
5   Unpublished notes on the Venn family, compiled by Ruth Gervis.
6   *A Vicarage Family*, Collins, 1963.
7   'I remember, I remember', *P.N.E.U. Parents' Review*, October 1964.
8   Notes for a talk by N.S., 1953.
9   *The Noel Streatfeild Birthday Story Book*, Dent, 1973.
10 Unpublished notes on the Venn family, compiled by Ruth Gervis.

CHAPTER 3
1   Talk given by N.S. to Brighton Girls' Club, 30 April 1959.
2   *By Special Request*, Collins, 1953.
3   Notes for a talk by N.S., 1953.
4   Talk by N. S. for American Women's Clubs. 1956.
5   Ibid.
6   'Copy-Cats', *The Spectator*, 19 September 1952.
7   *The Noel Streatfeild Christmas Holiday Book*, Dent, 1973.
8   *The Years of Grace*, Evans, 1950.
9   Unpublished notes on the Streatfeild family, compiled by Ruth Gervis.
10 *The Day before Yesterday*, Collins, 1956.
11 'My favourite town, Westerham', *Homes and Gardens*, March 1967.
12 'Families', *Chicago Sunday Tribune*, 27 August 1963.
13 Talk Given by N. S. to Brighton Girls' Club, 30 April 1959.

CHAPTER 4
1   *A Vicarage Family*, Collins, 1963.
2   *Myra Carroll*, Collins, 1944.
3   *The Years of Grace*, Evans, 1950.
4   Quoted by courtesy of Mrs Olive Poole.
5   *A Vicarage Family*, Collins, 1963.
6   *The Day before Yesterday*, Collins, 1956.
7   *A Vicarage Family*, Collins, 1963.
8   *A Young Person's Guide to the Ballet*, Frederick Warne, 1975.
9   'Two Child Dancers', *The World of Ballet*, Collins, 1970.

CHAPTER 5

1   *The Day before Yesterday*, Collins, 1956.
2   *Magic and the Magician*, Benn, 1958.
3   Quoted by courtesy of Mr John Stevens.
4   Quoted by courtesy of Mrs Joan Davies.
5   *Parson's Nine*, Heinemann, 1932.
6   *The Years of Grace*, Evans, 1950.
7   Ibid.
8   Quoted by courtesy of Mrs Ethel Baker.
9   Quoted by courtesy of Mrs Ethel Goldsmith.
10 Quoted by courtesy of Mrs E. Smith.
11 Quoted by courtesy of Miss G. Groome.

CHAPTER 6

1   *The Noel Streatfeild Summer Holiday Book*, Dent, 1973.
2   *My Drama School*, Robson Books, 1978.
3   *The Day before Yesterday*, Collins, 1956.
4   *The Whicharts*, Heinemann, 1931.
5   'Stage Door', *Collins Girls' Annual*, 1954.
6   Lecture notes.
7   *Ballet Shoes*, Dent, 1936.
8   *Curtain Up*, Dent, 1944.
9   Ibid.
10 *Away from the Vicarage*, Collins, 1965.

CHAPTER 7

1   Quoted by courtesy of Miss Betty Drury.
2   Preface to *The Amber Gate*, Kitty Barne, J. Curwen & Sons.
3   *By Special Request*, Collins, 1953.
4   Quoted by courtesy of Miss Naomi Stubbs.

CHAPTER 8

1   *Beyond the Vicarage*, Collins, 1971.
2   *Away from the Vicarage*, Collins, 1965.
3   *The Conti Story*, Joan Selby-Lowndes, 1954.
4   'Writing for Children', *The Schoolmaster*, 3 November 1956.
5   *The Whicharts*, Heinemann, 1931.
6   Talk given by N. S. at Lady Margaret School, Parson's Green, 28 February 1962.
7   Ibid.
8   *Away from the Vicarage*, Collins, 1965.
9   Ibid.
10 Interview with N. S., *Rhodesia Herald*, 24 September 1970.
11 'So you want to be an Author', *Sheffield Telegraph*, 22 August 1952.
12 Ibid.
13 Quoted by courtesy of Mr John Stevens.
14 Quoted by courtesy of Mrs Joan Davies.
15 *Beyond the Vicarage*, Collins, 1971.

CHAPTER 9

1   Unpublished lecture notes.
2   Interview with Valerie Fea, November 1969.
3   *Sunday Times*, 20 September 1931.
4   *Scots Observer*, 26 November 1931.
5   *Sunday Times*, 20 September 1931.
6   *The Years of Grace*, Evans, 1950.
7   *By Special Request*, Collins, 1953.
8   *Daily Mail*, 29 June 1933.
9   *Surrey Weekly Press* on *Tops and Bottoms*, 4 August 1933.
10 *Quiver* on *Shepherdess of Sheep*, March 1935.
11 *News Chronicle* on *Parson's Nine*, 20 June 1932.
12 *Everyman* on *Tops and Bottoms*, 22 July 1933.

CHAPTER 10

1   Quoted by courtesy of Mrs Sybil Sandison.
2   'Why did I ever write a children's book?', *The Writer*, December 1949.
3   'Two Child Dancers', *The World of Ballet*, Collins, 1970.
4   Ibid.
5   Ibid.
6   'My Moment of Success', *Books and Bookmen*, December 1958.
7   *Magic and the Magician*, Benn, 1958.
8   *Beyond the Vicarage*, Collins, 1971.
9   *Nottingham Guardian*, 3 December 1936.
10 *Daily Mirror*, 3 December 1936.
11 *The Guider*, November 1936.
12 *Manchester Guardian*, 4 December 1936.
13 *London Mercury*, December 1936.
14 'My moment of Success', *Books and Bookmen*, December 1958.
15 *August Adventure*, M. E. Atkinson, 1936.
16 *Family Footlights*, Kitty Barne, 1939.
17 *The Children who lived in a Barn*, Eleanor Graham, 1938.
18 *Jam Tomorrow*, Monica Redlich, 1937.
19 *More Ponies for Jean*, Joanna Cannan, 1943.
20 *A Very Ill-Tempered Family*, Juliana Ewing, 1876.
21 For example – *The Abbey Girls go back to School*, Elsie J. Oxenham, 1923.
22 *Jessica's First Prayer*, Hesba Stretton, 1867.
23 *A Peep behind the Scenes*, Mrs O. F. Walton, 1877.
24 Unpublished lecture notes.
25 *By Special Request*, Collins, 1953.

CHAPTER 11

1   Talk given by N. S. to London Writers' Circle, September 1937.
2   Ibid.
3   *The Years of Grace*, Evans, 1950.
4   *Look at the Circus*, Hamish Hamilton, 1960.
5   *Beyond the Vicarage*, Collins, 1971.
6   *Time and Tide*, December 1938.

7   *Yorkshire Post*, December 1938.
8   *Beyond the Vicarage*, Collins, 1971.

CHAPTER 12

1   *Away from the Vicarage*, Collins, 1965.
2   Unpublished notes, written during the war.
3   Ibid.
4   *Saplings*, Collins, 1945.
5   *Evening News*, 26 January 1943.
6   Quoted by courtesy of Mrs Elsa Dunbar.
7   Notes for a talk by N. S., 1953.
8   *WVS Bulletin*, July 1946.

CHAPTER 13

1   Quoted by courtesy of Mrs C. Boret.
2   Talk given by N. S., Manchester, September 1937.
3   N. S.'s Diary, 26 September 1940.
4   Ibid., 13 September 1940.
5   *Journal of the National Book League*, October 1950.
6   Unpublished letter, 1 September 1953.
7   *Times Literary Supplement*, 24 January 1942.
8   *John o' London's Weekly*, 30 November 1945.
9   *Books for Today*, May 1947.
10 'A Letter to the Reader', *Party Frock*, Collins, 1946.

CHAPTER 14

1   N. S.'s Diary, 1 September 1940.
2   *Beyond the Vicarage*, Collins, 1971.
3   N. S.'s Diary, 20 February 1946.
4   Ibid., 26 February 1946.
5   Ibid., 1 March 1946.
6   *The Painted Garden*, Collins, 1949.
7   'Writing for Children', *The Schoolmaster*, 30 November 1956.
8   *By Special Request*, Collins, 1953.
9   'A Garden in Miniature', *Homes and Gardens*, January 1965.
10 Unpublished notes, 1953.
11 *Smith's Trade Circular*, 22 September 1951.
12 *Punch*, 7 December 1949.
13 *Collins Magazine for Boys and Girls*, November 1948.
14 'Two Child Dancers', *The World of Ballet*, Collins, 1970.
15 *Glasgow Citizen*, 21 September 1949.
16 *Noel Streatfeild's Easter Holiday Book*, Dent 1974.

CHAPTER 15

1   *Church of England Newspaper*, 15 November 1957.
2   Unpublished article, 1953.
3   *Grimsby Evening Telegraph*, 17 February 1972.
4   Quoted by courtesy of Gina Wilson.
5   *Radio Times*, September 1952.

Notes

6   *Desert Island Discs*, BBC radio, 17 January 1976.
7   'How I came to write *White Boots*', *Radio Times*, 20 June 1960.
8   *Sunday Times*, 10 January 1954.
9   Book Buyer's Forecast for W. H. Smith, 27 July 1961.
10 Talk given by N. S. at King's College, London, 6 January 1953.
11 Ibid.
12 Article by Enid Blyton, *Church of England Newspaper*, 1950.
13 *The Spectator*, 19 September 1952.
14 *By Special Request*, Collins, 1953.
15 Ibid.
16 N. S.'s Diary, 9 March 1942.
17 'Sounds and Scents of Childhood', *The Book Window*, Autumn 1953.
18 *Time and Tide*, 29 December 1953.
19 *Times Literary Supplement*, 27 November 1953.
20 *Daily Mail*, 9 December 1954.
21 *Times Literary Supplement*, 11 April 1958.

CHAPTER 16

1   Quoted by courtesy of Mabel Esther Allan.
2   Talk given by N. S. at Derry and Toms, 27 October 1965.
3   *The Spectator*, 21 November 1947.
4   *Beyond the Vicarage*, Collins, 1971.
5   N. S.'s Diary, 12 September 1940.
6   *Confirmation and After*, Heinemann, 1963.
7   Quoted by courtesy of Mrs C. Boret.
8   N. S.'s Diary, 15 November 1928.
9   Introduction to *Away from the Vicarage*, Collins, 1965.

CHAPTER 17

1   *By Special Request*, Collins, 1953.
2   Quoted by courtesy of Miss Rachel Leigh-White.
3   *Times Literary Supplement*, 24 November 1966.
4   *Daily Telegraph*, 1 December 1966.
5   *Illustrated London News*, 3 December 1966.
6   *Majorca Daily Bulletin*, 8 August 1968.
7   *Times Literary Supplement*, 30 October 1970.
8   *The Observer*, 22 October 1972.
9   *Sunday Times*, 3 October 1971.
10 *The Observer*, 22 October, 1972.
11 *Irish Independent*, 25 November 1971.
12 *Desert Island Discs*, BBC radio, 17 January 1976.
13 *Majorca Daily Bulletin*, 8 August 1968.

Bibliography

1931	The Whicharts	HEINEMANN
1932	Parson's Nine	HEINEMANN
1933	Tops and Bottoms	HEINEMANN
1934	The Children's Matinee	HEINEMANN
	Shepherdess of Sheep	HEINEMANN
1936	It Pays to be Good	HEINEMANN
	Ballet Shoes	DENT
1937	Tennis Shoes	DENT
	Caroline England	HEINEMANN
1938	The Circus is Coming	DENT
1939	Luke	HEINEMANN
	Dennis the Dragon	DENT
1940	The House in Cornwall	DENT
	The Winter is Past	COLLINS
1941	The Children of Primrose Lane	COLLINS
1942	I Ordered a Table for Six	COLLINS
1943	Harlequinade	CHATTO and WINDUS
1944	Myra Carroll	COLLINS
	Curtain Up	DENT
1945	Saplings	COLLINS
1946	Party Frock	COLLINS
1947	Grass in Piccadilly	COLLINS
1949	The Painted Garden	COLLINS
1950	Mothering Sunday	COLLINS
	The Years of Grace	EVANS
1951	White Boots	COLLINS
1952	Aunt Clara	COLLINS
1953	The Fearless Treasure	MICHAEL JOSEPH
	By Special Request	COLLINS
1954	The Bell Family	COLLINS
1955	Growing Up Gracefully	BARKER
1956	Judith	COLLINS
	The Day Before Yesterday	COLLINS
	The Grey Family	HAMISH HAMILTON
1957	Wintle's Wonders	COLLINS
1958	Magic and the Magician	BENN
1959	Bertram	HAMISH HAMILTON
	The Royal Ballet School	COLLINS
	Noel Streatfeild's Ballet Annual	COLLINS
	The January Baby,	

	The February Baby, etc.	BARKER
1960	Look at the Circus	HAMISH HAMILTON
	New Town	COLLINS
1961	The Silent Speaker	COLLINS
1962	Apple Bough	COLLINS
1963	Lisa Goes to Russia	COLLINS
	A Vicarage Family	COLLINS
	The First Book of Ballet	EDMUND WARD
	Confirmation and After	HEINEMANN
1964	The Children on the Top Floor	COLLINS
1965	Away from the Vicarage	COLLINS
	Let's go Coaching	HAMISH HAMILTON
1966	The Thames	MULLER
	Enjoying Opera	DOBSON
	The Growing Summer	COLLINS
	Old Chairs to Mend	HAMISH HAMILTON
1967	Before Confirmation	HEINEMANN
	Caldicott Place	COLLINS
1968	Nicholas	BENN
	The Barrow Lane Gang	BBC, JACKANORY
	Gemma	ARMADA
	Gemma and Sisters	ARMADA
1969	Gemma Alone	ARMADA
	Goodbye Gemma	ARMADA
1970	Thursday's Child	COLLINS
1971	Beyond the Vicarage	COLLINS
1972	The Boy Pharaoh, Tutankhamen	MICHAEL JOSEPH
	Ballet Shoes for Anna	COLLINS
1973	The Noel Streatfeild Summer Holiday Book	DENT
	The Noel Streatfeild Christmas Holiday Book	DENT
1974	When the Siren Wailed	COLLINS
	The Noel Streatfeild Easter Holiday Book	DENT
1975	A Young Person's Guide to Ballet	WARNE
1976	Gran-Nannie	MICHAEL JOSEPH
	Far to Go	COLLINS
	The Noel Streatfeild Birthday Story Book	DENT
1977	The Noel Streatfeild Weekend Story Book	DENT
1978	Meet the Maitlands	W. H. ALLEN

Index

Index

Index